THE STATE OF THE SYSTEM

The State of the System

A Reality Check on Canada's Schools

PAUL W. BENNETT

McGill-Queen's University Press
Montreal & Kingston • London • Chicago

ISBN 978-0-2280-0083-9 (cloth)
ISBN 978-0-2280-0084-6 (paper)
ISBN 978-0-2280-0226-0 (ePDF)
ISBN 978-0-2280-0227-7 (ePUB)

Legal deposit third quarter 2020
Bibliothèque nationale du Québec

Printed in Canada on acid-free paper that is 100% ancient forest free
(100% post-consumer recycled), processed chlorine free

| Funded by the Government of Canada | Financé par le gouvernement du Canada | Canada | Canada Council for the Arts | Conseil des arts du Canada |

We acknowledge the support of the Canada Council for the Arts.

Nous remercions le Conseil des arts du Canada de son soutien.

Library and Archives Canada Cataloguing in Publication

Title: The state of the system: a reality check on Canada's schools / Paul W. Bennett.

Names: Bennett, Paul W., 1949– author.

Description: Includes bibliographical references and index.

Identifiers: Canadiana (print) 20200238701 | Canadiana (ebook) 20200238868 | ISBN 9780228000846 (paper) | ISBN 9780228000839 (cloth) | ISBN 9780228002260 (ePDF) | ISBN 9780228002277 (ePUB)

Subjects: LCSH: Public schools—Canada—Evaluation. | LCSH: Education—Canada—Evaluation.

Classification: LCC LA412 .B42 2020 | DDC 371.010971—dc23

This book was typeset by Marquis Interscript in 10.5 / 13 Sabon.

To Dianne and our children – and to all those
committed to meaningful education reform

Contents

Figures and Tables

FIGURES

TABLES

Acknowledgments

School reform is in my blood and it's been a passion of mine ever since I entered the teaching profession. Over the decades, my wide-ranging educational career has provided unparalleled opportunities to study, teach, and write in three different provinces: Ontario, Quebec, and Nova Scotia. First as a student, then as a history teacher, department chair, academic director, and school head, I came to know Canadian schools from the inside. Taking up educational causes, serving as an elected school trustee, and advocating for democratic reforms all opened my eyes to the tantalizing prospects for re-engineering the System. Years in the making, this book represents a distillation of lessons learned and a prescription for repurposing the Canadian K–12 system.

The "organizational factor" looms large not only in the shaping of history, society, and systems, but in my perspective on the System. Contemporary power structures, bureaucratic change, organizational theory, and reforming the social order were vitally important topics first introduced to me by the late York University historian Robert D. Cuff (1941–2001), a brilliant Princeton-trained scholar, truly fine teacher, and quintessential family man. As an education policy researcher, the American Enterprise Institute's Frederick Hess, author of *The Same Thing Over and Over* (2010) and the Cage-Busting Leadership series, sets a high standard which has sharpened my intellectual focus, clarified my thinking, and challenged many of my previous assumptions. Coming at education from a radically different perspective, Canada's best-known academic publisher on the Left, Errol Sharpe, is owed a debt of gratitude. It was a pleasure working closely with Errol to thrash out and refine my emerging synthesis, field-tested in my 2011 book, *Vanishing Schools, Threatened Communities: The Contested Schoolhouse in Maritime Canada, 1850–2010.*

Many academic mentors, fellow educators, and policy researchers have shaped my thinking and provided inspiration along the way. My dear friend, the late Desmond P. Morton, was always a constant inspiration by sheer example, even when he was chiding another of my most influential York University mentors, Jack Granatstein. As a doctoral student at the Ontario Institute for Studies in Education (1984–91), Alison Prentice drew me out of my comfort zone with total immersion in women's studies, while Harold Troper delighted in testing my mettle and exposing me to the depth, mysteries, and richness of race and ethnic studies. While on the editorial board of *The History and Social Science Teacher* (1986–92), the late Geoffrey Milburn of Althouse College, Western University, sharpened my wit, and kept me abreast of broader trends in history teaching. Fellow Canadian education historian Paul Axelrod and I share much in common, including the distinction of working closely at York University with the late John T. Saywell, whom I admired from his marvelous Canadian history textbooks. No high school teacher had a bigger influence on my life and teaching than Donald Bogle, an outstanding Ontario history and social science teacher. When Dean Axelrod invited me back in 2010 to the Canadian History of Education Association (CHEA/ACHE), I came to appreciate even more the marked influence of R.D. (Bob) Gidney, Peter Sexias, Ruth Sandwell, Amy Von Heyking, Bruce Curtis, and, more recently, Ted Christou, of Queen's University's Faculty of Education.

Most of my education policy research is informed by active engagement on the frontlines. Education reform spirit and determination were forged in Ontario during my York Region years as an activist Thornhill public school trustee and co-founder of the Coalition for Education Reform (1992–97). Back then, I was drawn to Bill Crothers, Malkin Dare, William Robson, Andrew Nikiforuk, and Doretta Wilson while we were campaigning for public accountability, better schools, and standards reform. Former Director of the Council of Ministers of Education Dr Paul Cappon impressed me greatly, and deserves far more recognition for putting Canadian K–12 education on the global map. Studying school closures drew me into the Canadian small schools movement and research community, starting in Nova Scotia, then right across the nation. Much of that public-interest policy research, featured in the book, was generated with such inspirational allies as Leif Helmer, Michael Corbett, Sheree Fitch, and Kate Oland.

Education policy research is a relatively small pond, especially in Canada. Working with the Atlantic Institute for Market Studies (AIMS), I found a home for my independent research with the consistent support of Charles Cirtwill, Marco Navarro-Genie, and Alex Whelan. Manitoba social studies teacher Michael Zwaagstra deeply influenced my thinking on teacher-guided instruction, evidence-based analysis, and giving voice to teacher concerns. The current head of the Canadian Education Association, Max Cooke, and the founder of VoicEd Radio, Stephen Hurley, always provided a sounding board and constructive advice on approaching educational issues. More recently, my research, writing, and commentary benefited enormously from the stimulating work of Michael K. Barbour and Can-e-Learn, the teen mental health research of Stanley Kutcher, the professional encouragement of Avis Glaze, and the editorial support of Jackson Doughart, editor, *Telegraph-Journal* and *Brunswick News*.

Friends and close colleagues have noticed a recent uptick in my spirit, energy, and output, roughly coinciding with discovering the marvels of researchED, the UK–based teaching research organization. Since falling in with founder Tom Bennett at researchED New York in May 2016, I have been totally energized by ground-breaking, evidence-based research generated by a brand new group of colleagues, including Martin Robinson, Eric Kalenze, John Mighton, Robert Pondiscio, Daisy Christodoulou, Barbara Oakley, Dan T. Willingham, and Dylan Wiliam.

This book would not have been possible without the highly professional team headed by Jonathan Crago at McGill-Queen's University Press. My sincere and committed senior editor, Jacqueline Mason, believed in the project, steered it through the approvals process, cleared away any potential obstacles, and kept it nicely on track. Sound, reliable, and accurate copy-editing was provided by Grace Rosalie Seybold, and my MQUP in-house editor Natalie Blachere managed to transform the edited manuscript, first into proofs, then a polished book.

While this is my tenth book, it might well be the one that summoned up all of my energies and absorbed extraordinary amounts of otherwise precious family time. Living with Dianne for all these years has forged deep bonds, and has taught me that the finest things in life are those that one shares. Our grown children, daughter Kelly and son

Blair, mean the world to us, and more so as our life goes on. I can never thank them enough for giving me the freedom to roam – to raise fundamental questions, range widely, and think freely on educational issues that matter.

THE STATE OF THE SYSTEM

does he speak to social purpose of
education or primarily as an
individual benefit?

Rousseauian but to exams

class books, bottom up, but
with commerce standards

Paul Bennett "drains the swamp"

Close Encounters and Brick Walls

Being ranked among the world's leading education nations on international student tests produces a wave of chest-thumping national pride in education circles. One positively gushing August 2017 *BBC News* story went so far as to anoint Canada as an "education superpower" on the basis of its recent Program of International Student Assessment (PISA) scores in mathematics, science, and reading. Upon closer scrutiny, most such public claims that the Canadian education system is either "world-class" or simply "pretty good" compared to other Western industrial nations are overblown and tend to emanate from those inside the system.[1]

From the outside, looking in, the System looks much different. Since the rise and expansion of the modern bureaucratic system over the past hundred years, public education in Canada has grown far more distant and much less connected with students, families, teachers, and communities. Voicing concerns about the state of our public schools can be exceedingly frustrating – and more often than not, an exercise in futility. Parents advocating mathematics or reading curriculum reforms, families seeking improved special needs programs, or communities fighting small school closures regularly hit brick walls and glass ceilings. Our public schools, initially established as the vanguard of universal, accessible, free education, have lost their way and become largely unresponsive to the public they still claim to serve. What *The State of the System* seeks to provide is a reality check on what's happened to Canada's Kindergarten-to-Grade-12 schools, and a plan to reclaim them for students, parents, teachers, and communities alike.

Close encounters with the System awaken engaged parents, teachers, and communities to the underlying sources of unease. Today's schools have been swallowed up by provincial ministries and regional school authorities. Everywhere you look, the march of urbanized, bureaucratic, centralized κ–12 education is nearly complete, marking the triumph of the System over students, parents, teachers, and the engaged public.[2] Putting students first has little meaning in a system that gives priority to management "systems," exemplifies top-down decision-making, thwarts community-based schools, and processes students like hamburgers in a fast-food operation. Graduation rates have risen so dramatically that high school diplomas are awarded to virtually everyone who meets attendance requirements.

The System, originally conceived as a liberal reform enterprise aimed at expanding mass schooling and broadening access to the populace, largely achieved its goals twenty-five years ago. Having achieved near-universal access, school authorities in the 1980s began to pivot toward introducing bureaucratic managerialism in the form of what American education administration experts Donald Peurach, David Cohen, and James Spillane term "instructionally focused education systems."[3] In a North American wave of structural reform, the systematizers saw the "incoherence" of instruction from one classroom to another as a problem and teacher autonomy as an obstacle to further modernization. School change came to mean supplanting didactic instruction, knowledge-based curricula, and the teaching of basic skills, while embracing "ambitious instructional experiences and outcomes for all students." At the school district level, it was reflected in new forms of school consolidation aimed at turning loose aggregations of schools into school systems. The teaching of foundational skills and knowledge was subsumed in a new school system improvement agenda focused on "educational excellence and equity." The shift also exemplified the logic of standards-and-accountability, resisted by classroom teachers as another encroachment on their prized autonomy as professionals. Centrally established accountability infrastructure continued to encounter resistance when it came to penetrating the "black box" of the classroom.[4]

Today's central administrative offices, layers of administration, big-box elementary schools, and super-sized high schools all testify to the dominance of the trend. Elected school boards, a last vestige of local education democracy, are now considered simply nuisances and fast becoming a threatened species. Critics of educational bureaucracy and even quiet doubters are either ignored or dismissed as turn-back-the-clockers in our twenty-first-century universe. Growing

numbers of classroom teachers are drawing the line in defense of
what's left of teacher autonomy and breathing life into a movement
for education on a more human scale.

The modern school system tends to function much like the prover-
bial "iron cage." Over the years, the famous German sociologist Max
Weber's conception of the iron cage of rationality and bureaucracy has
found concrete expression in what might be termed the "School
System." In its original form, it was applied broadly by Weber to
explain the tyranny of rationalization in the modern transformation
of social life, particularly in Western capitalist societies. The iron cage,
in his view, trapped individuals in systems purely driven by teleologi-
cal efficiency, rational calculation, and control.[5]

The original German term was *stahlhartes Gehäuse*, translated as
"iron cage" and given much wider expression after its appearance in
American sociologist Talcott Parsons's 1930 translation of Weber's
classic work, *The Protestant Ethic and the Spirit of Capitalism*. Weber's
most brilliant insight was seeing, in the future, the potential "bureaucratization" of the social order into "the polar night of icy dark-
ness." More recently, sociologists have interpreted the term a little
differently, as meaning "shell as hard as steel."[6] Whatever the precise
meaning, the term has great utility in assessing school systems and
advocating for root-and-branch reform of the modern bureaucratic
education state. The time for cage-busting education reform has come.

The conventional view of Canadian public education and its safe
assumptions was initially challenged in George Martell's 1974 collection of essays, *The Politics of the Canadian Public School*. In his
opening chapter, "The Schools, the State and the Corporations,"
Martell appropriated the term "iron cage" and proposed looking at
the system through the lens of its structure and context rather than
its passing and ephemeral policy preoccupations. A more recent for-
mulation of this structural critique can be found in David Clandfield's
2010 work, "The School as a Community Hub: A Public Alternative
of the Neo-Liberal Threat to Ontario Schools."[7]

The actual diagnosis of what's wrong with the System is not really
new. More than two decades ago Jennifer Lewington and Graham
Orpwood's *Overdue Assignment* (1993) identified the crux of the problem and sketched the outlines of a better path forward. With the Ontario
public school system facing calls for greater public accountability,
Lewington and Orpwood saw public education as a "closed system"
or "fortress" with "insiders" and "outsiders."[8] Ministry of Education

Figure 0.1 German Sociologist Max Weber, 1918

The renowned German sociologist Maximilian Karl Emil Weber
(1864–1920) applied the term "iron cage" in his analysis of the increasing
rationalization of social life in Western capitalist countries. The process
of bureaucratization, in his view, trapped individuals in systems based
purely on mechanical efficiency, rational calculation, and control.

bureaucrats occupied the top rung in the hierarchy, which functioned
top-down through school board administrators in the middle, to school
principals and classroom teachers at the bottom. Excluded from the
System were most groups seeking to represent the public interest, including parents, business organizations, and special interests.

    Since the 1990s, teachers' unions have grown considerably in
influence, but their access to education policy-makers is highly

dependent upon the orientation of the government in power. Under friendly regimes, such as Kathleen Wynne's Ontario Liberal government (2013–18) and Rachel Notley's Alberta NDP (2015–19), union leadership enjoyed ready access and collaborated with the education ministries on curriculum reform, student assessment, and classroom conditions.[9] Radical changes in government, such as the 2018 Doug Ford revolution in Ontario, can result in the unions being frozen out and compelled to take job actions to protect class sizes or to fend off education cuts threatening to destabilize public education.[10] Whatever government is in power, classroom teachers still rank at the bottom of the pecking order and are often excluded from decision-making processes.

Reinventing the System will involve confronting directly the "fortress" and the "edu-culture" that supports and sustains its authority, as most Education Ministers eventually discover, often to their dismay. Six inhibitors to change identified by Lewington and Orpwood remain virtually unchallenged: the dominance of a rigid, centralized bureaucracy; the focus on managing people and buildings rather than student learning; the confusion and lack of consensus on educational goals; the tendency to excuse declining student results; the impenetrable language or "eduspeak" of the teaching "priesthood"; and the inability of the System to renew itself. International, national, and provincial testing, first introduced in the 1990s, may have produced more measuring of student progress, but with little discernable impact on improving achievement levels. Complacency at the highest levels and the cult of "pretty good" remain very much intact more than two decades on.

Today's school system is an integral part of the modern bureaucratic state, and its influence is so pervasive that it's next to impossible to identify who is actually in charge of running the schools. Former American Education Secretary William Bennett was the first to identify (back in 1987) the existence of a shadowy, comfortable education establishment, which he dubbed, perhaps unfairly, "the blob." The so-called "blob," according to Bennett, was composed of "people (superintendents, district office staff, and school trustees) in the education system who work outside the classrooms, soaking up resources and resisting reform without contributing to student achievement."[11] Provincial systems of education in Canada remain totally dominated by what St. Francis-Xavier University political scientist Peter Clancy aptly termed "the core interests," namely education's insiders – senior provincial officials, superintendents, principals, and in-house consultants.[12]

"Sorry, we seem to be unable to foster any real thirst for knowledge in your kids right now... But we have developed 25 brand-new modules on the Importance of Cultural Safety..."

Figure 0.2 Ministry of Education and the Masses

A satirical look at the modern face of education bureaucracy –
the Ministry of Education. It also lampoons the focus on brand-new
instructional modules to the exclusion of a knowledge-based curriculum.

For Canadian public education in the twenty-first century, there is a better way. Lessons are still to be learned from David Osborne and Ted Gaebler's 1992 book, *Reinventing Government*, one of the best guides to revitalizing public management and public services. The best approach, as expressed by American public administration professor E.S. Savas, of Baruch College, CUNY, is one where governments learn to "steer, not row the boat."[13] In the education sector, that means concentrating on setting the general policy direction and leaving it to others, namely front-line teachers and engaged parents, to sort out the means of getting there. Flipping the system has considerable appeal among front-line teachers, but education reform agendas driven solely by teachers tend to foreclose on the meaningful participation of those served by the system – students, parents, and local communities.[14] A fully inclusive public school system has a place for everyone.

American educator Eric Kalenze, founder of researchED US, comes closer to the mark with his diagnosis and prescription. His 2014 book

Education Is Upside Down seeks to reframe education reform to focus on the right problems – the dominance of unproven theories, flawed instructional practices, misguided systemic reform efforts, and a fundamental misalignment between the educational institution and the society it is intended to serve. Challenging the conventional wisdom of educational progressivism, he calls upon Americans concerned about the plight of public education to turn the whole system right side up.[15]

Bureaucratic rule is alive and well in the System. The gradual fusion of public and private systems has produced a corporate bureaucratic culture that has spread from boardrooms to government and school district offices. The two top layers of education, provincial bureaucrats and school board administrators, still persist in trying not just to set the direction but also to implement it with a web of rules and regulations.[16] Teachers work in a world full of constraints – specifying the preferred curricular philosophy and teaching pedagogy, dictating class sizes and classroom seating configurations, determining which instructional materials to use, when an assembly or announcement will interrupt class, what technology they can access, the quality of professional development, and how often students receive tests and report cards. From a teacher's vantage point, the routines, rules, and expectations come to resemble the bars of a cage in a system that can exhaust teachers' time, passion, and energy. It also explains why so many educators close their doors and keep their heads down.[17]

The System, as it has evolved, is not working for students or teachers in the classroom. Educational gurus spawned by the school improvement industry have succeeded not only in commandeering school districts, but in promoting a succession of curricular and pedagogical changes floating on uncontested theories and urban myths.[18] This trend is most visible in the development and provision of resources by commercial purveyors closely aligned with learning corporations, curriculum developers, and teacher training schools.[19] The recent growth and expansion of researchED among classroom teachers and policy researchers suggests that sound, evidence-based teaching practice is on the upswing and beginning to engage more classroom practitioners.[20]

Top-down education is running its course, and the time has come to re-engineer K–12 education from the schools up. This book makes the case for reconstructing the System by entrusting more to those in the schools better able to respond to local needs and flexible enough to respond to emerging issues and unanticipated problems. For that to happen, the walls must come down, and those closest to students must be given more responsibility for student learning and the quality of public education. It is my hope that this book helps to point us in that direction.

1

A School System under Stress

Public school systems right across Canada are facing big, mostly unspoken challenges on many different fronts. Official education pronouncements and reports produced by provincial ministries of education, reaffirmed by the Council of Ministers of Education, Canada (CMEC), convey the distinct impression that public education is in pretty good shape, obscuring the nature and extent of those challenges. Teaching in today's classrooms, full of children with learning challenges and complex needs, is harder than ever. Many classroom teachers are being asked to do too much with limited time and too few resources. Parents are looking for straight talk about how their children are performing in school. Employers claim that recent graduates cannot read or write properly. Students want a high school education that provides a ticket to those disappearing secure, decently paying jobs. Concerned taxpayers jump on the latest international and provincial student test results and see them as confirmation that they are not getting good value for all those education dollars.[1]

Champions of public education tend to dominate public discussion and exert inordinate influence over the mainstream Canadian media. Provincial education advocacy groups, led by Ontario's People for Education organization, champion the public schools and can be counted upon to support most, if not all, initiatives promising to invest more in the education system based upon the assumption that funding is the solution to most of the system's challenges. Popular books on Canada's K–12 school system embrace those same core assumptions. One of the most recent books, *Pushing the Limits*, published in September 2017, by two educators aligned with People for Education, Kelly Gallagher-Mackay and Nancy Steinhauer, demonstrated the current educational fetish – the pursuit and promotion of "21st century skills." The book had a tone which might be described as "Pollyanna-ish" and it highlighted success stories and trumpeted isolated classroom innovations. Instead of addressing the system's challenges squarely, the book focused on "how our schools [can] prepare children for the challenges of tomorrow." Most of the vignettes tended to reaffirm support for mainstream provincial curriculum initiatives underway, particularly in Ontario, Alberta, and British Columbia.[2]

Futuristic prescriptions such as this are inclined to build upon illusions. The overriding assumption in *Pushing the Limits* is that schools exist to "prepare our students for the future" and to equip them with "21st century skills." One Grade 7 teacher featured in the book, Aaron Warner, promoter of the two-hour-per-week Google Genius Hour, claims that teaching subject content is no longer important because "sixty per cent of the jobs of the future haven't been invented yet."[3] That oft-repeated assertion, it turns out, does not stand up to close scrutiny at all. Two British education researchers, reporting for the BBC, Daisy Christodoulou and Andrew Old, were unable to verify the origin of that factoid, and, based upon their calculations, only 33 percent – not 65 percent – of all jobs today are actually "new," even by the most generous definition. They also point out, quite correctly, that such a claim is insufficient justification for turning the entire school system upside down. When asked whether "21st century skills" would last, Christodoulou responded that, in her judgment, "the alphabet (language) and numbers (numerology)" would outlive us all.[4] Pursuing futuristic generic skills, then, is likely problematic and no substitute for cognitive learning and foundational knowledge in our schools.

What's really wrong with our schools? School systems across Canada are under stress, more intense than it was twenty years ago. Education reform has never been more urgent, nor is the need for an informed public to take more responsibility for turning the system around. It can and should no longer be the preserve of those who currently write, and sometimes manipulate, the education reform agenda. Much as it was two decades ago, those accustomed to running the system, mostly provincial bureaucrats and school district administrators, trumpet a steady succession of "innovations" – often rebranded and recycled initiatives – while holding fast to the traditional bases of the power structure.[5] The shadowy, largely invisible

Appeal to populism

education establishment shows little interest in sharing its authority, engaging the public, or deviating from the command-and-control model of operations. Removing the walls and establishing public accountability will only come through taking back the schools in the public interest, so as to ensure that students, parents, teachers, employers, and local communities are more fully engaged in education policy-making, from the school level up.

Our bureaucratic education system, from the outside looking in, resembles a fortress. Toronto *Globe and Mail* education reporter Jennifer Lewington and York University professor Graham Orpwood produced a revealing diagram likening the Ontario school system in the 1990s to "Fortress Education" – a closed-system world divided into insiders and outsiders. That diagram (Figure 1.1) remains relevant today, more than twenty-five years later. Reforming the K–12 education system involves, to a surprisingly large degree, reclaiming it from these interests. Teachers' unions remain, for the most part, on the outside, except during rare periods when provincial authorities rely heavily on their political support and grant them access to the inner circles. With rare exceptions, the diagram is still useful in explaining how the System acts to guard its boundaries and keep the public at a safe distance.

This simplified model illustrates how provincial school systems tend to operate right across the country, because the School System exhibits common characteristics throughout. First, the insiders operate within a closed, top-down, delineated structure. From Ministry of Education bureaucrats at the top, through school board administrators in the middle, to school principals and teachers in the classroom, all have been socialized though the same career development process to fit the expected mold. Entry into the system is through paper teaching qualifications and moving up the ladder is managed through graduated steps. Moving up the hierarchy, in rank and salary, is generally tied to acquiring additional specialist qualifications. Maintaining that order effectively excludes new blood at management levels and insulates the system against radical ideas that might threaten the status quo. Changing such a system requires overcoming edu-culture and can be next to impossible, as a succession of activist education ministers, in various provinces, have learned over the years.

Second, and equally important, education insiders tend to associate mostly with one another, and not with the outside public, and so the hierarchy tends to shape and circumscribe their professional conduct

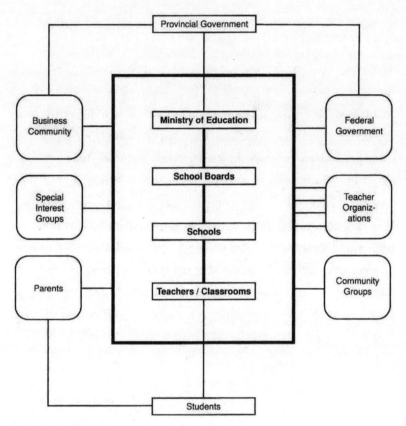

Figure 1.1 Fortress Education: Insiders and Outsiders in Education

A simplified model of the School System and how it actually works, first
presented in Jennifer Lewington and Graham Orpwood, *Overdue Assignment:
Taking Responsibility for Canada's Schools* (1993), 42.

and behaviour. Education policies are set at the top and mostly delivered top-down, in the form of "mandates," the politically correct term
for directives. From their initial teacher training onward, teachers are
schooled to essentially fall in line with both provincial/district mandates and teacher union rules. It is considered unwise and perhaps
risky to speak out of turn or to tell tales out of school. New directions
or ideas, packaged as "innovations," generated at the top, are explained
in greater detail as one moves down the system, until classroom teachers translate them into actual practice. However, ingenious teachers
find ways of circumventing the mandates and confounding the factory
model of school organization. Many educators, at all levels of the

system, can – and do – safely ignore edicts from above. Once the classroom door is closed, it is quite common for teachers to carry on with practices that work.

Third, and finally, parent groups, public interest groups, and business associations are mostly treated as outsiders, especially between provincial and municipal (school board) elections. Since the 1990s, the authority and influence of elected school trustees as public representatives has waned significantly almost everywhere, except in the major metropolitan school boards. School administrators and principals are remarkably skilled at managing and limiting parent engagement and influence at all levels of the system. Parent involvement is carefully managed so as to build support for provincial initiatives and to tap into new sources of funds for enhanced resources. Some of the more effective education advocacy groups, such as People for Education (Ontario, 2003 to 2018) and the Association for Community Living (New Brunswick), enjoy more access, but even their influence tends to be narrowly circumscribed and channelled into support for current or emerging policy initiatives.

Changes in the political winds can make or break education advocacy groups. Ontario's People for Education enjoyed unprecedented access to the Ministry of Education during the fifteen-year run of the Dalton McGuinty–Kathleen Wynne Liberal government. When governments embrace inclusive education, certain advocacy groups, such as Inclusive Education Canada, gain greater influence. Higher math standards advocates associated with the Western Canada Initiative for Strengthening Mathematics (WISE Math) tend to wield more influence when their positions are aligned with the agenda of an incoming regime. Lobbying elected school boards can be frustrating because the remaining regional boards have lost public legitimacy and only allow for set-piece formal delegation presentations. Competing groups petition the elected boards, but it takes a parent uprising to stall, let alone alter, senior staff recommendations, and public meetings rarely provide openings for wide-ranging discussion of major policy matters. While their exact connections vary from province to province, the most effective teachers' unions operate entirely through partnerships forged within the system. When marginalized and excluded or embroiled in bitter contract disputes, teachers' unions resort to direct action, mounting organized protests and mobilizing a range of system partners, including parent and student groups.

FORTRESS EDUCATION

Most of what Lewington and Orpwood identified as the iron rules of protection maintaining "Fortress Education" still hold true. Here they are, slightly reworded to fit in today's education context.

1. *Centralized, rigid bureaucracy*

All Canadian provincial systems exhibit a similar structure, though the degree of centralized control varies from one jurisdiction to another when it comes to producing provincial curricula, overseeing student assessment, and regulating teacher certification. With few deviations, the systems are bureaucratic and unresponsive to parent or public concerns, largely because the province is the sole institution responsible for setting the agenda for schools.[6] Parent concerns and advocacy gradually cracked through the prevailing one-size-fits-all model and alternative school programs began to pop up, mostly in major metropolitan school districts. In the province of Alberta, the ministry of education gave ground in May 1994 by sanctioning a limited number of charter schools, publicly funded and parent-run, but outside the school board system.[7]

Though society changed dramatically over the next twenty-five years, regular high schools and elementary schools remained sheltered and interchangeable, carrying out mandates and delivering a curriculum provided by ministries and branded by regional school districts. The Edmonton Public Schools pioneered the development and implementation of School-Based Management (SBM), decentralizing decision-making to principals and school governing councils. While it sparked studies and pilot projects in Quebec, Nova Scotia, and Newfoundland, education administrators never really embraced the model.[8] School superintendents consolidated their control and successfully staved off any and all restructuring projects aimed at either busting bureaucracy or decentralizing school governance and management.

2. *Resistance to learning and teaching research*

The regular classroom remains a black box protected from, or immune to, the latest research discoveries in teaching and learning.[9] While educational fads come and go, what goes on inside the classroom remains mostly unchanged, sometimes for the better. New theories about how children and teens learn are introduced, then abandoned, in a continuous loop of passing "innovations," leaving a trail of half-baked projects and failed experiments.

A succession of new information technologies, from video projectors to SMART Boards to iPads and mobile devices, have been used mostly to augment traditional teaching methods. Outside innovations such as Khan Academy video lessons and "flipping the classroom" tend to be rejected like poorly executed heart or lung transplants. Many high school subject specialists resist teaching only relevant topics because they find the recommended resources faddish, superficial, and lacking in substance. More recently, teachers are beginning to call into question unproven theories supporting "student-centred" progressive education that tend to denigrate research-proven explicit instruction.

3. Teaching as secular priesthood

Educators – or so it seems from the outside looking in – speak their own unique, almost indecipherable language best described as "edu-speak" and flock together exchanging edu-babble at conferences or on social network sites.[10] Many of the terms appropriated by education professionals, often shortened to acronyms, make it difficult to understand, let alone engage in, the swirl of discussion filling what are now called "education echo chambers." Grasping the meaning of "child-centred learning" is relatively easy compared to confronting the mysteries of popular panaceas such as DI (differentiated instruction), PBL (project-based learning), and SEL (social and emotional learning), and if you find yourself engulfed in the special education world, be prepared for IEP (individualized education plan), ASD (autism spectrum disorder), or Self-Reg (Self-Regulation/Mindfulness). Student reports are rife with learning outcomes language that speaks more to justifying the program of study than how your child is actually performing in the course.

Honest and open discussion of ideas and choices rarely happens when educators seem oblivious to the language barrier. Faddish language tends to breed public mistrust because it plants in the public mind the notion that the system feeds on fads, not facts or substantive knowledge. Education experts and consultants argue incessantly over the same issues, particularly the merits of child-centred learning, the value of PISA tests, and the impact of de-streaming classes, leaving the sometimes-exasperated public on the sidelines.

4. *Stagnation of teacher training and development*

Teaching and learning research lags significantly in Canada, where
– with few exceptions – faculties of education are simply not producing ground-breaking, evidence-based research on critical curricular
and pedagogical issues. Compared to Britain and the United States,
where the education debate has spawned hundreds of governmental
and independent research institutes, Canada continues to show a
dearth of research activity, especially outside the University of Toronto
orbit of the Ontario Institute for Studies in Education (OISE).[11] Most
faculties of education are dominated by mentor teachers with little
or no scholarly research interest or expertise. Our national research
umbrella association, the Society for the Study of Education (CSSE),
sponsors a journal and hosts an annual conference, but most of the
published works consist of small-sample studies addressing micro-
scopic and school- or system-limited topics.

Much of the lively policy debate in K–1 2 education is now generated
by "crossover" research institutes such as the Atlantic Institute for
Market Studies (AIMS), the Canadian Centre for Policy Alternatives
(CCPA), and the Fraser Institute, all operating outside the system. That
is indicative of a central problem – the preoccupations of faculties of
education are disconnected from the concerns of the informed public.

5. *Use and abuse of student results*

Student assessment and standardized testing has expanded greatly
since the early 1990s in all Canadian provinces, except for
Saskatchewan. While public education was once an accountability-
free zone when it came to student performance assessment, provincial
authorities gradually, one at a time, adopted their own province-wide
student testing programs. In the case of Ontario, the predominance
of a child-centred educational philosophy stalled the introduction of
provincial monitoring of student achievement and then the implementation of test-based provincial achievement assessment.[12] Prodded
by the Council of Ministers of Education, Canada (CMEC) under
Dr Paul Cappon, Ontario eventually joined the School Achievement
Indicators Project (SAIP), and senior education bureaucrats, somewhat
reluctantly, responded to active parent advocacy for accountability
for student results. In designing more sophisticated forms of provincial
assessment, education consultants and teacher advisory bodies

attempted to introduce "outcomes-based education" methods and student reports that brushed aside the public's expressed desire for clarity, simplicity, and comparability.

Testing and accountability eventually emerged as the principal means of assessing student progress. Lagging student performance levels, particularly in Alberta and Ontario, raised serious questions about the reliability of teachers' marks in student assessment.[13] Teacher resistance to standardized testing of any kind gradually subsided in the late 1990s, but cross-country comparisons of student performance did not appear until after 2000, and systematic, comparative studies of course content and teaching practices never really materialized. Provincial education ministries, supported by teachers' unions, successfully stymied quality education advocates pushing for the full, government-sanctioned disclosure of student results on a school-by-school basis.[14]

THE TOP-HEAVY AND UNRESPONSIVE SYSTEM

Much of the administrative build-up in the System occurred between 1980 and 1990. In the case of Ontario, the ranks of administrative, non-classroom personnel mushroomed, while the student population grew by only 6 percent. Mandating of provincial programs demanded more supervision, co-ordination, and central office administrative assistance. The number of board consultants and supervisory officers rose by 22 percent, and then jumped by 1993–94 to 27 percent. All of this was on top of the existing complement of board staff responsible for designing and implementing board-specific programs of study and extending special education through the provision of teaching assistants and staff psychologists.[15] That bulge resulted in more and more board employees, employed in and around schools, but not in the classroom.

Deep and intractable conflicts emerged in public education during the 1990s. In early 1993, an Angus Reid / Southam News survey of 1,507 Canadians found that nearly half (46 percent) of those polled believed that the quality of education was worse than it had been twenty-five years earlier. The distinct impression left by this survey, and others that followed every few years, was that the quality of education was on a downward slide. School leaders and educators react defensively to such surveys and, with the best of intentions, busy themselves trying to address the contradictory expectations and

*read
later*

demands of competing interest and advocacy groups,[16] ranging from Ontario's People for Education and Canadian Parents for French (CPF Canada) to the Society for Quality Education (SQE Canada). In spite of the efforts of teachers, school administrators, and board members, the conflict over conflicting priorities remains unresolved and feeds public cynicism. Parents and students as well as educators are caught in a world of educational paradox.

Far too many parents are kept at a distance and feel unwelcome when they approach their schools with questions or concerns. Our school system, in theory and on paper, attempts to reach out and involve them in the education process. Under pressure to be more open and transparent, schools everywhere purport to favour parent involvement and many attempt to listen to parents and to seek their advice. It is now common for school principals to enlist parent advisory councils or parent volunteers in drafting school improvement plans. One of the most popular buzzwords is "partnership" and it is used to demonstrate a willingness to overcome the usual divide of "them" versus "us" separating parents and teachers. It works as long as parents accept the limits of parent involvement and respect the defined parameters.[17] Those who seek genuine engagement quickly discover the limits of parent participation and either find themselves marginalized or become frustrated and drop by the wayside.

Public satisfaction with the System can be difficult to gauge, and the best-known annual survey, conducted by the Ontario Institute for Studies in Education (OISE), is limited to Ontario. The fortieth annual OISE Survey of Educational Issues, released in June 2018, provided some indication of a continuing decline in satisfaction with schools.[18] In 2012, some two-thirds of those surveyed reported that they were satisfied with the school system, but by 2017, the figure had declined sharply to half of respondents. Overall, Ontario public satisfaction levels have declined to levels not seen since the mid-1990s, and that was most clearly reflected in the erosion of satisfaction with teachers' performance. In 2017, just over half (54 percent) were satisfied with the job teachers are doing, down from over two-thirds in 2015. Public support for higher spending on schools had also fallen sharply, and most parents reported seeing little or no increased emphasis on mathematics in their school communities in spite of this being identified as a province-wide curriculum priority. In hindsight, these were possibly early signs of a growing discontent that provided fertile ground

Table 1.1
Public Satisfaction with the School System and Teachers' Performance, 1980–2017

| | PUBLIC | | | PARENTS | | |
| | Percentage Satisfied with System and Teachers' Performance | | | Percentage Satisfied with System and Teachers' Performance | | |
Year	System	Teachers	Count	System	Teachers	Count
1980	51	–	–	–	–	–
1982	55	–	1050	–	–	–
1986	42	–	1042	–	–	–
1988	36	–	1011	–	–	–
1990	47	–	1032	–	–	–
1996	50	–	1000	–	–	–
1998	44	62	1007	51	65	317
2000	44	63	1002	50	67	271
2002	43	67	1054	53	71	317
2004	56	69	1002	64	72	228
2007	61	68	1001	69	69	207
2009	63	67	747	70	71	266
2012	65	70	1016	77	76	284
2015	60	69	753	70	77	206
2017	50	53	1529	61	58	419

The OISE survey for 2018 entitled *Public Attitudes Toward Education in Ontario* provided an overview of public satisfaction trends from 1998 to 2017. Public satisfaction with the system and with teachers dropped between 2015 and 2017 to 50 percent and 53 percent respectively, as did parent satisfaction, which stood at 61 percent and 58 percent.

Source: OISE 2018.

for the June 2018 Doug Ford–inspired populist upheaval with its explicit "back-to-basics" education agenda.

Students who occupy the mainstream rarely encounter the paradox affecting a sizable proportion of the student population. Millions of education dollars are spent on communications campaigns and programs designed to make schools inviting, stimulating, and engaging places for students. Yet, for far too many, the daily reality is quite different. Boredom, indifference, and low expectations are still all too common. In a 1991 survey of school leavers, Statistics Canada found that three out of ten students cited boredom as their main reason for leaving school before graduation.[19] For former home-educated students such as Zander Sherman, author of the 2012 book *The Curiosity of School*, institutionalized education, and particularly high school, has a deadening effect on human creativity. While graduation rates are climbing, surprising numbers of graduates enter college, university, and the workplace with marginal skills. Today one in ten Canadian students at graduation have "a capacity to deal only with simple, clear material involving uncomplicated tasks."[20]

Classroom teachers and school principals, occupying the educational front lines, confront their own paradox. A majority of teachers, right across Canada, complain that their voices are not heard in a system that, on the surface, promises consultation and involvement on class-room issues and conditions that affect the quality of learning for all students. Only 17 percent of 17,000 teachers surveyed in 1992 by Queen's University researchers felt they had "meaningful dialogue" with government over education issues.[21] Increasingly, teachers feel singled out and held responsible for the system's deficiencies, and can become alienated in a system that expects them to be system champions and advocates, especially to parents, for what happens in today's increasingly complex and challenging classrooms. Teaching the way teachers aspire to teach seems to be getting more difficult. A May 2012 national Canadian Teachers' Federation survey, poll-ing 4,700 teachers, identified the main obstacles impeding teacher effectiveness and job satisfaction.[22] Most expressed concern over the encroachments on teacher autonomy and the loss of control caused by a variety of factors, including provincial mandates, standardized testing, and more complex class composition.

SIGNS OF DISSATISFACTION AND DISSENT

Today the school population is gradually declining, and, when it comes to publicly funded schools, parents and students are beginning to vote with their feet. The Canadian K–12 school-age population has now dropped below 5 million students, and the number of Canadians aged 5 to 17 attending school declined by 6.6 percent from 2000 to 2015. Over that fifteen-year period, every province except Alberta (up 11.6 percent) recorded a decline in its school-age population. While public schools remain the dominant form of educational provision in all ten provinces across Canada, student enrolment in independent and alternative schools is steadily growing. Where funded or tax-subsidized independent schools are available, as in British Columbia and Quebec, non-public school enrolments now exceed 12 percent of the total population. In Alberta, the only province authorizing direct-grant charter schools, the proportion of parents choosing alternative schools is growing rapidly, including the independent sector, which grew from 2005 to 2015 by 40 percent to 4.4 percent overall.[23]

Dissent with mainstream public education is more pronounced in rural and small-town Canada. Outside the major metropolitan centres, the system not only exemplifies but promulgates a dominant metro-centric outlook. Although only about one in five Canadians lives in a rural community (in Atlantic Canada and the Prairie West, it is more than two in five), most Canadian schools are still found in rural areas. Today small rural schools are under threat, very often depicted by school authorities as declining, inefficient, and old-fashioned locations for the education of modern children. For more than a century, Acadia University's Michael Corbett reminds us, they have been targeted as "places in need of modernization, reform, professionalization, specialization and greater efficiency." The very strengths of smaller schools, urban as well as rural – their embeddedness in community and their deep, supportive educational relationships – stand in defiance of an expanding bureaucratic school system.[24] Not only is there little evidence to support the case that small schools are either more expensive to run or inferior in programs, but, given that many serve disadvantaged communities, a strong case can be made that they produce more successful graduates and better life outcomes.

Today's major metropolitan school systems have grown so large that they resemble a colossus from the outside. Canada's largest school system, the Toronto District School Board (TDSB), is the fourth biggest in North America and dwarfs all others in its sheer size and scale of operations. Formed in 1998 through the amalgamation of six Toronto-area boards, the TDSB is a $3.2 billion operation with some 246,000 students attending nearly 600 schools. Of these schools, 451 offer elementary education, 102 offer secondary-level education, and there are five adult day schools. The TDSB also operates 16 alternative elementary schools as well as 20 alternative secondary schools. The gigantic system employs some 31,000 permanent and 8,000 temporary staff, including 10,000 elementary school teachers and 5,800 at the secondary level.[25] Ten years ago, then–Ontario Education Minister Kathleen Wynne, a former TDSB trustee, claimed that the board's size did not allow it to operate "in an agile way," that student test scores lagged compared to other boards, and that decision-making at the top was more difficult. When the TDSB faced a leadership crisis in January 2015, critics, most notably Dr Charles Pascal of OISE, claimed that the TDSB was dysfunctional in its board leadership and too big to operate effectively.[26] Managing such an education behemoth continues to pose challenges, and serious questions remain about its capacity to be flexible and agile in response to parent concerns and student needs at the school level.

Underlying dissatisfaction with K–12 education periodically erupts into a full-blown backlash against the prevailing ideology of "progressive" reform and the unwavering commitment to invest more heavily in support of existing programs. One prime example of that populist resistance was the meteoric rise to power in June 2018 of the Ontario Progressive Conservative government of Doug Ford, ending fifteen years of Liberal rule.[27] Campaigning with the slogan "Ford for the People," he pledged to reform the school curriculum, defend provincial testing, introduce a moratorium on school closures, and consult more with disaffected communities. Most of these planks in the Ontario PC education "promise package" were presented in plain and simple language that appropriated "back-to-basics" philosophy and "common-sense" reform.[28]

The Doug Ford government's educational philosophy not only represented a complete rejection of the Toronto-centric vision of the Wynne Liberal government, but took dead aim at what was labelled an "education-guru–driven" brand of "identity politics" in education.[29] "At one time, Ontario schools focused on teaching the skills that matter: reading, writing and math," the PC manifesto declared. "This approach helped to prepare our kids for the challenges of work and life. Today, however, more and more of our schools have been turned into social laboratories and our kids into test subjects for whatever special interests and so-called experts that have captured Kathleen Wynne's ear." The "Ford Nation" appeal tapped into a groundswell of public dissent over top-down decision-making and the tendency to exclude parents favouring higher standards, teaching the fundamentals, or making sex education the sole prerogative of parents rather than schools. That view was expressed in no-nonsense fashion: "By ignoring parents and focusing on narrow agendas or force-feeding our kids experimental curricula like 'Discovery Math' the Liberals are leaving our children woefully unprepared to compete with other students from across Canada and around the world. And instead of helping our kids pass their tests, the NDP want to cancel the tests altogether."[30] Whatever one might think of the Ford education agenda, it did not spring out of nowhere.

Figure 1.2 Doug Ford Populism in Action, Tillsonburg, Ontario, May 2018

Doug Ford's 2018 "For the People" campaign mobilized "Ford Nation" and attracted throngs in rural Ontario communities such as Tillsonburg in the heart of Conservative south-western Ontario.

Student preparedness for university or college is also being called into question. An April 2019 study conducted at four Ontario universities – York, Western, Waterloo, and Toronto – provided troubling evidence that secondary schools were falling significantly short in providing graduates with the necessary academic skills to succeed in post-secondary education.[31] Initially administered in late 2017 to 22,000 York University undergraduates, the questionnaire was then conducted a year later at the three other universities, yielding similar results. The key findings: only about 44 percent of students felt they had the generic skills needed to do well in their academic studies; some 41 percent were classified as at-risk because of limited levels of basic academic skills; and 16 percent lacked almost all of the skills needed for higher education. More than one-third of the professors interviewed reported that fewer than 10 percent of their students were "fully engaged." Four out of five professors said that they had dumbed down their course work and reduced the frequency and difficulty of assignments. "Students with high self-esteem based on false feedback [in high school]," the authors claim, "are much more difficult to teach because many cannot take criticism without assuming it is personal." The research merely corroborated the earlier findings of

James Côté and Anton L. Allahar's 2007 book *Ivory Tower Blues*.[32]
It all raised serious questions about not only the quality of high school
education, but the impact on universities of pushing up high school
graduation rates.

Education officialdom has refined the art of putting a shine on the
apple and concealing any imperfections. Concerned parents, special
needs advocates, private-sector employers, and threatened school
communities grumble and complain that the education bureaucracy
does not listen to them. Classroom teachers, speaking out-of-school
and on social media,regularly express frustration over feeling powerless in a system that imposes mandates and ignores their concerns.[33]
Small-school advocates are fighting rural and small-town school
closures and actively resisting the incursion of district consolidation
and metrocentric forces threatening the very existence of their communities.[34] When and where education consultation occurs, or official
surveys are administered, the framing of the questions and the top-
down nature of that engagement tend to promote or deepen public
skepticism about the hidden motives of system thinkers. Consumers
of public education, when asked directly, express rising levels of either
dissatisfaction or skepticism about whether the system is delivering
on its promises.[35] That's why the system is now under stress.

2

Shaping of the System

The Modern Bureaucratic Education State
in Formation, 1920–93

Today's modern bureaucratic education state did not emerge, fully formed, out of nowhere. Massive administrative reorganization can be traced back to the origins of school consolidation at the turn of the twentieth century. With the advent of the Consolidated Schools Project between 1903 and 1905, launched by Montreal tobacco manufacturer William Macdonald and agricultural scientist James W. Robertson of Ottawa's National Experimental Farm, the one-room schoolhouse era gradually yielded to larger units of administration (regional school districts) and more centralized schools offering a wider range of educational services.[1] While Macdonald and Robertson set the wheels in motion, larger-scale school consolidation, spearheaded by provincial authorities, did not really materialize until the period between 1913 and 1919.[2] A broader Canadian movement toward what was termed the "Larger Unit," encompassing administrative centralization and the consolidation of schools, began gathering steam from the 1920s onward and achieved dominance from the early post-war years to the late 1960s.[3] Driven by the arrival of the post-war Baby Boom children, provincial school systems modernized and ballooned in the 1960s, taking on much of their present-day form. The creation of a unified Quebec Ministry of Education (MEQ) in 1964 marked the beginning of the end of an ecclesiastical system and brought Quebec more into line with other Canadian provinces.[4] What emerged in this transformation was the modern Canadian bureaucratic education state.

State schooling, in each of Canada's provinces, was the product of an earlier phase of state formation, conceived as modernist initiatives to bring social order to the populace and serving to advance what

Ian McKay has termed "the project of liberal rule."[5] While state schooling had its origins in the 1840s, centralization (and the attendant full-scale bureaucratization) was largely a creature of the fifty-year period from the 1940s to the 1990s. This phase represented, in my view, the triumph of the modern bureaucratic liberal state.[6] School consolidation expanded as the outward manifestation of state expansion, drawing sustenance from expanding school enrolment levels until the mid-1970s, and then became a matter of financial necessity amidst a phase of radically contracting enrolment. Ontario's Royal Commission on Learning from 1993 to 1995 may well have been the tipping point, alerting provincial politicians, parents, and citizens to the hard reality that the system functioned much like a fortress – well-funded and bloated at the centre, but not particularly accountable to students, parents, or anyone.[7] It all proved to be a harbinger of the more recent wave of bureaucratic management, student testing, and accountability, often labelled "neo-liberal reform."

SCHOOL CONSOLIDATION AND THE RISE OF THE LARGER UNIT

The gradual migration of rural people to urban places after 1920 gave rise to a wave of consolidation into larger units of administration, signalling the beginning of the end of small, mostly one-room rural schools. Teachers' college officials such as W.E. MacPherson, writing in 1924, identified what was known as "the rural school problem."[8] Educational commissions in Manitoba (1923) and later in British Columbia (1938) identified wide rural-urban disparities and recommended changes, including complete provincial tax support for education and the elimination of small administrative units. The Saskatchewan government fell into line, passing the *Larger School Units Act* in 1944 and, one year later, placing all northern schools in one giant administrative district, funded entirely by the province.

The appeal of larger organizational units, along with the financial difficulties besetting poor rural districts, gave impetus to the Alberta consolidation drive. In 1929, Perren Baker, Alberta's Minister of Education under the U.F.A. government, attempted in vain to reorganize the province's 150 school districts into twenty large divisions.[9] The reorganization was eventually implemented by the Social Credit government of William Aberhart, which swept into office in 1935 committed to the large-unit scheme. A "Consolidation College" was

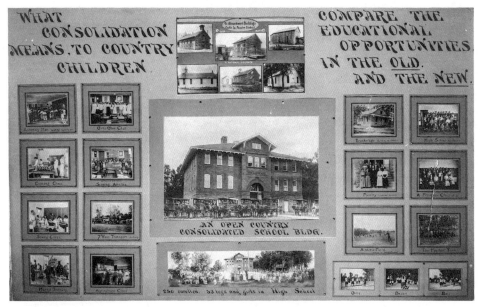

Figure 2.1 A "Consolidation College" Exhibit Poster, 1936

A poster depicting the Consolidation College's activities aimed at educating "country folk" about the advantages of merging schools.

established in 1936, and it featured a touring exhibit extolling the advantages of the "new" system over the "old" one for "country children." The division system was introduced, and in 1937, 774 rural districts were amalgamated into 11 divisions; by 1941, school governance was organized into 50 large divisions. In 1950, Alberta's *County Act* gave county councils the powers of divisional school boards, and by 1965, 28 county boards had been established.[10]

School consolidation came to the fore in Nova Scotia in November 1938 when the Council of Public Instruction initiated a Commission on the Larger School Unit. It reported that, as of 1940, the provincial school system remained predominantly rural and still essentially organized in one-room school sections. Of the province's 1,758 total school sections, 1,490 (84.7 percent) were rural sections, 233 (13.3 percent) were village sections, and 45 (2.5 percent) were urban, located in incorporated towns and cities. The fate of the one-room schools would ultimately come down to a matter of dollars and cents. The financial advantages of consolidation were presented without any reference to social costs in terms of lost identity or community stability.

In 1946, Nova Scotia's Angus L. Macdonald government followed up with a plan to develop a provincial system of rural and regional high schools. Consolidating schools and centralizing administrative facilities to achieve financial efficiencies became official Nova Scotia Department of Education dogma after the publication of the 1954 Pottier Commission report. The old one-school sections, with boundaries dating from the founding of the Common School system in 1864–65, were eventually swept away.[11] Despite the existence of a fair number of school officials championing consolidation, public opinion in rural Nova Scotia and elsewhere remained steadfast in its support of the small, local unit of organization.

TRANSFORMATION OF TEACHER ORGANIZATION – GROWTH OF TEACHERS' UNIONS

School consolidation and administrative centralization had a ripple effect and it directly affected teacher organizations. The first teachers' unions emerged alongside, and almost in parallel with, the organizational evolution of the System. While teachers began to organize in the 1890s, the first province-wide unions and national organizations did not appear until the period from 1918 to 1920, sparked in some cases by the labour activism of the Winnipeg General Strike.[12] In Ontario, the first teachers' labour union to be formed was the Federation of Women Teachers' Associations of Ontario (FWTAO) in 1918, closely followed in 1919 by the Ontario Secondary School Teachers' Federation (OSSTF). Male public school teachers explored working with the OSSTF, but were ultimately left to form a union of their own, the Ontario Public School Male Teachers' Federation (OPSMTF).[13] The predominance of small schools in rural districts posed organizational challenges and, in the early years, membership was voluntary, so the numbers were thin in many jurisdictions.

A fledgling national organization got its start in October 1919 when four teachers from British Columbia and Manitoba took time out from a Conference on Education, Character and Citizenship to meet in a "little lumber room" at the Winnipeg Board of Trade. In the year that followed, the prime movers, Henry Charlesworth of the British Columbia Teachers' Federation and E.K. Marshall of the Manitoba Teachers' Federation, set out to establish a federation of teacher organizations in the Western provinces. A founding meeting was held on 27 July 1920 at the Calgary Public Library, attended by Western representatives and two delegates from Ontario. The Western alliance was set aside in favour of a national organization with support from Quebec and the Maritime provinces. Out of that gathering emerged the Canadian Teachers' Federation (CTF), which claimed an initial membership of 9,000 teachers. Incorporated under the Companies' Act in 1948, the CTF opened its central office in January 1948, staffed by a full-time secretary-treasurer.[14]

A critical turning point for teacher organization came with their formal recognition as a profession with the legal right to levy membership dues. In the case of Ontario, that came in 1944 when the Ontario Conservative government of George Drew passed the *Teaching Profession Act*. The Ontario Teachers' Federation (OTF) replaced the Ontario Teachers' Council and included L'association des enseignants francontariens (AEFO) and the Ontario English Catholic Teachers' Association (OECTA) as affiliates. Most significantly, it conferred "statutory recognition to the federations as professional organizations" and made membership in the unions mandatory for all Ontario teachers.[15] With membership fees secured, teachers' unions were able to match the organizational muscle of provincial and regional education authorities.

The closure of one-room schoolhouses and the transition to modern classrooms profoundly altered the working lives of teachers, and teacher organizations responded by establishing larger professional offices and more extensive professional services and programs. In the case of Alberta, the phenomenal growth of the school system from 1950 to 1968 was reflected in the size of the teacher force and in higher salary scales. In 1950, Alberta enrolled 173,000 students in 2,136 elementary and secondary schools taught by some 6,500 teachers earning an average salary of $2,500. By 1959, the student population had grown to 273,000 attending 1,318 schools, taught by 11,000 teachers who earned $4,700 a year. The centralization of school facilities exerted a profound impact. Out of 1,545 one-room schools in 1950, there were only about 275 remaining by 1959. School board budgets soared from $29 million in 1950 to over $85 million in 1959.[16] Teacher contract negotiations were conducted on a much larger scale. When the Alberta Teachers' Association celebrated its fiftieth anniversary in 1968, it did so in much larger provincial headquarters at Barnett House in the west end of Edmonton.[17] This was another transformation associated with the growth of the modern education state.

ADMINISTRATIVE CENTRALIZATION AND ITS PROGENY –
SCHOOL FINANCE AND FACILITIES PLANNING

School consolidation gradually came to be seen by the rising class of school finance managers as an organizational panacea. Much of the rationale for, and momentum behind, consolidation was driven by a new breed of North American educational planners. Foremost among them was Dr Edgar Morphet, a leading American professor of educational administration who rose to be Chief of School Finance in the US Office of Education. Morphet exerted considerable influence on Canadian education planners and administrators. His papers and textbooks extolled the virtues of larger administrative units and school consolidation.[18] Morphet's planning principles and models were widely accepted and embraced by aspiring principals and administrators, as demonstrated in a 1969 Atlantic Provinces Development Board paper.[19] In applying educational finance principles, he and his academic disciples did much to entrench a new bureaucratic ideology based upon economies of scale, operational efficiency, optimal school size, and the allocation of pupil places. It was top-down organizational planning in its rawest form.

School system expansion and district consolidation produced the first generation of senior education administrators. One of those, Wesley C. Lorimer, superintendent of Winnipeg School Division No. 1 from 1953 to 1966, epitomized the new class of bureaucratic leaders who guided the transition from a collection of schools to an integrated system.[20] While overseeing the Winnipeg school district, he confronted and tackled major organizational challenges, including an unprecedented explosion in student numbers, a lack of adequate facilities to accommodate the boom, a shortage of qualified teachers, the reorganization of the administration, and provincial efforts to change the district's boundaries. Without much public fanfare, Lorimer preserved, protected, and strengthened the division by creating a favourable public image, building his own leadership cadre, and cultivating support among external constituencies, including the province and the Winnipeg Chamber of Commerce.

One of Morphet's Canadian disciples was Professor George E. Flower of Toronto's Ontario Institute for Studies in Education, a staunch advocate of larger school districts. He welcomed the prevailing trend toward larger local education authorities with their advantages for financial control and educational planning. In 1964, he published a widely read textbook, *How Big Is Too Big?* and adopted that theme for his Quance Public Lecture that year on the challenges facing public education.[21] Reacting to the common criticism that smaller units fostered closer personal relationships, he began to argue that public accountability could be decentralized and preserved within the larger local unit. "Larger and fewer school districts," he wrote in December 1967, were the wave of the future as the "tiny horse-and-buggy district" gave way to "the larger motor-car area." Every possible objection to "bigness" was summarily dismissed, even public concerns that larger districts were "too monolithic, too impersonal," and he relished the prospect of "greater centralization" in the form of provincial control over local school authorities.[22]

THE "BIGGER IS BETTER" PHILOSOPHY, SCHOOL REORGANIZATION, AND SYSTEM EXPANSION

The "Bigger Is Better" philosophy in education gave a powerful, unrelenting impetus to the next phase of massive school consolidation. This consolidation movement was signalled by the introduction of regional schools, a modernist invention marking the arrival of what John Kenneth Galbraith once called the "technostructure"[23] and only compounding the problem of rural depopulation. Such bureaucratic systems and ways of thinking were highly incompatible with the prevailing values in most local communities. It took a young economics professor, Jim McNiven, to see, back in 1978, that the advance of systematized forms of organization, including larger school districts, was a harbinger of fundamental social change. "School reorganization," he contended, exemplified "a multi-faceted attempt to remould the nature of rural society, and failing that, to depopulate those rural areas where resistance to this process is greatest."[24]

Ontario experienced what Robin S. Harris aptly described as a "Quiet Evolution" in public education.[25] After the unceremonious shelving of a 1950 Royal Commission report produced by Justice John A. Hope, calling for major restructuring, organizational change came gradually, in stages. Under Minister of Education and later Premier John Robarts (1959–62), a massive school building boom was initiated and the high school program completely organized into three divisions: academic; commercial; and science, technology, and trades. His successor, William G. Davis, presided over a massive integrated K–13 education budget, and authorized the establishment of the Ontario Institute for Studies in Education (1965) and a new community college system, known as the Colleges of Applied Arts and Technology. The school system was regionalized, with townships as the smallest units of administration, and as of January 1969, county-size school boards were established, promising a greater range of program services in rural communities.[26] Even though the June 1968 report *Living and Learning*, popularly known as the Hall-Dennis Report, spelled the end of the Robarts Plan of 1962 and encouraged more "child-centred learning," the trend toward regionalization and bureaucratic management remained unabated.

Maritime advocates of the Larger School District model drew inspiration from New Brunswick's 1962 Royal Commission on Finance and Municipal Taxation. The Byrne Commission proposed a sweeping reorganization of that province's school system. It recommended a drastic reduction in the number of school districts from 422 to just thirty-three, and the total takeover by the province of the funding of education. The Louis Robichaud government endorsed the plan in January 1962 and gave it a name, The Programme of Equal Opportunity. In the Maritimes, New Brunswick would lead the way in consolidating the entire system, cutting back significantly on the responsibilities of local school authorities.[27] The Byrne-Robichaud plan drew heavy critical fire as a centralizing scheme but was implemented after Robichaud won re-election in October 1967. It was welcomed by consolidators such as Flower as a needed dose of "fiscal reality" which would "make sure that total available revenues for education" were "expended equitably over the whole province." The appealing popular mantra of equitable "educational opportunity for all" was beginning to morph into "one-size-fits-all" to provide "educational value for every dollar spent."[28]

Nova Scotia responded with a Comprehensive School System Plan of its own. Larger school units were identified as the solution for many of the system's ills, particularly at the senior and junior high school levels. In 1968, Premier G.I. Smith's government passed legislation to permit the amalgamation of school boards in selected regions designated as "amalgamation areas." Municipal authorities were authorized to enter into negotiations aimed at securing amalgamation agreements.[29] Instead of imposing a New Brunswick–style regime, the province attempted to "broker" agreements between the Urban and Rural School Boards Association and the Nova Scotia Teachers' Union. Unlike New Brunswick, Nova Scotia inched toward "unified comprehensive services" through a protracted series of negotiations. The "let's make a deal" approach guided by Education Minister Gerald Doucet secured compliance while ruffling fewer feathers.[30]

In Prince Edward Island, the long-delayed consolidation of schools was achieved through a virtual "educational revolution" aimed at eliminating small rural schools and extending high school education. A Royal Commission on educational finance again laid the groundwork. After years of vacillation, Conservative Premier Walter Shaw finally moved to build a network of regional comprehensive and vocational high schools, and by 1963, fifteen rather standardized brick-box high schools were scattered across the Island.[31] A youthful and dynamic Liberal premier, Alex Campbell, toppled the Shaw government in July 1966 and unleashed a torrent of organizational change, thereby stirring up an Island hornet's nest. A Toronto-based firm, Acres Research and Planning, guided by researcher Dr Alan F. Brown of OISE, produced an August 1967 consultant's report which claimed that the public school system was full of antiquated one-room schools. Out of 25,265 elementary school children, nearly 16,000 attended schools judged physically inadequate.[32]

PEI's Comprehensive Development Plan, guided by General Manager Del Gallagher, plowed ahead with a ten-year timetable (1966 to 1976) eliminating all 252 one-room schools and all 258 two-to-five-roomers, sending shock waves through many villages and rural communities. For a whole generation of students, consolidation brought a first encounter with school buses, children of other faiths, and schoolyard cuss words.[33] In the case of PEI, the number of districts was slashed from over 400 to 5, sweeping away the province's deeply rooted one-room school system.

STRUCTURAL REFORM – QUEBEC'S QUIET REVOLUTION IN EDUCATION

Significant structural change came to Quebec state education in the 1960s. In April 1963, a Quebec Commission of Inquiry on Education, headed by Msgr Alphonse Parent, vice-rector of Laval University, charted the course. After seven months of public hearings, 325 individual briefs, and junkets across North America and into Europe, Parent and his eight fellow commissioners recommended the creation of a Quebec Ministry of Education. In merging the existing Council of Public Instruction with the Department of Youth in the new mega-department later that year, Quebec began its transition to a more secular, modernized education state.[34] Swept up in the buoyant spirit of the so-called Quiet Revolution, most Quebeckers welcomed the change, responding favourably to this modernization project without worrying about its potential, largely unintended consequences.

Establishing a Quebec Ministry of Education was a response to grave public concerns being voiced about the former education regime. The mounting criticism can be traced back to a stinging 3 November 1959 letter to the newspaper *Le Devoir*, written by an obscure Catholic brother using the name "Frère Untel" (Brother Anonymous) to protect his identity, and blaming the schools for being archaic and out of touch with the emerging modern urban industrial society. Five months later, encouraged by *Le Devoir* editor André Laurendeau, the vocal priest expanded his critique in *Les insolences du Frère Untel* (*The Impertinences of Brother Anonymous*).[35] This *cri de coeur* tapped into deep discontent over the excesses of clerical rule, selling 100,000 copies in the first four months. Laying aside the "delicate" and "nostalgic" temperament of his religious order, Brother Anonymous claimed that the Department of Public Instruction, controlled by clerics, was insular and inefficient and, for twenty years, had failed to provide "civic or patriotic education." He called for closing the old Department and retiring the officials with new medals, including one for "Solemn Mediocrity." Overall, he claimed that religious authority had produced pious, isolated teachers and bred a fear of liberty and freedom of expression. "Education for Heaven" was not good enough and, according to Brother Anonymous, only served to perpetuate what he termed "shrivelled, timid, ignorant Catholicism reduced to a morality" that retarded social advancement.[36]

Elected with the famous slogan *il faut que ça change* ("It has to change"), Jean Lesage and his Liberal government did succeed in modernizing Quebec public education between 1960 and 1966.[37] Under a new Minister, Paul Gerin-Lajoie, a series of educational reforms were initiated that not only laid the foundations for a modern education state, but also closed the gap between Quebec and other Canadian provinces. Government grants were made available to school boards; all parents, not just property owners, secured the right to vote in school board elections; compulsory school attendance was extended by a year to age fifteen; free public education was finally extended to the end of high school; and initial moves were made to improve technical and vocational education.[38]

Figure 2.2 Creation of Quebec Ministry of Education: Paul Gerin-Lajoie
Quebec's Minister of Education Paul Gerin-Lajoie unveils the new school system
organization, 1964.

The key Quebec education reform initiative, Bill 60 (1964), placed
education more directly under civil rather than religious authority,
but measures still had to pass through the Superior Council of
Education, where the old Catholic and Protestant clerical elites still
held sway. Subsequent reports from the Parent Commission, issued
in 1964 and 1965, paved the way for a reorganization of elementary
and secondary education, and the establishment of a new polyvalent
college system, later named *Collèges d'enseignement générale et pro-
fessionale* and commonly called CEGEPs. While the Lesage reforms
met stiff resistance and eventually sank the government, the education
reforms survived. In 1967, the Superior Council approved the "neutral
state" system recommended by the Parent Commission, and in June
of that year, all schools were given the right to declare, within one
year, whether they wished to remain denominational. Religious

instruction was made optional at the secondary level, but remained at the core of the elementary curriculum, unless parents chose to exempt their children.[39] General implementation of a more secular school system, while underway, would take considerable time to come to full fruition.

SYSTEM EXPANSION – THE BABY BOOM AND THE "THREE BS" – BIGGER, BETTER, BUREAUCRACY

School consolidation in PEI represented a radical shift, but in Canada's urban and suburban communities bureaucratic forms of school organization and management grew more naturally out of post-war prosperity and expansion. Major metropolitan areas came to be served by mammoth, sprawling school bureaucracies.

The emergence of the Dartmouth, Nova Scotia school system provides a typical example. Up until 1960, Dartmouth was an incorporated town – and the Town and the outlying suburbs operated their own schools. The completion of the Angus L. Macdonald Bridge spurred a Dartmouth population explosion and gradually changed the small-town atmosphere. The days of long line-ups and daily conversations at the Dartmouth Ferry dock came to an end. School consolidation in the booming municipality of Dartmouth did not come easily. Beneath the veneer of solidarity, local Dartmouth councillors were unsettled by the bewildering changes and muttered about "losing a feeling of family" in the old town. Mayor I.W. Akerley rose above the fray, forged alliances, and pursued consolidation with vigour. His successor, Mayor Joe Zatzman, promoted system expansion from a businessman's point of view.[40] The biggest test came in 1966–67 with amalgamation of the former Catholic schools and integration of the oft-forgotten Department of National Defence schools. School board politics added to the unpredictability, especially after elections, when half the municipal representatives might turn over. School superintendents such as Carmen F. Moir of Dartmouth came to exert considerable influence over an increasingly complex, bureaucratic local education system.[41]

School promoters and consolidators in the 1960s and early 1970s believed that "Bigger Is Better" in public education. School superintendents in Canada, with few exceptions, accepted the trend toward larger administrative units and were completely swept up in modernizing the entire school system. Swollen student enrolment, driven by the arrival of the Baby Boom generation, produced massive expansion, raising concerns about the rising cost of education. Cost-conscious Canadians were concerned about bringing a system that now consumed a much greater share of taxes under some kind of control.[42] Further school system consolidation was spurred in the 1960s by the need to wring more operational efficiency out of a system growing like an untended weed. In all Canadian provinces, elementary and secondary education came under more direct provincial control and the number of school districts was reduced drastically.

CHALLENGING THE NEW ORTHODOXY
OF MODERNIZATION

Most political leaders and education bureaucrats in Canada's English-speaking provinces heralded the modern education state as the wave of the present and future, but a few scholars did begin challenging the orthodoxy. One of the first academics to do so was an American revisionist educational historian, Professor Michael B. Katz. After recently arriving at the Ontario Institute for Studies in Education (OISE) from Harvard University, he wrote a controversial 1968 article calling into question the ideology and objectives of modern public education.[43] His fresh perspective not only cut against the grain of the Canadian educational establishment, it also encouraged a flurry of critical thinking. Small bands of academic skeptics, based in Toronto at OISE or associated with *This Magazine Is about Schools*, began to question their previous assumptions about the beneficence of public education.

Traditional education historians such as Willard Brehaut saw the Ontario system as the "House of Ryerson," a universal, free, publicly accessible system of schools built upon the common school edifice created by the first superintendent, Egerton Ryerson.[44] Katz proposed a new way of looking at the origin and motives of publicly funded education. In "Class, Bureaucracy and Schools," he contended that school reform since the mid-1900s had actually been driven by "conservative social forces" who created and upheld a system expressing and reflecting their aspirations, fears, and interests. Public school systems, he argued, represented "the attempt of the 'better people' to do something to the rest." From the 1880s onward, Ryerson's Ontario model, like its American counterpart, had assumed a fixed form, remarkably resistant to change. The whole system exemplified the following core characteristics, as expressed in Katz's words: "it was universal, tax-supported, free, compulsory, bureaucratic, class-based, and racist."[45] From the beginning, the school system promoted middle-class or "bourgeois" social values, and favoured bureaucratic regulation over the fostering of individual rights. While public school promoters professed to support "equal opportunity" for all, Katz claimed that they acted differently, favouring bureaucracy as a means of controlling or strictly limiting the potential for social mobility among the common people.

CONFRONTING THE EDUCATIONAL BULLDOZER –
LOCAL RESISTANCE TO CONSOLIDATION

Few Canadians were influenced by Katz and the academic skeptics, but similar sentiments were voiced by those local citizens steamrolled by the educational bulldozer otherwise known as school consolidation. Closing down schoolhouses and introducing families to the joys of school bus transportation aroused anger, frustration, and feelings of powerlessness in many small communities.[46] Education critic Richard Wilbur, a well-known writer-broadcaster in Caraquet, New Brunswick, voiced his deep concern in 1970 about the aim and orientation of a school system preparing high school students for "factory jobs." Aligning himself with rural New Brunswickers, he was skeptical about "mass education" and the centralization of school services in designated "growth centres" far removed from the heart of the rural and small-town Maritimes.[47]

Most teachers were rooted in, and often strongly attached to, the rural school communities, even though larger consolidated schools and junior high schools did open up wider career opportunities and the potential for higher salaries. Expressing skepticism about "bigger and better" schools was frowned upon by the authorities, so it was best kept to oneself. Away from the school and in retirement, rural schoolteachers such as Dorothy Elderkin Lawrence, editor of *Telling Tales Out of School* (1995), were more candid in their views about the loss of community identity incurred through the passing of the one-room schoolhouse.[48]

The public mood in Canada's English-speaking provinces, as in Quebec, remained fairly buoyant in the late 1960s and early 1970s. A Centennial Year commemorative booklet, *Nova Scotia: Three Hundred Years in Education*, captured well the spirit and temper of the times. Modernizing forces were in the ascendancy and voices of dissent were muffled in the effervescent, celebratory atmosphere.[49] Consolidated schools had arrived or were coming to most small towns and larger villages, and hundreds of older abandoned wooden schools were facing extinction or an uncertain future. Older teaching philosophies and methods were also under attack. Amidst all the clamour, William B. Hamilton of the Atlantic Institute of Education was one of the few educational insiders who openly expressed his reservations about the new directions. The overriding theme was "bigger is better," he wryly observed in 1979. "Whether that system is superior," he continued, "is a matter to be decided by some future historian."[50]

CHALLENGING CENTRALIZED ADMINISTRATIVE AUTHORITY

The dominant pattern of centralized administrative decision-making began to unravel in the 1960s and 1970s. A better-educated Canadian public, and one generally more conscious of individual rights, began to take a greater interest in the behaviour of public institutions and, in particular, in the school's role as a fundamental social institution. As part of the great political awakening that swept Canada and the United States, traditionally quiescent parent-teacher associations were gradually swept aside by an array of special interest groups and organizations that were considerably more vocal in nature, and more intent on challenging the way that long-standing school policies and practices were controlled. Parents, taxpayers, business leaders, and others dissatisfied with the direction and quality of public schooling petitioned provincial and local governments for greater direct involvement in school decision-making. Their influence exerted an impact upon education policy. By the late 1970s, new programs and avenues for consultation were created to deal with these new constituencies, who represented special needs children, the socially disadvantaged, the cause of gender equity, multiculturalism, and other social justice issues.[51] The doors had swung open for everyone, it seemed, except for parents and concerned citizens.

THE RISE OF PARENT VOICES – AND SCHOOL ADVISORY COUNCILS

Public concerns that provincial and school district bureaucracies had grown too large and complex eventually found expression in growing community demands for greater parental involvement in schools. Such concerns were strongly voiced throughout the 1980s in presentations to various government-appointed education commissions. British Columbia's 1984–85 Provincial School Review Committee, for example, found that more than 80 percent of the approximately 6,000 written responses they received called for greater public and parental participation in school matters, and 75 percent of respondents supported the notion that school councils, composed of parents and other community members, should be established.[52] Two years later, these views were echoed in the findings of the Province's 1987–88 Royal Commission when it recognized the public appetite, particularly on the part of parents, for more active "participation in local school affairs," and proposed the establishment of parent-community advisory committees. The 1989 *School Act* reform directed BC's 75 school districts to authorize the formation of a parents' advisory council in each school to advise "the local board of school trustees, the principal, and staff, on any matter relating to the school."[53]

Developments in British Columbia reflected broader changes across Canada that aimed at shifting the locus of school district governance downward to local school levels, attempting to secure more democratic control closer to the people. In Newfoundland, the importance of expanding parental and public involvement in educational decisions was likewise emphasized by that province's 1992 Royal Commission. "If the school system is to reach its maximum potential with the resources available," the report noted, "it is essential to establish the means for effective parental involvement in the governance of the province's schools." School councils were recommended, consisting of "elected representatives of parents and teachers, the school principal, as well as appointees from the churches and members of the business community selected by the council itself."[54]

Securing more parental involvement in educational decision-making proved to be a formidable challenge. While Alberta enacted *Education Act* reforms in 1988 encouraging greater parental participation in school-level decision-making, a 1992 Department of Education survey on the state of school councils in the province revealed that no school board had delegated any significant authority to school councils, thus defeating the spirit of what the government originally intended.[73] To overcome the resistance, Alberta passed a *School Amendment Act* in 1994 which, as in Quebec, made school councils mandatory, albeit in an advisory rather than a governance role.[55] With the exception of Quebec, school councils across Canada were all consigned to an "advisory role" so as to contain and limit their influence on the shaping of school, board, or provincial policy or practice.[56]

THE HARDENED SHELL – QUEBEC'S CENTRALIZED AND REGULATED SYSTEM

Schooling in Quebec after the Quiet Revolution became an instrument for state creation. The Ministry of Education (MEQ) morphed into a highly centralized, regulated system with a burgeoning administrative bureaucracy, a remarkably standardized curriculum, and provincial student examinations at the secondary level. Language and culture loomed large in education policy reform, especially following the November 1976 election of René Lévesque's Parti Québécois government. In the largely French-speaking province, the right to have one's children educated in English was restricted by Bill 101 (1977), formally known as the *Charter of the French Language*. Under Bill 101, in order for a student to receive English language school instruction, a "certificate of eligibility" was required, and initially these were extended only to those with one parent educated in English in Quebec. In 1993, the Quebec government relaxed that requirement to include children with one parent educated in English elsewhere in Canada.[57] Such measures exemplified the central role education played in state policy aimed at safeguarding the French language and culture in the province.

The Quebec government attempted, not all that successfully, to counter the centralization of educational administration. A 1978 MEQ Green Paper generated an "Education Project" initiative that sought to balance "centralization" of curriculum and assessment in relation to increasing community demands for "school and board-based autonomy." Facing increasing pressure for conformity, school districts, principals and parents were clamouring for schools to be given more latitude to "expand beyond the dictates of MEQ policy." Education policy analysts Gary J. Anderson and Janyne M. Rahming claimed that the Project plan amounted to "a formula for rating school excellence" rather than "a policy for effecting school improvement."[58] Provincial regulation continued to exert a predominant influence over curriculum and school organization. Prominent McGill University education historians Norman Henchy and Donald Burgess put it bluntly: "Freedom was replaced by control, individuality was replaced by the need for equality, and choice was replaced by restriction, all undertaken in the name of improving the quality of education."[59] In short, the Education Project was little more than an "elaborate smoke-screen" designed by the MEQ to conceal the centralist nature of education policy.

Matters of language and culture took precedence in the Quebec school system. While Quebec retained its traditional Catholic and Protestant religious and linguistic dualism, secular and linguistic influences gradually superseded the confessional tradition in the schools. A 1991 study of the multicultural/intercultural policies of the two largest school boards, la Commission des écoles Catholiques de Montréal (CECM) and the Protestant School Board of Greater Montreal (PSGM), illustrated how it worked in practice. "Despite differences in religious and political orientations, administrative structures, programs and scope," Rosalind Zinman observed, "both Boards adhere to a liberal humanist framework with reformist, idealist and normative tendencies, and are not inclined to change."[60] Language issues involving the dominant French and minority English communities dominated policy discourse, extending beyond education, shaping provincial and school district policy with regard to immigrant acceptance and the promotion of cultural integration.

SIGNS OF A SEA CHANGE IN ONTARIO EDUCATION

Out of all the primarily English-speaking provinces, Ontario stood out in the early 1990s for its overgrown, inwardly focused, and largely unaccountable public school system. In late 1992 and early 1993, public confidence in the Ontario school system was badly shaken. A public outcry about education costs, school trustee spending habits, and school administrators' smug complacency about student performance standards all spelled trouble for the Ontario NDP government of Bob Rae.[61] A former Ministry of Education researcher and assessment expert, Dennis Raphael, identified the crux of the problem afflicting the provincial system: Ontario was so committed to a child-centred educational philosophy that it lacked any means of assessing how students were actually performing in the schools. "If students enjoyed working with science-type materials such as magnets or mirrors," one Ottawa teacher told Raphael, "I really don't care if they learned anything."[62] As one of only two provinces without an every-student achievement assessment program, it had become an outlier in an educational world increasingly engaged in national and international assessments.

Assessing student performance outcomes in response to account-ability concerns, Raphael discovered, ran smack up against resistance from Ontario school administrators, particularly in the elementary school division. A provincial test bank, the Ontario Assessment Instrument Pool (OAIP), developed by Raphael and others, was estab-lished, then essentially abandoned, even though Ontario students were faring poorly on comparable international assessments. "The Ontario education bureaucracy," he claimed in the spring of 1993, "still marches to the tune of the child-centred drummer, even though this tune is no longer popular with the public and is abandoned almost everywhere else in the world."

THE LEGACY — A CRISIS OF PUBLIC CONFIDENCE

From 1920 to the early 1990s, consolidation, bureaucracy, and public education came to be so closely intertwined that in Canadian provinces outside Quebec it became impossible to answer the question "Who's in charge?" Modernization had further accelerated the trend toward a new form of administrative centralization and state managerialism without much public accountability or attention to student perfor-mance results. Prominent education analysts such as Toronto *Globe and Mail* education reporter Jennifer Lewington and OISE professor Stephen B. Lawton had come to describe the school system as a "bureaucratic fortress" maintaining strict boundaries between "insid-ers" and "outsiders" in education.[63] Public education in the early 1990s was now said to be impenetrable and facing "a crisis of public confidence." Leading education critics such as Lewington, Graham Orpwood, Andrew Nikiforuk, and parent advocacy groups such as the Ontario Coalition for Education Reform confronted the modern bureaucratic education state, largely erected since the 1960s, and called for "the walls to come down."[64]

The Ontario education reform wave had echoes in other provinces. Parents, chambers of commerce, and advocacy groups were clamour-ing for higher standards, provincial testing, and more public account-ability. By 1992, the Quebec Ministry of Education was facing increased public pressure to significantly change its direction. A new Plan of Action, *Joining Forces* (1992), recognized the limits of central-ized direction and the need to "make the education system more flexible in order to give freer rein to those who work closely with the student."[65] A subsequent MEQ reform strategy, *Moving Ahead* (1993), proposed a shift in focus from the role of central manager to facilitator of more school-level activity among those closest to the student. While the Quebec Ministry vowed to step back, it was only to help the school system "deliver the goods" in terms of improved student progress and achievement.[66] An Ontario Royal Commission on Learning, appointed in 1993, was about to hear, during its 1993–94 consultations, a groundswell of support for reforms.[67] Out East in Nova Scotia, education reform rumblings found concrete expression in 1994 when newly elected Premier John Savage and his Liberal government released a White Paper calling for the reinvention of the education system.[68] Education reform agitation signalled that the tide was about to turn in favour of restructuring, student achievement testing, and accountability.

3

Testing Time

The Triumph of Testing, Accountability, and Systems, 1993–2015

The crisis of public confidence in the system broke out into the open in the early 1990s. Concerned parents began asking hard questions about the quality of education and speaking out, first in hushed tones in school parking lots, then more openly in the public domain. One of the catalysts for the quality education movement in Ontario education was Maureen Somers-Beebe, a thirty-three-year-old mother of three boys, who rocked the system by asking her board of education in Peterborough, Ontario, four pointed questions.[1] It all started when one of her sons, Adam, finishing Grade 3 at South Monaghan Public School, came home with "above average" grades, even though he, and several of his peers, could barely read and had trouble spelling two- and three-letter words.

Somers-Beebe's son and his classmates were being immersed in "progressive" activity-centred learning. Instead of being taught through explicit instruction, children were encouraged to discover math in sandboxes, to explore their feelings through books, and to move from one play-based activity to another around the room.[2] Their teacher moved about the room doing more nurturing than actual teaching. The classroom, Somers-Beebe was convinced, resembled a social laboratory where the children were essentially guinea pigs.

Sensing that something was wrong, Somers-Beebe then discovered that the Grade 3 class did not seem to have a written curriculum. After forming a local group called Parents for Education, she asked the principal and then the district superintendent these four questions:

What are our children learning?
How will they learn it?

When will they learn it?
How will you know, the teacher know, and the parent know that
the child has learned it?

What Somers-Beebe and her group encountered was symptomatic
of what had gone wrong in the system since the 1960s. She and the
others received a long talk on early child development theory and a
copy of *The Formative Years*, a provincial curriculum guideline overflowing with educational jargon associated with early childhood education. Then they heard the standard brush-offs: parents worry too
much; trust us, we're the professionals; modern schools are not as you
remember them; every child develops when ready at his or her own
pace. Relax, leave it to us, and your child will eventually blossom.

The South Monaghan parents' group, led by Somers-Beebe, were
not satisfied with the answers and persisted in repeating the questions.
After one meeting with the director of education and curriculum
superintendent, they were told that only the provincial Ministry of
Education could answer her. When the group presented to senior
administration, Somers-Beebe was barred from attending because she
exhibited "hostile body language." Finally, the board promised to
look into developing an elementary curriculum, but advised them it
would take a year. To placate the group, the board held a Learning
Symposium at which experts from other boards tried to answer the
questions. When the board tested the twenty-one children in Adam's
Grade 4 class, twelve were found to be at a Grade 2 reading level and
some were still unable to write in sentences. The board's only response
was to authorize a remedial reading program, and advised them that
if they were looking for "direct, sequential instruction" it would have
to be provided by fee-for-service tutoring outside of school hours.

The Parents for Education group eventually hit a brick wall. The
board tried to bow out, saying they had answered Somers-Beebe's
"deceptively simple questions" and explaining that the staff had been
placed "under severe stress" caused by the active parents. Over the
summer break, the principal transferred and half the teaching staff
turned over. Fed up with the board's inability to fix the problem,
Somers-Beebe moved Adam to a nearby Catholic school. Her son was
immediately assessed, removed from the activities-format classroom,
and given direct instruction in reading, writing, and math. Two years
after the protest, Adam was reading at a 7.1 grade level in Grade 5

and the mother who started it all was providing home tutoring to meet the unmet needs of other local children falling through the cracks.

WHAT HAD GONE WRONG?

The inability of educators to answer Maureen Somers-Beebe's fundamental questions and to deliver the basics was all too common in the early 1990s in province after province, right across Canada.[3] The mushrooming of the modern bureaucratic education state also coincided with the spread of what was termed "educational progressivism." A whole generation of teachers, imbued with the progressive theories of American educator John Dewey, frowned upon traditional teaching and spouted "sweet-sounding progressive dogma."[4] In place of purposeful, orderly classroom practice, elementary education was being transformed into nurturing childcare centres overflowing with hands-on, "learn by doing" activities. Providing children with life-relevant experiences, Somers-Beebe and thousands of other parents discovered, now took precedence over providing them with sound foundations. A flexible, adaptable curriculum had emerged in place of systematic, sequential learning, and in the relative absence of standardized assessment, no one seemed to know what children were learning at each grade level. In the vast majority of school districts, as Somers-Beebe's little crusade revealed, schools had become essentially "accountability-free zones" for students and teachers.

What had gone wrong? Canada's school system in the early 1990s was well on its way to demonstrating what Toronto *Globe and Mail* education columnist Andrew Nikiforuk aptly described as a tragedy of the commons. Parents, teachers, and school administrators, he claimed, could be likened to fifty families who own a community pasture. In the beginning, the pasture (school system) had a well-defined public purpose: the sustenance of fifty cows. As long as each member of the community placed only one cow on the common, all was well. But when members of the community began to increase their share of the common by adding more cows, the pasture became overgrazed and gradually depleted. The additional cows multiplied and consumed more and more of the dwindling patches of grass down to their roots. Gradually the pasture eroded and became less productive.[5]

In the public education sphere, placing more and more cows on the limited land was roughly equivalent to loading more and more mandates on the schools. Overloading the system with a seemingly endless array of competing project initiatives, services, and curricula was depleting a vitally important community institution with finite resources. Trying to be all things to all people had led to "overgrazing" and contributed to what Nikiforuk characterized as "the aimlessness of the modern school."[6] While the existential crisis did not lead to catastrophe, it did spark a dramatic shift in the direction of reaffirming the academic focus of schooling and the primacy of shoring up the foundations of teaching and learning. It also tipped the balance in favour of introducing far more rigorous student assessment and public accountability for improving student achievement.

High schools in the early 1990s remained much like those described in Theodore Sizer's American education classic, *Horace's Compromise.* They were too often bleak places where teachers and students formed a unique social compact Sizer described as "a conspiracy of the least."[7] Tired and jaded teachers expected little mental work (such as writing two or three sentences about a full book), while students agreed, in return, not to cause too much trouble. During the class, students slumped in their seats, ate snacks, listened to their Walkmans, and ambled around the classroom. Seasoned high schoolers learned that doing a bare minimum would still yield a high school diploma. Without being challenged to improve their grades, students marked time and the pall of mediocrity hung over regular high school life.

Prominent education critics such as Nikiforuk pointed to warnings about declining expectations from the renowned American poet, novelist, and cultural critic Wendell Barry. Lowering of expectations started in the universities and colleges, Barry claimed, and then had the effect of lowering standards in the schools. In shaping the school to fit the students, he predicted that we "can maintain no standards" and will "lose the subjects and eventually will lose the students as well." While Barry abhorred discrimination of any kind, he feared that the absence of standards made it more difficult to "recognize, reward and promote good work." His greatest fear was that special pleading by "'disadvantaged groups' – whether disadvantaged by history, economics, or education – can make it increasingly difficult for members of that group to do good work and have it recognized." Most Canadian educators, including the vast majority of education professors, initially resisted the call for standards of any kind. The standard line of defense was "education must always look to tomorrow's horizons rather than backwards to yesterday's standards."[8]

Figure 3.1 Andrew Nikiforuk, Toronto *Globe and Mail* Education Columnist
Toronto *Globe and Mail* columnist Andrew Nikiforuk emerged as the voice
of education reform. His popular "Fifth Column" ran from 1991 to 1994 and
also produced the raw material for a stinging critique, entitled *School's Out:
The Catastrophe in Public Education and What to Do about It* (1993).

Senior education bureaucrats in the 1990s inhabited radically different planets from most parents advocating quality education reform.
A survey of Ontario's chief education officers (CEOs) conducted in
1991 by OISE professor Mark Holmes revealed a startling ideological

gap between the educators who formed the leadership cadre and the parent advocates.[9] Most CEOs favoured the progressive, child-centred model of education, even though they devoted only about twenty percent of their time to delivering and assessing school curricula and personnel. Parents surveyed ranked cultural or technocratic priorities highest, and progressive ideology near the bottom. Only 11 percent of the CEOs thought it necessary to annually test students on their basic skills, while fully 60 percent of the non-educators supported regular student assessments. Progressive educational sympathies, Holmes found, were so entrenched among system leaders that they were a factor in determining who got promoted to principal, the gateway to higher school administration. Changing the system would require a turnover at the top and the entry of new system managers more attuned to the winds of change in education reform.

The cover of *Maclean's* on 14 March 1994 was emblazoned with the headline "Are we cheating our kids?" and the feature story drew national attention to the crisis in confidence. Surveying K–12 education across Canada, *Maclean's* reporter Victor Dwyer found that the school system was "not making the grade" and was depriving students of a good education. Personal stories rounded out the picture of a system that had lost its way. When *Toronto Star* reporter Janice Dineen looked into what her Grade 5 son was doing in school in February 1992, she was appalled to learn that, over a three-week period, her son's class watched Friday movies, saw an English cartoon in French class, went on a ski trip, heard a nurse talk about puberty, and visited the kindergarten class. On the same day that Dineen was writing her piece, the second International Assessment of Educational Progress (IAEP II) came out, showing that Ontario, one of Canada's best-endowed school systems, finished in the bottom tier among Canadian provinces as well as compared to other nations.

An Education Report Card, published by the Coalition for Education Reform in 1994 in the booklet *Could Do Better*, did not mince any words in explaining why Ontario's schools were now a "D-Minus system." That book laid out, in painful detail, the scope of the problem, supported by research findings:

- Failure to Produce Good Students
- Failure to Produce Good Citizens
- The Growth of Public Dissatisfaction

The stinging critique then provided a diagnosis of the roots of the problem, captured in crystal-clear topic headings:

- No Curriculum – Common or Otherwise
- Teaching to the Test – Not!
- Deliberate Suppression of Data
- Advancement without Achievement
- Dim Prospects for Reform from Within
- Disagreement about the Purpose of Schooling

That little CER booklet served as manual for parents, teachers, and ordinary taxpayers demanding more from the school system. It recognized that, while there was no consensus on the best way forward, "inaction is tantamount to giving the status quo free rein – and Ontario students deserve better."[10]

The absence of clear goals had left the system adrift and eroded public confidence in the overall public education enterprise. Concerned parents associated with advocacy groups such as the Ontario Coalition for Education Reform and leading business advocacy groups began to demand clarity on the core mission of schools and challenged those running the system to sharpen their focus, uphold higher standards, and be prepared to demonstrate what students were learning in schools.[11] Without a national presence in education, the struggle for quality education was waged, province-to-province, throughout the latter half of the 1990s. One intergovernmental body, the Council of Ministers of Education, led by Dr Paul Cappon, raised awareness of the "achievement gap" among OECD countries and the provinces and nudged provincial authorities in the direction of testing and accountability. Leading educators, right across the country, began, finally, to begin defining what Canadians expected of their schools. One Ontario director of education, Veronica Lacey of the Toronto region North York school board, led the charge in promoting national standards and more regularized, standardized testing of students. "We must be the only country in the world," she stated, "that can't get its act together as a nation to talk about educational issues."[12] Eventually the barriers fell by the wayside, and the system gradually accepted the necessity of being more open, transparent, and accountable to the public for student learning and achievement.

WHAT COULD BE DONE TO RESTORE
PUBLIC CONFIDENCE?

Identifying the problem proved far easier than producing viable policy responses and solutions. Education reformers claimed, first and foremost, that insufficient provincial funding was not a factor in the underperformance of students, particularly in Ontario, and international comparisons revealed that Canada, in 1989, spent a higher proportion of its gross domestic product on education, compared to Japan and higher-performing European states. They also rejected the notion that somehow Canadian students were less able or more disabled than those in other countries. Most of their criticism centred on what was termed the debilitating effect of the dominant "child-centred" model of education. Active parents looking for dramatic improvement pointed to authoritative research, such as Project Follow Through, and their own school experience in advocating for a shift from "child-centred" approaches to "teacher-directed" instruction. Three out of five parents surveyed in the 1990s saw student testing as the only reliable way of assessing whether children were actually learning and as the best means of measuring the impact of proposed changes in core philosophy, curriculum, and instruction.[13]

Student assessment and testing became the primary battleground in the struggle to uphold and reaffirm education standards. Storm warnings signalled by the parent-driven education reform movement began to come from all segments of society – as parents, business owners, and taxpayers coalesced around a common agenda seeking reliable evidence that the system was delivering results. As public concern over the state of the schools rose, fuelled by widespread media coverage, system managers were facing increasing pressure to find new ways to demonstrate improvements. Teachers' organizations initially resisted the public demand for student testing and accountability and, together with some elements of the education establishment, fought a rearguard action, leaving the distinct impression that they had something to hide.[14] While that anti-testing faction never really disappeared, the opponents ended up on the losing end of the struggle in the 1990s to introduce higher standards, core curriculum, and large-scale student assessment.

The fierce public debate over student testing provided a glimpse of the underlying discord within the system. Given the lack of consensus around the goals of public education, it was hardly surprising that the disagreements surfaced over the matter of testing. Most educators were leery of standardized tests because doing well on those tests tended to become an end in itself. Much of the public and many in the popular media, hungry for some concrete evidence of how students were performing, seized upon student performance rankings and international comparisons of student achievement.[15] Promoters of large-scale student assessment made a compelling case as to why it was necessary and how it would be of longer-term benefit to the system. Gradually, most parents and a large segment of the public came to see the prime advantages: the provision of a more reliable, objective measure of student progress; the diagnosis of individual learning difficulties; the acquisition of feedback on the adequacy of course curriculum and teaching methods; and the gathering of intelligence about how a province's students measured up in terms of others.

Standardized testing was no panacea for an education system under stress. The challenges of reforming education lay deeper and proved more difficult to tackle because of the depleted state of liberal education and the challenge of resuscitating standards. Establishing national and provincial standards in an education world committed to child-centred learning posed significant problems. Two independently minded Canadian academics, Peter C. Emberley and Waller R. Newell, identified the nub of the problem – the decline of the liberal education and its virtual abandonment in the public schools. Progressive education approaches as exemplified in Ontario's 1992 *Common Curriculum*, in their view, favoured process over knowledge and left students intellectually "impoverished" rather than providing a well-rounded education grounded in subject disciplines and rooted in "philosophical reason."[16]

THE MODERN CLASSROOM – A MICROCOSM OF AIMLESS EDUCATION

The triumph of the education state had transformed the school into an entirely different species. While the school of the 1950s had expanded in size and was bulging with Baby Boom children, teachers and principals still occupied the centre of the enterprise. The urban metropolitan school of the 1990s was more bloated, was insulated by outer layers of bureaucracy, spouted progressive rhetoric, embraced brave new curricula, and adhered to union contracts. The student body was far more diverse, comprising rich and poor, English-speaking and non-English-speaking, black and white, straight and gay. In the midst of this pluralistic mass, it was harder to identify school leadership because the centre of authority had disappeared.[17] In far too many cases, principals were being crowded out by a new class of school consultants and specialists, floating about, here and there, and heading up initiatives, often at cross purposes.

Once the anchor of the community, the modern school had evolved into a bureaucratic nerve centre that was the complete antithesis of a community.[18] With layers of administration, assistant principals, social workers, psychologists, language consultants, multicultural experts, full-time teaching aides, and on-duty policemen, the regular junior and senior high school did not convey a sense of community but rather the impression of being a proliferation of competing professional cultures. Expanding its role meant the modern mega-school was expected to be a universal receptor, absorbing more and more civic and social responsibilities. In the relative absence of strong school leadership, each professional group in the school took on more and more mandates, most notably in the field of special education services. While parents came to rely, more and more, on daycare and pre-school services, regular day schools took on the job of accommodating everyone and keeping them happy, regardless of the consequences for students, teachers, or the school community itself. Few stopped to ask the really fundamental question posed by Denis Cassivi in his fascinating expose *Education and the Cult of Modernism*: "What difference do elaborate buildings, nifty class schedules, and computerized timetables make if the children are not learning?"[19]

The education policy ground first began to shift in Ontario when the New Democratic Party government of Bob Rae started to respond to the mounting demand for education reform. Two critical turning points in the shift were the January 1993 launch of an independent education commission, the Royal Commission on Learning, and the appointment of a reform-minded Education Minister, Dave Cooke, sympathetic to the calls for significant change.[20] Minister Cooke was openly skeptical about the philosophy and language of a rewritten version of *The Common Curriculum* and in April 1993 ordered a more robust provincial review of Grade 9 reading and writing skills, including a system-wide assessment of every student. The January 1995 report of the commission, *For the Love of Learning*, tilted the policy debate more in the direction of system reform. The commission, co-chaired by Gerald Caplan and Monique Bégin, was critical of the

Figure 3.2 Announcement of Ontario Royal Commission on Learning, 1993

The official response to Ontario's education crisis was the Royal Commission on Learning (1993–95), appointed by Education Minister Dave Cooke. Here Cooke poses with the members, flanked by co-chairs Gerald Caplan and Monique Bégin. Back row (left to right): Monsignor Dennis Murphy, Banisha Bharti, and Avis Glaze.

province for its lack of leadership and for abdicating its responsibility for education. It recommended a wide range of changes, including "system-level monitoring" to ensure improved accountability to the public. Education reformers hailed the report as a breakthrough and it did mark the turn of the tide.

THE RADICAL TURN – "COMMON SENSE" REVOLUTIONS IN EDUCATION

Provincial governments in Ontario and far beyond felt the public pressure from quality education advocates to reform their school systems and demonstrate more accountability for improving student results. System-wide school reform surfaced first in Nova Scotia, where the John Savage Liberal government, elected in May 1993, was heavily influenced in their thinking by David Osborne and Ted Gaebler's *Reinventing Government* (1993), the most influential public policy reform tract of the time.[21] His Minister of Education, John MacEachern, a former Glace Bay high school math and physics teacher, emerged as one of the Savage government's most energetic and articulate policy advocates. He won over Education Department officials and they responded by producing a creative spurt of educational change proposals, including school-based management and governing councils.

During the tumultuous year of 1994, MacEachern survived a severe test, achieving cost efficiencies by raising class sizes and improving public accountability by introducing school-level governance. When provincial bargaining with the Nova Scotia Teachers Union reached a stalemate, the Minister stood his ground. After several weeks of what St. Francis Xavier University political scientist Peter Clancy described as "brinkmanship," a teachers' contract agreement was finally reached in early June 1994, one that strengthened the province's hand on the education front.[22]

The most radical shift happened in Ontario with the 1995 election of the Conservative Mike Harris government championing an explicitly neo-conservative philosophy and program known as *The Common Sense Revolution* (CSR). Between June 1995 and the spring of 1998, the Harris government introduced changes in Ontario education that were extraordinary in scope, in sheer speed of execution, and in the turbulence they created in and around the schools.[23] While classroom funding was protected, the Conservatives sought to achieve more value for money in the education sector. The CSR clearly embraced the critique of education advanced by the CER and its supporters in the business community. "Ontario spends $14-billion a year on education – more per pupil than any other province – and still gets a failing grade," the CSR program declared. Conservative education policy targeted education bureaucracy in a system which was overburdened with education personnel who "don't teach" and one with "massive duplication of programs and services" among boards and between boards and the department. While board amalgamation was not proposed, the CSR identified savings to be made by trimming the salaries of trustees who acted like "full-time politicians with full-time salaries." High school would be reduced to four years, ending in Grade 12, and junior kindergarten would remain a local option. Most significantly, the Conservatives pledged to scrap *The Common Curriculum* and replace it with a core curriculum, supported by province-wide testing at regular grade intervals.[24] The overriding objective was to spend more efficiently while improving the quality of education.

Premier Harris swept into office determined to honour his CSR commitments, and his cabinet took the 1995 election victory as a license to effect sweeping change. The Harris Conservatives claimed that the education system was rudderless – and children were passing through with no useful measurement of their progress, or lack of it. Education Minister John Snobelen had set the tone in 1995 when he told senior bureaucrats that the way to achieve major change was to "invent a crisis."[25] Acting accordingly, the Harris government moved quickly to equalize funding for schools province-wide, introduce a better curriculum, and institute standardized tests. A provincial student assessment agency, first proposed by Cooke and the NDP, was established and named the Education Quality and Accountability Office (EQAO), albeit with a smaller budget ($15 million) than had been proposed by the previous government.[26] A new core curriculum was introduced and every high school course was eventually rewritten to solidify the academic standards and respect discrete subject knowledge. Following up on the Learning Commission recommendation, the government also established a College of Teachers aimed at upholding teaching standards, firming up teacher discipline, and providing public transparency in rare cases of misconduct.[27] The Ontario Parent Council, created in 1994, was beefed up with new appointees drawn from among the parent groups clamouring for a larger role on K–12 education. All school boards were required to establish school councils by June 1996, and a year later, all publicly funded schools were required to have functioning school-level governance.[28]

Cutting education spending sparked a real, full-blown crisis. While the Conservatives initially pledged to trim $400 million from the education budget, the final total was closer to $1 billion, representing a 22.7 percent cut in provincial operating grants. Starting in the late spring of 1996, Snobelen embarked upon radical restructuring, eventually reducing the number of school boards from 129 to 72 and removing their taxing powers. Massive changes ushered in by Bill 160 sparked confrontations with Ontario teachers' federations, education workers, and public sector unions. Spearheaded by OSSTF president Earl Manners, teachers held their ground and charged that the Harris agenda was threatening to "bankrupt education and destroy the teaching profession." After a boisterous Maple Leaf Gardens protest in October 1996, Snobelen was replaced by former Toronto East York Mayor Dave Johnson in an attempt to diffuse the labour conflict. When Johnson refused to bend, teachers resorted to a ten-day labour protest, an unofficial strike, lasting from 27 October to 7 November, while the Ontario Legislature stood in recess. The contentious bill, containing a few amendments, was passed into law on 1 December 1997, leaving lasting teacher-government wounds and a bitter residue of distrust.[29]

BREAKING THE GRIDLOCK – THE ALBERTA CHARTER SCHOOLS MOVEMENT

School reform emerged in a different form in Alberta. For Albertans, parental choice in education was the real trigger, and it inspired a movement strongly supported by leading business interests. One of the first to catch the reform bug was Dr Joe Freedman, a Red Deer radiologist and father of two girls, who travelled extensively and was attuned to educational developments around the world. When Freedman received a local school board survey to fill in, the simple-minded questions stuck in his craw and he replied with a stinging letter reminding the board that parents were the school system's clients and deserved better. Looking further into what was going on in high school, he discovered that the curriculum expectations in mathematics and science were far below those in European and Asian schools. Together with Alberta Education Minister Jim Dinning, he engineered a 1991 Alberta Chamber of Resources research study, *International Comparisons in Education*, that compared textbook content in Alberta with that in Japan, Hungary, and Germany and pointed out the glaring deficiencies. He formed his own Society for Advancing Educational Research and self-published a 1993 book, *Failing Grades: Canadian Schooling in a Global Context*, accompanied by a booklet and instructional video. Some 5,000 copies of the book set were distributed in Alberta and across North America.[30]

Education reform was championed in Alberta by Freedman, the Calgary-based Toronto *Globe and Mail* education columnist Andrew Nikiforuk, and their group, Albertans for Quality Education. That group raised public awareness about international test scores and then began to challenge the "monopoly" of public schools over education.[31] Freedman was drawn to the idea of charter schools as a way of breaking what he termed the "educational gridlock" standing in the way of better schools and higher quality education for children. After studying charter laws in Minnesota and eight other American states, the group successfully lobbied then–Education Minister Halvar Jonson to introduce legislation authorizing the creation of charter schools. The Alberta charter law passed on 25 May 1994, and the first three such schools opened in September 1995. Freedman, a tireless champion of the cause, published a second book, *The Charter School Idea* (1995), and travelled across Canada seeding the concept.[32]

Alberta's Education Department embraces a "school choice" philosophy and, since 1994, charter schools have formed one of those alternative programs. Charter schools are publicly funded schools which have a greater degree of autonomy than normal public schools. Provincial approval is conditional upon the schools offering alternative programs that are significantly different from the regular public schools operated by district school boards. Under Alberta law, they report directly to the province, bypassing their local district school board, but are limited in number and may not exceed their assigned quota of students.[33] While the charter school vision shook the educational establishment, it never caught on outside Alberta, where regulations today limit the number of charters to fifteen province-wide.

GLOBALIZATION, INTERNATIONAL TESTING, AND THE SCHOOLS

The advent of Alberta's charter school movement coincided with a dramatic shift in education associated with the phenomenon of globalization. From the early 1990s onward, Canadian education authorities and provincial education policy were increasingly dominated by global trends, particularly in North America, Europe, and Latin America, and among countries associated with the Organization for Economic Cooperation and Development (OECD).[34] Educational leaders across Canada, encouraged by the Council of Ministers of Education, Canada and the Conference Board of Canada, drew regular attention to international student assessments and claimed that Canadian students must be competitive in their performance. Critics of globalization claimed that it represented the dawn of a new "neo-liberal era" in education. Serious concerns were raised over the promotion of management innovation and market solutions in the education sector. In public education, neo-liberalism was seen as a new threat in the form of "an explicit belief in consumer choice and

market freedom" coupled with a fear that it represented "the dominance of private interests over the state."[35]

Provincial education departments, once bastions of child-centred
education, gradually embraced the global trends and began to reorient
school systems to prepare students for success in the twenty-first-
century global economic world. Vocal critics on the Canadian left
attempted to refute claims that Canada's schools were failing and
claimed that it was a thinly veiled movement to "privatize" public
education.[36] Slowly the focus of education shifted to become not only
more aligned with a so-called knowledge-based society, but increasingly driven largely by the high-technology economy. A new mantra
emerged along with what become known as "21st century learning":
critical thinking, creativity, competencies, innovation, and cooperative
forms of work. In the neo-liberal narrative, systems were focused on
being "globally competitive" and responsible for preparing students
with twenty-first-century skills while demonstrating a competitive edge
and entrepreneurial competencies.[37] The once-mighty education state
was to "steer not row" the system and to ensure that parents were
offered more program choices for their children both inside and outside
the public system. In both Alberta, where charter schools exist, and in
British Columbia, where private schools are provincially funded, school
choice became an accepted and integral part of an education domain
offering students and families four or five different school options.[38]

Large-scale standardized tests gradually became the norm between
2000 and 2012 in all Canadian provinces, except for Prince Edward
Island and Saskatchewan. The OECD's flagship international test, the
Program of International Student Assessment (PISA), administered
to fifteen-year-olds once every three years, became the benchmark for
student achievement. While Quebec had its own system-wide secondary school examinations, province after province in English-speaking
Canada followed Ontario in introducing their own standardized tests
at regular grade intervals. With the support of the CMEC, the provinces
collaborated in building a national testing program known as the
Pan-Canadian Assessment Program (PCAP).[39] All of these testing
regimes focused on three core competencies: literacy (reading and
writing), numeracy (mathematics), and science (applied mathematics).
Critics of student testing saw standardized student assessment as
insidious because it began to drive teaching practice and encouraged
students to value math and science over the humanities and the arts.
From 2000 onwards, the PISA rankings were treated as Canada's

version of the "league tables," and student achievement rankings were regularly used in rating the quality of education between and among the provinces. Education policy-makers caught a fever known as "PISA envy" and scrambled to see why first Finland, and later China (Hong Kong/Shanghai) and Singapore, produced the world's top-performing students.[40]

TECHNOLOGY AND THE CORPORATE EDUCATION HYDRA

Most teachers who were early adopters of classroom technology applied student-centred, constructivist approaches and utilized computers and laptops to facilitate active learning. Introduced as a learning tool, technology's use mushroomed, which only facilitated the spread of neo-liberal values and entrepreneurial aptitudes among students. While teachers tried to counter that influence by utilizing critical pedagogy, that effort fell short amidst the onslaught of technological tools, from computers to laptops to mobile devices. Huge learning corporations such as Pearson International expanded from textbooks to electronic resources and student assessments. Along with large-scale assessment came administrative data systems such as *Power School* and the widespread collection and use of "big data" exerting an impact upon regular teachers everywhere.[41]

Twenty-first-century skills were closely aligned with technology and learning, branded in Canada as Information and Communications Technology (ICT) and packaged as meeting the needs of the "next generation" of learners. A national organization, C21 Canada, emerged in 2011–12 to promote "new models of public education" in response to "the advent of the knowledge and digital era."[42] In May 2012, C21 Canada released a futuristic blueprint, *Shifting Minds*, proposing "a go-forward 21st Century learning framework for Canada's public education systems" founded upon a set of seven declaratory principles, endorsing freer access for students, encouraging more "personalized" learning, and pledging support for "educational leaders" committed to digital learning initiatives. While the C21 Canada policy paper purported to be "Canadian" in origin, it mirrored the American Partnership for 21st Century Skills (P21) approach and was buttressed with mostly US technology-in-education research studies.[43]

Working with CMEC and Canadian branches of the international learning corporations, C21 Canada held regional conferences and attempts to "seed" "21st Century learning," mainly through provincial and territorial departments of education. In British Columbia, the BC Learns initiative, first proposed in late 2010 and known as "Personalized Learning," won the support of C21 Canada and, in 2015–16, was piloted in sixteen elementary schools. Ontario's eLearning initiative from 2011 to 2014 drew in part on C21 Canada's work. In other provinces, such as Nova Scotia, the "21st Century learning" promoters secured some regional school board support, but gained little traction with budget-conscious provincial education departments.[44]

More recently, Google Apps for Education (GAFE) has made significant inroads into Canada's K–12 school systems. When it comes to digital learning, Google has enjoyed much more success than Microsoft and smaller players in the growing market for software in elementary and secondary schools. First introduced in 2006, GAFE made its first big breakthroughs from 2012 onwards. Public concerns that Google was mining student e-mail accounts for ad-targeting purposes represented a setback, but that problem was squarely addressed in April 2014. In Nova Scotia, GAFE was adopted, piloted during 2014–15, and then approved for a rollout to all four hundred public schools in the province. By the end of 2015, it was spreading quickly and teacher training summits had been held or were scheduled to be held in Ontario, Alberta, Quebec, and BC as well as Nova Scotia.[45] In schools across the country, it is becoming increasingly essential for students to have access to the internet in order to be successful. Homework, projects, and even information and advice from teachers are now transmitted online, and are more readily accessible to those with the electronic tools to access the information.

SYSTEMS CREEP AND ITS IMPACT ON LEARNING

Systemic changes wrought by globalization have dramatically altered the state of Canadian K–12 education. The advent of large-scale student assessment has shifted the focus from student-centred learning to boosting student achievement and measuring success at every level. Educational policies reflecting the neo-liberal policy agenda have sought to raise achievement levels and to reinvest savings from any management efficiencies into the classroom. Students are being tested far more in our schools, but gains in student learning are difficult to see, let alone measure. Large-scale student assessments were harbingers of a wider range of machine-driven technological solutions impacting education management and the working life of teachers.[46] Teachers' unions have emerged in the forefront of the battle to curtail or redirect the advance of system-wide reforms that impinge upon teachers' autonomy and freedom in the classroom. Most teachers express concerns about how globalization is affecting children and the connected, internet-saturated lives they lead. They feel intense pressure to meet rising societal expectations – or demands – that teachers can overcome all the obstacles, hardships, and barriers that children bring to school.

System-wide change is stalling because principals and teachers, working on the front lines, are pushing back against further systematization. Today's complex classrooms are making it far more difficult to teach, let alone raise academic achievement, and class composition is the biggest concern of educators at every level. Standardized testing, student tracking, and the computerization of reporting have made teaching more challenging and increased its so-called "bureaucratic paperwork."[47] While educational austerity is more of a threat than a reality, judging by rising spending levels, those fears add to the anxieties felt by teachers faced with constant pressure to master new testing and tracking systems, all with different reporting requirements. The greatest concern of all is the unrealistic demands made to prepare students for a radically different twenty-first-century world that has not yet arrived – a "techno-immersive world with jobs that have not yet been identified." The BC Teachers Federation's lead researcher Larry Kuehn captured well the angst about where society and education are heading: "Much of the hype (about the twenty-first-century workplace) fails to recognize that, for many, the jobs of the future will be service jobs, not skilled trades, not new-economy high-tech jobs."[48] Techno-automation and data analytics, education critics warn, stand to benefit the few far more than the many.

4

Consolidate and Control

School Consolidation and Bureaucratic Managerialism

Consolidation is a favoured strategy used by business management to advance uniformity and reduce costs of operation. Since the origins of school planning in the 1920s, public education has generated its own managerial class of "educrats" firmly committed to the ideal of "progress and efficiency" and relentless in pursuit of education district and school consolidation. The assorted collection of late-nineteenth- and early-twentieth-century school communities, organized around urban collegiates, county academies, and one-room schoolhouses, was gradually transformed into "systems" of schools. By the early 2000s, the reigning TED Talk education rock star Sir Ken Robinson was packing auditoriums and churning out videos claiming that the modern school system had essentially adopted a "fast food" industry model by embracing organizational efficiency, mass production, and uniformity.[1]

Schooling in the System, according to Robinson and his followers, has been transformed into a factory-like operation driven by an unwavering and resilient one-size-fits-all philosophy of production. If so, then the actual operating system is much like that of one of the great marvels of the machine shop, the repetitive part-cutting machine. Entering the school system, children progress in batches in orderly, lock-step fashion, grade by grade, one year at a time, from kindergarten to graduation. Waves of heavily promoted school reforms come and go, but the system continues to click along relatively undisturbed on its programmed course.[2] Imaginative reformers with Big Ideas run smack up against what American education professor Larry Cuban terms the "black box of the classroom" and end up almost spinning their wheels "tinkering toward utopia."[3] Unable to correct its "learning path error," the system just keeps pumping out a consistently branded, remarkably standardized supply of students at the end.

One of the implicit goals of centralization and consolidation was to reduce the "span of control" in the management of schools. Small schools scattered and organized as a multiplicity of units present problems of management for high-level managers,[4] in this case provincial and district superintendents. Consolidating schools and establishing bigger district units narrows the span of control and makes the individual units and their employees easier to manage and direct for system-wide purposes. While district consolidation can yield more schools to manage from the central office, that challenge can be overcome by adding a new cohort of middle managers. Very large school districts tend to employ large central office staffs and generate layers of bureaucracy.[5] There are some benefits to consolidating operations, but only to a certain point. When school districts become so massive that they dominate an entire region, they can and do begin to function as a public monopoly with little or no incentive to improve their operations or performance.[6]

Centralized decision-making in education has tended to be aligned with "command-and-control" management. School administrators in expanding systems found themselves on what Anthony Normore once described as the "edge of chaos" and under pressure to adopt new and expanded administrative roles driven by student, teacher, and school accountability.[7] One of Canada's recognized assessment experts, Lorna Earl, examined the impact of the public accountability movement in Ontario in the 1990s. Educational accountability, from the school administrator's perspective, meant "being responsible or obligated to report and to justify one's actions to those who are entitled to the information."[8] Some administrators resisted the push toward quality assurance, closer oversight, and order compliance; others embraced school improvement, public reporting of results, and communicating of action plans. The primary challenge for education administrators lay in meeting the state policy and professional demands without losing sight of the system's core mission – to meet the needs of children and act in their best interests. With the arrival of education technology, digital surveillance, and data collection, the problem has become more acute. Today's school district superintendents have come to rely increasingly upon algorithmic decision-making systems, and school-level managers are absorbed in bureaucratic managerialism.[9]

CREEPING CENTRALIZATION
AND SCHOOL DISTRICT CONSOLIDATION

School district consolidation is a striking phenomenon not only from province to province in Canada, but across the United States as well. Two levels of consolidation, encompassing the merging of smaller schools and the collapsing of school districts, lead to the centralization of management. It also rests primarily on two presumed benefits: (1) *fiscal efficiency* and (2) *higher educational quality*. The sheer scale of district consolidation is staggering. Driven largely by the pursuit of financial economy and efficiency, district consolidation swept across the United States and reduced the number of K–12 districts from 117,108 in 1939–40 to 13,862 by 2006–07, a decline of 88 percent. The rate of consolidation has slowed over the past decade, but at least a few districts consolidate every year in many states.[10] While comparative Canadian data is not readily available, it is relatively safe to assume the existence of a similar pattern.[11]

School district consolidation in Canada is driven by provincial education authorities looking for cost reductions, but in some cases, the trigger factor is eliminating local education authorities who are obstructing education initiatives. Provincial announcements authorizing educational restructuring, such as the 1996 Ontario School Reduction Task Force, justify the school district consolidation as a cost reduction measure and commit to redirecting any savings into the classroom. Declining student enrolments, demographic trends, out-migration, and duplicated functions are among the common factors cited in making the case for consolidation.[12]

In the case of Prince Edward Island, provincial education authorities claimed that district consolidation was aimed at providing clarity of direction rather than any economic benefits. In October 2011, for example, the PEI Education Governance Commission recognized that the evidence of "operational efficiencies and net savings" is mixed, based upon previous ventures in Prince Edward Island and elsewhere. "There is a risk," the Commission report recognized, "that any savings that may result from elimination of duplication in some areas could be offset, initially by transition costs, and in the longer term by rising expenditures in other areas such as increased specialization and more hierarchy."[13]

In most places, however, school district consolidation is still primarily justified as a way to cut costs. These cost savings arise, the argument goes, because the provision of education is characterized by economies of scale, which exist whenever the cost of education per student declines as the number of students goes up. In this context, the cost of education is not the same as education spending, but is instead the amount a school district would have to spend to obtain a given level of performance, as measured by test scores, graduation rates, and perhaps other output measures. To put it another way, economies of scale exist if spending on education per pupil declines as the number of pupils goes up, controlling for school district performance. Because consolidation creates larger school districts, it results in lower costs per pupil whenever such economies exist.[14]

The potential advantages of school district consolidation are:

Indivisibilities: First, the school services provided to each student by certain education professionals may not diminish in quality as the number of students increases, at least over some range. All districts require a superintendent, and the same central administration may be able to serve a significant range of enrolment with little change in total costs.

Increased Dimension: Second, education requires certain physical capital, such as heating systems and science laboratories, which require a certain scale to operate efficiently and therefore have a high cost per pupil in small districts.

Specialization: Third, larger districts may be able to employ more specialized teachers, putting them in a better position to provide the wide range of courses required by public accountability systems and expected today by students and parents.

Innovation and Learning: Finally, teachers in larger districts have more colleagues on whom to draw for advice and discussion, interactions that presumably lead to improved effectiveness.[15]

POTENTIAL MITIGATING FACTORS

Popular assumptions about economies of scale have been challenged by researchers focusing on the relationship between school and school district size and student performance and well-being. Rural education studies have demonstrated that the sizes of the school district and the high school are highly correlated, and, in many cases, cost savings are rarely realized and larger schools can have a detrimental impact upon student performance and engagement. Effective schools research also tends to show that small to moderate-sized schools are more successful than mega-schools at retaining students through to high school graduation.[16] Leading American experts on school district consolidation William Duncombe and John Yinger have found that extremely large districts (those enrolling 15,000 or more students) are likely to be fiscally inefficient because consolidation has proceeded beyond the point of a favourable cost-benefit ratio.

Four identified disadvantages of excessive consolidation are:

Higher Transportation Costs: First, consolidated school districts usually make of larger schools, which implies that average transportation distance must increase. As a result, consolidation might increase a district's transportation spending per pupil.

Levelling Up of HR Costs: Second, consolidating districts may level up salaries and benefits to those of the most generous participating district, thereby raising personnel costs.

Lowering of Staff Morale: Third, administrators and teachers tend to have a more positive attitude toward work in smaller schools, which tend to have more flexible rules and procedures.

Less Student and Parent Participation: Finally, students can be more motivated and parents more comfortable with interacting with teachers in smaller districts, which tend to have a greater community feel. These attitudes, and closer student-faculty relationships generally, may result in higher student performance at any given spending level. Longer school bus rides also have a detrimental impact upon student engagement and achievement (further explored in chapter 5).

Overall, the net impact of consolidation on education costs per pupil *is not always clear.* The consolidation of tiny school districts of 1,500 students or fewer is likely to tap into economies of size and thereby lower these costs, but, beyond those numbers, consolidation might actually cause costs per pupil to rise.[17] The most recent research literature review, published in 2011 by the US National Education Policy Center, concluded that "claims for educational benefits from systematic state-wide school and district consolidation are vastly overestimated and, beyond school districts of 1,500, have actually been maximized years ago."[18]

BIGNESS, BUREAUCRACY, AND SCHOOLS

Everywhere you look across Canada today, the march of urbanized, bureaucratic, centralized education is nearly complete, and we are

Figure 4.1 Early School Consolidators
School Inspector H.M. MacDonald and the Antigonish Municipal School
Board, 1942, strongly supported consolidation plans in Eastern Nova
Scotia.

approaching "peak consolidation."[19] Today's central administrative
offices, layers of administration, super-sized elementary schools and
big-box high schools all testify to the dominance of the trend toward
school consolidation. School finance directors and facilities planners,
following in the footsteps of American education finance pioneer Edgar
L. Morphet and OISE school administration professor George E.
Flower, have welcomed the prevailing trend toward larger local education authorities and bigger schools. In embracing Morphet's education
finance model and principles, they did much to entrench a new bureaucratic ideology based upon economies of scale, operational efficiency,
optimal school size, and the allocation of pupil places.[20] Today's space
optimization algorithms used to plan new schools and identify surplus
sites owe their origins to the work of Morphet and his generation of
school planners. Similar modes of top-down educational planning
remain the preferred methods in our provincial school systems.

ignores capacity issues

School consolidation is normally presented as a common-sense, practical solution to declining enrolment in small schools, whether located in urban neighbourhoods or rural communities. School consolidators, posing as modernizers and progressives, tend to rely upon a few standard lines. "Student enrolment has dropped, so we cannot afford to keep your small school open. Now don't get emotional on us. It simply comes down to a matter of dollars and cents." Both the logic and the accuracy of those claims are now being seriously challenged.

What's wrong with this conventional school planning and design logic? A growing body of North American education research on the "dollars and sense" of school size is exploding the myth, and now suggests that smaller-scale schools are not only better for students but, surprisingly, more cost-effective for school boards.[21] Whereas school consolidation and economies of scale were once merely accepted truths, supported by little evidence, newer studies are demonstrating that truly small schools also deliver better results in academic achievement, high school completion rates, student safety, and social connectedness.

School sizes continued to grow until the first decade of the 2000s with little research support, coherent analysis, or public scrutiny. One influential study, J.B. Conant's 1959 book *The American High School Today*, fed the up-sizing movement with a fateful recommendation that high schools required at least 400 students to offer a "comprehensive program" and no high school should have a graduating class of fewer than 100 students.[22] Following his recommendation, high schools were increasingly consolidated, and in the United States, the number of high schools with more than 1,500 students doubled within two decades. By 2010, 40 percent of America's high schools had enrolled more than 1,000 students apiece, and the die was cast.

The most popular, safest, and single most effective model of schooling, the small schools model, was not only overlooked but effectively marginalized by policy-makers and school facilities planners. Independent scholarly research in support of smaller schools, especially for secondary school students, gradually began to surface;[23] such empirical research, however, rarely made it to the table where policy is made – in the Ministry of Education, the superintendent's office, the school architect's workplace, or even the university faculties of education.

One of the first studies to challenge the prevailing orthodoxy was the 2002 Knowledge Works Foundation study *Dollars & Sense: The*

Cost Effectiveness of Small Schools.[24] Written by Barbara Kent Lawrence and a team of recognized experts, it very effectively demolished the central arguments made by large school defenders based upon so-called economies of scale. Small schools, the authors claimed, actually cost less to build per student. They made the compelling case that large schools, compared to small schools, have:

- Higher administrative overhead
- Higher maintenance costs
- Increased transportation costs
- Lower graduation rates
- Higher rates of vandalism
- Higher absenteeism
- Lower teacher satisfaction

In addition to dispelling myths about economies of scale, the authors proposed specific guidelines for ideal school sizes, specifying upper limits:

High Schools (Grades 9–12), 75 students per grade,
300 total enrolment
Middle Schools (Grades 5–8), 50 students per grade,
200 total enrolment
Elementary Schools (Grades 1–8), 25 students per grade,
200 total enrolment
Elementary Schools (Grades 1–6), 25 students per grade,
150 total enrolment

The authors of *Dollars & Sense* also rejected claims that the benefits of "smallness" could be achieved by designing and creating schools-within-a-school (SWaS). They recognized that turning oversized facilities into SWaS design schools may be practical, but recommended against designing new schools where large numbers of students (Grades K–12) were reconfigured into divisions in particular sections or linked buildings.

A landmark 2008 *Educational Planning* article, "Don't Supersize Me," written by Craig B. Howley, provided the concrete evidence that building small schools was more cost-effective.[25] Comparing 87 smaller Grade 9–12 schools with 81 larger schools, Howley's research demonstrated that the smaller schools (138 to 600 students) were, on average, no more expensive per student to build than the larger schools (enrolling 601–999 students), and were actually less costly per square foot ($96 vs. $110). Furthermore, planned larger "new build" schools were routinely oversized when actual enrolments were considered, making them, on balance, more expensive per student, the key cost metric.

During a nine-year period, from 2000 to 2009, the Bill and Melinda Gates Foundation took a $2 billion run at the problem with mixed results.[26] Comprehensive high schools were declared harmful to the academic advancement and welfare of American students. Mega–high schools with as many as 4,500 students educated under a single roof were found to be breeding apathy, sapping students' motivation to learn and teachers' commitment to teaching. Beginning in 2000, the Gates Foundation poured hundreds of millions of dollars into replacing these dropout factories, funding 1,600 new, mostly urban high schools of a few hundred students each, some of them in restructured comprehensive high schools, others in new locations.

The massive Gates Small School Initiative, centred in Portland, Oregon, ran into structural barriers, sparked teacher union resistance, and did not produce quick results.[27] Trying to resize schools and reinvent decadent school cultures proved more challenging than expected, and the Gates Foundation ran out of patience when student test scores remained stagnant. "Many of the small schools that we invested in did not improve students' achievement in any significant way," Bill Gates wrote in 2009. The foundation then made a sharp turn and shifted its attention and resources to teacher quality reform strategies.

The campaign for more personalized urban and regional high schools – structured and designed to forge more meaningful connections between students and adults in a concerted effort to boost student achievement – is still supported by a raft of research and student and teacher surveys. American authorities on student dropouts consistently report that students don't care because they don't feel valued. "When adolescents trust their teachers ... they're more likely to persist through graduation," claim the University of Michigan's Valerie Lee and Julia Smith of Western Michigan University. While smaller size was not a determinant of student learning, it can be a "facilitating factor" for creating a positive learning environment, especially for socially disadvantaged students.[28]

The Gates experiments did provide some vitally important lessons. Reducing school sizes alone is not enough to turn around under-performing schools. In the case of New York City, shutting down twenty large, under-performing high schools worked better in improving graduation rates (from 47 to 63 percent) because the principals of the two hundred new smaller schools that were created as replacements had the power to hire their own teachers and staff.[29] The Knowledge Is Power Program (KIPP) charter schools, created on the small school model, also fared much better than the mainstream reconfigured urban high schools.[30] Principals and teachers at KIPP schools, for example, pride themselves on knowing every student's name – something the schools are able to do mostly because they're small, with average enrolments of three hundred. Even in his 2009 critique of the Small Schools Initiative, Bill Gates praised the small-scale KIPP schools. Their strong results may reflect the combination of smaller size, high standards, longer school days, and employing their own teachers and staff.

THE DOLLARS AND SENSE OF SMALL SCHOOLS

Creating smaller schools and a more intimate school climate in the absence of high standards and good teaching isn't enough. There's no guarantee that small schools, in and of themselves, will create good climates. Having said that, smaller schools are more likely to create the sense of connectedness among students and teachers that motivates them both to work hard, according to the *Dollars & Sense* researchers.[31] The needed level of genuine caring and mutual obligation between students and teachers is also found far less frequently in large, comprehensive high schools. Small schools, in other words, are more likely to generate the conditions that make learning possible.

Breaking up super-sized, dysfunctional high schools proved to be much easier said than done in the United States. Writing in the July/August 2010 special edition of *Washington Monthly*, Thomas Toch put it best.[32] Creating smaller units within oversized high schools may not work miracles, but is likely a step in the right direction. Smaller school settings are still proving to be one of a number of important means to the desired end: getting students and teachers in impoverished neighbourhoods or marginalized rural communities to invest more in their work still looks like the best route toward "lifting achievement" and getting "a far wider range of students" through high school and on to post-secondary education.

Building super-sized schools is frequently presented as a further "progressive" step in modernizing the system. Yet leading thinkers such as Robert D. Putnam claim that bigger schools and increasing bureaucratization have served to undermine both civic engagement and social connectedness. "Smaller schools, like smaller towns," as Putnam pointed out in his bestseller *Bowling Alone* (2001), "generate higher expectations for mutual reciprocity and collective action. So de-concentrating mega-schools or creating smaller 'schools within schools' will almost certainly produce civic dividends."[33] Bigness and bureaucracy are not always good for students, teachers, or schools. It is not a matter of returning to a simpler time, but rather one of regaining control over our schools, rebuilding social capital, and revitalizing local communities.

EDUCATION CENTRES AND EMPIRE-BUILDING

Centralizing school administration represents the highest stage of educational consolidation. Inside the system, erecting Education Centres to house central administration is presented as a natural evolution of modernization; from the outside, it often looks like a visible manifestation of empire-building. From 2005 to 2012, right across Canada, building oversized central office complexes or leasing space for super-sized corporate headquarters was in vogue among major metropolitan school districts. The most ostentatious example of the so-called "edifice complex" was the Calgary Board of Education's move in February 2011 into a 180,000 sq. ft. corporate headquarters in South West Calgary, leased for twenty years, for $5.5 million in 2011, escalating to $11 million or more in subsequent years.[34] Two other urban boards that moved out of their downtowns to occupy more palatial Education Centres in the suburbs were the Halifax Regional School Board and the Hamilton-Wentworth District School Board. Both of those moves sparked local controversy centred on the question of priorities and the impact of moving farther away from downtown schools.[35]

The fateful Calgary decision was made five years earlier by a CBE board of trustees chaired by Gordon Dirks, a future Alberta Minister of Education, before the 2008 global financial meltdown. When the grandiose headquarters opened, it provoked a loud public outcry because it coincided with news that the CBE was cutting 200 full-time teaching jobs and 85 student support positions in the throes of a budget crunch. The CBE teachers' union president, Jenny Regal, was not only dumbfounded by the cost of the new building, but alarmed about "the way money has to go to the lease instead of the classroom." Public concern found a voice in the form of a Calgary public education watchdog group, ARTICS, the Association for Responsive Trusteeship in Calgary Schools. The chair of ARTICS, Larry Leach, publicly criticized the secretive deal and the lack of public accountability. "It was all done behind closed doors," he told CBC News. "We want the CBE to be more accountable … and transparent," Leach stated. "This is public education, these are public dollars."[36] Such concerns found further confirmation in an April 2018 provincial audit that showed the CBE claiming $9.1 million of office rental fees as instructional costs. It was also revealed that the board was spending 3.3 percent on administrative costs, while running a $15 million budget deficit.[37] Legitimate concerns over excessive spending tended to obscure public discussion of underlying trends indicative of centralization and the so-called controlling politics of the "new managerialism" in public education.

Some thirty years after the advent of School-Based Management (SBM), this school board, like many across North America, remained wedded to system-wide management of virtually every aspect of educational service. While more advanced senior administrators claim to be modelling "distributed leadership," they remain resistant to more democratic, school-level decision-making models and tend to spend most of their time within their bureaucratic cocoons. New York teaching veteran Thomas Whitby, initiator of #edchat, is one educator who has expressed concern over the trend toward centralizing board operations in Education Centres farther and farther away from classroom teachers. After visiting a Long Island school district headquarters, a few years ago, he noted that they can function as a world apart from front-line teachers in the schools.

Administrative build-up is one of the main consequences of district consolidation. A Nova Scotia education administration review, conducted in 2017–18 and led by Canadian education consultant Avis Glaze, turned up some telling statistics. The province's eight school districts, serving 118,000 students in 395 schools, employed 38 senior administrators at a salary cost of $4.7 million a year, and 6.7 percent of the total staff based in the schools were classed as administration. Furthermore, some 100 teaching support specialists housed in seven English-language district offices rarely visited the schools because they were overburdened with paperwork, data entry, and administrative tasks. As a corrective measure, Glaze recommended that they be redeployed for four days a week to work with teachers in the classrooms.[38]

A succession of system-wide education reforms since the early 1990s have also changed the very nature of the principalship and school leadership. Student testing, accountability, and measurement systems have revolutionized school-level administration. A new form of managerialism has come to the fore as a manifestation of neo-liberal ideology in an age of global competitiveness. Growing demands for educational efficiencies and accountability for student outcomes arose at the very time when principals' and teachers' capacity to manage the factors that affect these dimensions of learning were diminishing.[39] One leading Australian researcher, Bruce Johnson, has not only flagged, but registered concern over the sociopolitical phenomenon of educational managerialism. "Bureaucratic managerialism," according to Johnson, has been used to "construct a seemingly irresistible top-down juggernaut of reform that largely excludes the possibility or desirability of local agency." School-based management had considerable appeal because it fostered a positive politics of "negotiation, collaboration, and conflict resolution to address issues of local concern in schools." He longed for the day when teachers, as well as parents, could enjoy a "more positive framework" with ongoing opportunities to participate in the "school improvement journey."[40] In practice, the advance of managerialism significantly altered school culture, affecting principals and staff alike, as they gradually adapted to a more assessment-driven, competitive organizational order.[41]

Managerialism has had a profound influence on educational practice in schools. While its impact has been more pronounced at the university and college level, provincial school systems and school boards since the mid-1990s have embraced large-scale student assessments and have begun producing school-by-school student performance accountability reports. With few exceptions, school authorities have resisted releasing provincial or district rankings based upon student assessment results.[42] School-based management and block-funding of schools, pioneered in Edmonton Public Schools, have not gained much traction elsewhere. Published rankings of schools do appear annually, but they are produced by independent market-oriented policy institutes such as the Fraser Institute, the Montreal Economic Institute, or the Atlantic Institute for Market Studies.

What has changed is the higher echelons of educational leadership. Senior education bureaucrats and district superintendents are increasingly drawn from management schools instead of from education faculties specializing in teaching subject disciplines. From 1998 to 2001, former British Columbia Deputy Minister of Education Charles Ungerleider reported that only one or two of his ten provincial counterparts had a formal background in education. In place of people like Ungerleider, governments were turning more and more to experts in management or administration. These practitioners of "new managerialism," he claimed, lacked the requisite educational knowledge and an intimate understanding of public schooling, which limited their capacity to speak authoritatively to one another and to the education ministers they served.[43] Driven more by globalization and new information technologies, school superintendents and administrators were gradually becoming system managers most comfortable in organizational culture and skilled in training up principals in the art and science of organizational learning.[44] Successful school leaders, for better or worse, were those who were the most effective at marketing their schools by showing responsiveness to public (i.e. consumer) demands.

CENTRALIZATION, BUREAUCRACY, AND SCHOOL LIFE

Teaching and learning in public schools, rural as well as urban, are now driven to a surprising degree by bureaucratic imperatives and the dominant educational accountability agenda.[45] Most of the provincial curricula and guidelines are interwoven with, and reflect standards reinforced in, a standardized, one-size-fits-all program of provincial testing and accountability. In rural regional high schools and even local elementary schools, educators are trained to implement standardized student assessments, outcome-based learning, and data-driven reporting. Child development philosophy, social justice and equity initiatives, and "success for all" programs tend to counterbalance somewhat the full force of system-wide testing and accountability in elementary schools.[46] Nevertheless, system-wide testing in mathematics and literacy has tended to cut into instructional time for supposedly soft subjects such as social studies and environmental science. All of this tends to erode the time remaining for local, place-based programs essential to what Australian rural educators term "education for sustainability." The priority, for them, is educating children prepared to meet "the crucial global challenges of sustainability and survival."[47]

Centrally developed and managed school curricula have come to serve the demands and needs of a corporatist, managed, and networked urban society, experienced most acutely in rural and small-town Canada.[48] Yet, as Acadia University's Michael Corbett has aptly observed, rural places will not go away. "Rustic spaces," he points out, "continue to haunt our global consumer society and our forward-looking modernist education system." Instead of fading from the scene, they persist and stand in the way of urban modernizers seeking to "develop" rural places as sources of resources and labour to fuel the urban, technocratic, globalized economy. Surrounded by a world too large to be controlled, rural dwellers seek to "shrink it back to their size and reach" and "anchor themselves in places" where they can "recall their historic memories." Small school advocates and rural educators, for that reason, favour place-based education, and that has given the rural education movement a new lease on life.[49]

Small school advocates and front-line educators are in the forefront of the resistance to the advance of the centralizing, bureaucratic education state. Confronted with globalization and the spread of neo-liberal competitive values, community school educators are reaffirming the importance of place-based history, culture, and tradition and promoting the advantages of a local community-based curriculum that speaks to the needs and aspirations of rural children.[50] Regular teachers find themselves on the front lines of a growing resistance to the spread of the new managerialism in the schools. With caring professions such as teaching being transformed into systems for the collection and assessment of student and school assessment data, they are seeing places of learning becoming service delivery operations with performance targets.[51] Close observers of advances in education technology are also awakening to the new realities of digital oversight exemplified in the emergence of electronic record systems, data-gathering networks, and algorithmic decision-making processes.[52] Glimmers of hope are appearing amidst an increasingly metrocentric, data-driven, systematized education world.

5

Education on Wheels

The Hidden Costs of Busing Schoolchildren

The yellow school bus rumbling along a winding country road is one of the most popular and enduring images of rural education. Since the inception of student busing, education planners and school administrators have portrayed the yellow buses as a harbinger of progress and a gateway for schoolchildren to improved school conditions, more variety in teaching, and better outcomes.[1] In the early 1990s, *The Magic School Bus*, a popular children's television series, romanticized the yellow bus as an imaginative journey through time and space. The show was revived in September 2017 in a modernized version for today's generation of youngsters.[2]

Those mythological images run smack up against the daily reality of longer and longer school bus rides for millions of children as young as four years of age and as old as eighteen in our K–12 school system. Today, roads full of school buses exemplify the dominance of a mode of transportation technology that enabled and advanced school consolidation and paved the way for bigger and bigger schools, known as "big box" elementary and "super-sized" high. Tougher questions are also being asked: Did the promised improvements materialize? And, where they did, were there hidden short-term and long-term costs?

Student busing is no longer strictly a rural phenomenon. North American public schools, urban, suburban, and rural, simply do not operate anymore without a ready fleet of yellow buses. More and more of our school tax dollars are going to provide services outside the classroom in the form of "Education on Wheels," otherwise known as daily student transportation. A January 2015 study published by the Atlantic Institute for Market Studies (AIMS) documented the shift in two of the Maritime provinces.[3] From 1987 to 2014, according to

School Bus Fleet annual reports, student enrolment in New Brunswick significantly declined but annual busing costs almost doubled, rising from $31.3 million to $58.7 million. In Nova Scotia, over the years from 2009 to 2014, student transportation costs (actual operating/per F/S) rose from $64.2 million to $71.2 million, an increase of 10.9 percent at a time when overall P–12 (pre-kindergarten to Grade 12) enrolment shrunk by 8.3 percent from 131,159 to 120,340 students. Student busing costs and numbers, it seemed, defied demographic gravity, at least in Maritime Canada.

BUSING STUDENTS TO SCHOOL –
A LASTING IMPACT OF SCHOOL CONSOLIDATION

School closures and consolidation are routinely implemented as austerity measures without any real disclosure of the impact on school board or provincial school busing costs. Small school advocates and community activists who ask questions about the added costs to taxpayers are assured either that they are of no concern or that more students can simply be added to existing bus routes.[4] Behind the scenes, school boards claim that costs are "at the breaking point" and lobby fiercely for increased grant support to maintain or augment their bus fleets. Transportation is, as a 2008 Alberta School Boards Association report quipped, "the stone in everybody's shoe."[5] Yet, in the case of a province such as Nova Scotia, closing schools and putting more students on buses has only compounded the problem. Nine years ago, three in five P–12 students (62.8 percent) were bused to school each day; by 2013–14, two-thirds (68.1 percent) of the province's students rode the buses and were travelling longer average daily distances. Expanding student bus transportation is closely connected with the process of school consolidation in rural and remote school districts.

Student transportation trends vary across North American states and provinces. Looking at the entire US kindergarten to Grade 12 student population, slightly over half (55.3 percent) of the 25.3 million students in 2004 were transported on school buses at public expense.[6] A 2009 American study of how that nation's elementary school students get to school demonstrated that, while the proportion of US K–12 students bused over the past forty years had remained about 39 percent overall, the percentage being driven by parents had jumped from 12 percent to 45 percent. Most significantly, the proportion of American students walking or bicycling to school had dropped from 48 percent to only 13 percent.[7] This pattern is not as evident in Maritime cities such as Halifax, Saint John, Moncton, or Fredericton. In the Halifax Regional School Board (2013–14), for example, 24,509 of the 48,596 students (or 50.4 percent) were bused, about 7.6 percent more than five years earlier. For small-town and rural Maritime children, student transportation by those distinctive yellow buses still predominates, with most school districts busing between 80 and 95.9 percent of their students to and from school each day from September to June.[8]

School closures mean longer and longer bus rides in rural communities across Canada. Ontario's Near North District School Board serves the Almaguin Highlands south of North Bay, and the experience of rural students there is quite typical. When the Magnetawan Central School was threatened with closure in April 2014, local school trustee Al Bottomley protested busing plans that would have scheduled high school students and a small number of elementary students for one-way rides of at least 75 minutes. "My main issue is how long can you put a kid on a bus before their brain falls out? That's my worry with little kids and even bigger kids," he told *Almaguin News*. "I think you have to think of what you want these kids to have," he added. "Do you want them to be in a central area that's going to cost them time on buses, time away from their homes and also at a cost to the towns they leave?"[9] Faced with a tight budget and limited options, the Near North Board was looking at closing schools and some less-than-desirable alternative student accommodation plans. Raised in the tiny hamlet of Loring, Bottomley was well-acquainted with waiting for the bus at 40 below zero, and with how hard getting to school could be when tired out or coping with a family crisis. Without many readily available studies assessing the impact on a child's ability to learn or participate in extra-curricular activities, school boards are essentially flying blind when it comes to busing more and more students.

Today student transportation is a major public expenditure for provincial authorities and school boards, and particularly in rural and small-town Canada, a higher proportion of students are transported to school each day. School bus expenditures, funded mostly through provincial grants, have rarely, if ever, been audited and remain largely unexplored by researchers. A Canadian Education Association (CEA) study in 1987 provided an overview of the national picture, covering 158 school boards, and documented wide variations in the operation, regulation, and funding of bus fleets from one province to another. In the case of the four Atlantic Provinces, the CEA reported that $99.3 million was spent during 1986–87 on pupil transportation, representing from 5.4 to 7.03 percent of total provincial education budgets.[10] Expanding student bus transportation was identified in comparative school board data as closely connected with the process of school consolidation in rural and remote school districts.

Comparative analysis of Canadian student transportation is a challenge in the absence of a federal presence in education and the limitations of the published data. A North American trade magazine, *School Bus Fleet*, provides annual summaries of Canadian Pupil Transportation Data by province, so there is some basis for comparison. Annual reports from 2007 to 2014 include New Brunswick and Nova Scotia, and report on the number of school buses, number of students transported, total kilometres of service, and, on a limited basis, provincial funding levels. In New Brunswick, from 1987 to 2014, student enrolment has significantly declined but annual busing costs have almost doubled, rising from $31.3 million to $58.7 million. In June 2013, the magazine reported that Nova Scotia had a total school bus fleet inventory of 1,376 buses, 149 (or 10 percent) more than six years earlier.[11]

A more detailed picture of the changes emerges from an analysis of the Nova Scotia data on student transportation. While school enrolments have plummeted in Nova Scotia, transportation costs per student have risen. Official Nova Scotia Education Department data covering the eight school boards for the five-year period 2009–14 contradicts the published *Bus Fleet* magazine information, showing slightly fewer buses (1,073 to 1,100), but reporting much higher costs per student transported and a growing proportion of all P–12 students (5.3 percent more) dependent upon daily bus transportation. (See Tables 5.1 and 5.2.)

CONTAINING RISING STUDENT TRANSPORTATION COSTS

Over the past thirty years, since the mid-1980s, provincial authorities and school boards outside of the Maritime region have become much more attuned to student transportation costs and the potential for cost efficiencies. Sharing of bus services between school boards and with other educational institutions surfaced in the mid-1980s, mainly in

Table 5.1
Student Transportation Expenditures, School Boards of Nova Scotia, 2009–14

School Board	2009-10	2010–11	2011–12	2012–13	2013–14
	(actual expenditures for full-time students)				
Annapolis RSB	8,600,769	8,663,909	9,372,417	9,195,532	9,009,089
Cape Breton RSB	7,240,446	6,896,728	7,287,239	6,919,774	6,698,234
Chignecto-Central	11,432,183	12,264,951	12,032,521	12,110,055	12,630,881
Acadien (CSAP)	5,449,673	6,015,747	6,239,478	6,474,827	6,633,266
Halifax RSB	14,110,959	15,815,391	16,588,051	17,501,098	17,977,039
South Shore RSB	5,524,123	6,077,649	5,780,174	5,703,634	5,746,905
Strait Region RSB	7,289,491	7,002,284	7,373,078	7,355,672	5,746,905
Tri-County RSB	4,591,907	5,128,587	5,217,892	5,064,626	5,097,544
Totals	64,239,551	67,865,244	69,890,850	70,325,218	71,241,213

A Table showing Student Transportation expenditures generated by the Nova Scotia Department of Education and Early Childhood Development, October, 2014.

Source: Atlantic Institute for Market Studies/Bennett and Gillis, 2015.

Table 5.2
Student Population Changes and Students Bused, Nova Scotia, 2009–14

School Board	2009-10	2010–11	2011–12	2012–13	2013–14
	(number of students; percentage bused in parentheses)				
Annapolis RSB	14,882 (85.1)	14,415 (83.0)	14,079 (82.7)	13,585 (87.5)	13,341 (84.8)
Cape Breton-Victoria RSB	16,312 (85.1)	15,307 (44.0)	14.575 (44.7)	13,977 (48.6)	13,673 (49.0)
Chignecto Central RSB	22,196 (76.3)	21,750 (77.2)	21,295 (77.8)	20,954 (78.7)	20,423 (82.3)
Conseil scolaire acadien provincial	4,227 (95.0)	4,316 (97.0)	4,415 (85.9)	4,556 (86.8)	4,718 (94.2)
Halifax RSB	51,388 (42.8)	50,480 (44.7)	49,552 (46.4)	49,027 (47.5)	48,596 (50.4)
South Shore RSB	7,347 (91.6)	7,307 (90.4)	6,949 (93.1)	6,864 (91.6)	6,681 (92.4)
Strait Region RSB	7,382 (96.2)	7,289 (96.0)	6,988 (95.7)	6,804 (96.2)	6,633 (95.9)
Tri-County RSB	7,425 (80.0)	6,938 (83.8)	6,680 (89.1)	6,401 (90.7)	6,275 (90.0)
Totals	131,159 (62.8)	127,802 (63.9)	124,533 (64.7)	122,168 (66.3)	120,340 (68.1)

Student Transportation Data generated by the Nova Scotia Department of Education and Early Childhood Development, October, 2014.

Source: Atlantic Institute for Market Studies/Bennett and Gillis, 2015

Ontario and rural Alberta. Joint Consortia for Transportation Services were established in four or five coterminous public and separate Ontario school board districts, including York Region and Sudbury School District. The Ontario School Bus Operators Association, based in Toronto, joined the collaboration when a number of boards began pushing for cost efficiencies. Such initiatives were accompanied by business plans incorporating computerized route scheduling, enforcement of walking distances, combining of routes, bulk purchasing, double runs, and staggered school times.[12]

A 2002 Ontario Education Equality Task Force recommended that the province create 8 to 10 joint transportation service boards. In 2006–07, the Ontario Ministry of Education took action, requiring school boards across the province to develop partnerships and combine school board transportation departments into separate fully integrated transportation organizations. The *Student Transportation Reform* initiative compelled all of the province's 72 boards to embrace the co-operative student transportation model and to combine in common, coterminous geographical areas.[13]

In the initial phases of coterminous sharing, millions of tax dollars were saved, but the entry of dominant bus industry players such as Laidlaw and Stock and the advent of preferred supplier arrangements tended to reduce price competition over time. While the initial cost efficiencies were dramatic, they did not apparently last. An Ontario Task Force report in June 2011 identified the problem of competitive procurement and revealed that school bus costs to serve 800,000 students had reached $845 million, representing 4 percent of the education budget. Based upon such findings, Ontario economist Don Drummond included reducing student transportation costs by 25 percent in his February 2012 report recommending province-wide austerity measures.[14] That recommendation was likely based upon the documented findings of Ministry of Education Effectiveness & Efficiency Reviews, conducted since 2008, and pointing out further potential cost savings among Ontario's 18 consortia operations.[15]

One research study, produced for the June 2012 Canadian Transportation Research Forum, provided a valuable critical economic market analysis of Canadian school bus transportation. Researchers Joseph Monteiro and Benjamin Atkinson offered an overview of student transportation, province by province, and then examined, in some detail, the school bus industry. They also provided an authoritative analysis of its structure, services, operations, market conditions, and concentration. Provincial regulations were examined to determine the impact on oligopolistic competition and entry into the industry. The researchers identified the need to further examine the impact of subsidization of pupil transportation, the privatization of school bus services, and the costs relative to the primary mission of public education systems. Serious attention was drawn to the potential for collusion between bus operators and "bid rigging" in the awarding of contracts.[16]

Transporting students to school is consuming more and more of the costs of public education in provincial school systems. Student transportation costs continue to creep up, particularly in the Maritime provinces, at a time when overall K–12 student enrolment continues to decline. While this is fast becoming a major challenge for provincial education authorities and school boards, the critical issues remain shrouded in mystery and largely hidden from the public. School board initiatives aimed at containing costs by fiddling with local busing regulations and enforcing walking distances have little effect when student transportation is taking a bigger and bigger bite out of provincial education spending.[17]

RIDING THE SCHOOL BUS: SHORT-TERM IMPACT

Generations of schoolchildren have ridden school buses, but research into the impact of long bus rides is mostly recent in origin. Education planners and student transportation managers treated the busing of students as an operational function and a matter of "moving people and goods" in an educational system. Moving students to and from schools efficiently and safely was the priority, and student health and wellness was a secondary consideration. Walking to school was, for most children, a healthy outdoor activity associated with what Cape Breton University's Catherine O'Brien has described as "wonder, joy, discovery and happiness."[18] Riding buses is part of the larger shift to motorized transportation. Compared to thirty years ago, children's daily trips, once taken by walking or cycling, are now taken by yellow bus or family car. Changes in school site planning, community land use, and transportation services have not only raised concerns about children's health but drawn attention to the need to protect and design more walkable, liveable communities.

Longer bus rides are common for rural children across North America. A 2001 US study covering rural and suburban schools in five different states demonstrated the challenges facing rural children

and teens riding school buses. Compared to their suburban counterparts, rural schools were: a) more likely to have longest rides of
30 minutes or more; b) more likely to have attendance areas greater
than 10 square miles; c) more likely to have bus routes with rougher
rides; d) less likely to have a full-time bus supervisor; and e) more
likely to group elementary to secondary students all together on bus
runs.[19] Such findings confirm the common concerns expressed by
rural parents and communities over the ride lengths and potential
dangers faced by students attending rural elementary schools.

Rural school advocates claim that long school bus rides have
the potential to rob children of the "joy of childhood." One of the
best-known case studies is West Virginia, where from 1990 to 1999,
more than a quarter of the state's 323 public schools were closed,
mostly in rural counties, and the state was reported to be providing the most expensive student transportation system in the United
States. Responding to the mass of closures, Beth Spence, a Challenge
West Virginia researcher, documented personal stories testifying to the
adverse impact of long school bus rides.[20] The smallest children were
left exhausted, high school students were too tired to complete homework, few could participate in extra-curricular sports or activities, and
most missed out on spending time on weeknights with their families.
School bus rides were depicted as dangerous adventures where sick
or injured children went unattended and some entertained themselves
vandalizing the bus or burning the bus seats. Students attending bigger comprehensive schools enjoyed greater class offerings but avoided
taking "hard courses" because they were too tired to do the required
homework when they arrived home. Families accustomed to long rural
bus rides testified to the time lost over the course of their education.
One Webster County mother claimed that, over four years of high
school, she spent 32 percent of her time on the bus, amounting to some
2,160 hours, roughly equivalent to 54 forty-hour work weeks. It was,
in Spence's words, a tale of "childhoods lost and dreams aborted" for
the rural West Virginian children who rode those yellow buses.

Similar adverse effects have been found in the best Canadian study
focused on rural families. Geographer Michael Fox interviewed
64 rural Quebec families in the mid-1990s, and, using the Household
Activity Travel Simulator developed at Oxford University, he assessed
the impact of long rides on household activities.[21] He found that long
bus rides reduced the number and variety of household activities and
reduced students' sleep time, homework time, and recreational time.

Students also suffered a variety of other school-related ill effects, including social isolation and disconnectedness at school. School busing schedules also played havoc with the regular and essential routines of farm family life. Rural school busing, Fox concluded, was "a costly and socially questionable activity" when it came to rural families.

Parental concerns and anecdotal evidence suggest that long bus rides may well affect student academic performance. Yet, in spite of the recent focus on student achievement factors, the impact of rural busing remains understudied. One pioneering American study, conducted in the early 1970s and using data collected from students in 27 Oklahoma school districts, found a small association between the length of students' bus rides and their academic achievement.[22] Studies of the impact of school consolidation on rural students of lower socio-economic status have proven more conclusive. In rural locales, where so many families' incomes fall below the national median, distant consolidated schools and long bus rides are part of the daily reality for schoolchildren. Smaller schools are positively associated with improved achievement for impoverished students, so it's reasonable to assume that attending larger, more distant schools would have a more detrimental outcome.[23]

Bullying on school buses is not new, but it surfaced in the early 2000s as a public issue of great concern to parents and teachers, right across Canada. One of Canada's leading authorities on bullying, Stu Auty, president of the Canadian Safe Schools Network, spent thirty years in education, and saw school buses as a source of a lot of the problems.[24] Being confined on the bus was a "big deal," he said in May 2014, because an hour's ride can be an eternity when you are a child being picked upon by peers. "School bus drivers are very concerned about it," he told *Global News*, "and, in some cases, it's been called 'recess in a can' where a driver has to control 30 kids behind them." It was, he added, more acute in rural areas "where kids are being bused and can't necessarily switch schools." One Calgary driver with three years' experience, Clarissa Rayner, provided a first-hand account of the real-life challenges. Transporting up to 68 Grade 5 to 8 students to a public school, she confronted children at an age when "bullying starts to become bigger." Typical of most drivers, she took on the job with little special training and was simply told to watch over the students, on her own, and if anything happened, to write up an incident report for the school to deal with. Looking back on the experience, she recalled that she had little interaction with the school beyond handing in the pink slips and was never informed of any results.[25]

Busing more and more students to school has very real but harder to identify longer-term human, social, and environmental costs. Although current Canadian research is sparse, existing research and anecdotal evidence is clear: Long bus rides affect children's health, erode family and play time, decrease physical activity, diminish participation in extracurricular activities, and may affect educational performance.[26] Back in 2005, Richard Gilbert and Catherine O'Brien did broaden the focus of study to assess the impact of land-use and transportation planning upon children and youth. The body of research produced to support the Ontario *Guidelines for Child and Youth Friendly Land-use and Transportation Planning in Rural Areas* clearly demonstrates the toll that transporting children takes on their health and overall well-being. Rural youth were shown to have a greater risk related to obesity and physical activity, and were more susceptible to health problems related to the poor air quality in buses and the length of time they are subjected to air pollutants. "While it receives little attention," the guidelines stated, "in-car air pollution may pose one of the greatest modern threats to human health."[27] Keeping schools within the local community, working towards shorter bus rides, and encouraging active transportation, rather than eliminating the opportunity for it, their research demonstrated, should be much higher priorities when planning for schools.

Two more recent Canadian studies have tackled head-on the health and safety effects of long bus rides. A Middlesex-London Health Unit report, prepared by Graham L. Pollett, MD, in October 2008, identified links between school bus time and physical activity, safety, bullying, air quality, and academic performance. Longer bus rides following the loss of community schools may well also increase rates of stress and anxiety in rural families. Bus fumes constitute a major pollutant in rural areas, and serious concerns have now been raised about air quality on school buses. "Given the evidence noted on air quality in school buses," Professor O'Brien of Cape Breton University insists, "not reducing children's exposure to pollutants in these vehicles could be more costly in the long run." In addition, longer hours spent on the bus translate into fewer opportunities for active, healthy living, and contribute to higher rates of obesity.[28]

Nova Scotia's Chief Medical Officer, Dr Robert Strang, supports this assessment of the health risks and favours active transportation that promotes the health and well-being of children and youth. Speaking in June 2014 at the Annual General Meeting of Community Transit–Nova Scotia, a non-profit transportation advocacy group, he supported not only easier access to affordable transportation, but a rethinking of school closures and the impact on student transportation. "Sedentary behaviour is a health risk," he stated, then posed the key questions: "How can we build in options for walking and cycling in daily life? In rural environments, how can we promote active as well as public transportation?" He also saw a constructive role for school boards. "What if we took a different approach to schools and made them the centre of the community," he asked. "Chignecto-Central Regional School Board (CCRSB) has 20,000 students, 83% of whom ride the school bus. Is moving schools closer to students part of the solution?" In his talk, Dr Strang issued a clear challenge: "Let's develop healthy communities in Nova Scotia: safe, affordable, and connected socially ... A piece of the puzzle is taking a different approach to transportation."[29]

TOWARD MORE WALKABLE SCHOOLS – THE SEARCH FOR ALTERNATIVES

Most student transportation departments in Canada and the US today focus primarily on getting students to school on yellow school buses. Aside from the metric dashboards and French-language signs, Canadian and US school buses are practically identical, produced by the same manufacturers. Looking at student transportation through the "yellow bus" lens tends to obscure the transportation departments' real role – providing students with access to education. They are entrusted, after all, with ensuring that students of all ages, urban and rural, travel safely to and from school. From one Canadian province to another, they also provide a way to get to school for students who live far away, as well as those with disabilities. By focusing solely on busing, however, student transportation officials miss a crucial opportunity to support students and communities.

Student transportation should be about more than school buses. Students are also getting to school by foot, bicycle, car, and public transportation; decisions about how students travel to school affect their health and safety, as well as traffic congestion, air pollution, and the health and safety of the community at large. Achieving cost efficiencies through improved operational effectiveness is only half of the equation. The North American Safe Routes to School movement, embraced by the Halifax-based Ecology Action Centre (EAC), is opening our eyes to a new vision of what is termed a "multi-modal student transportation system."[30] Taking a more holistic approach, it should be possible to transform existing operations into a support system that not only transports students safely, but is good for student health, academic engagement, community well-being, and environmental sustainability.

School buses certainly play a key role in getting students to and from school, but buses, like walking and bicycling, are only one piece of the school transportation puzzle. While titles such as "school transportation director" seem to suggest a position that oversees all transportation-related issues at a school or within a jurisdiction, in practice, these positions tend to focus heavily, if not solely, on bus-related transportation. School district policies give a clear indication of their current focus and priorities. Clause 1.1 of the Student Transportation Policy of the Halifax Regional Centre for Education (the largest school district in Atlantic Canada) reads "the Halifax Regional School Board will ensure that transportation service is provided in a safe manner to eligible students." Here, eligible students means bused-in students, despite the fact that the pertinent section of the Education Act reads "to provide for a publicly funded school system whose primary mandate is to provide education programs and services for students to enable them to develop their potential and acquire the knowledge, skills and attitudes needed to contribute to a healthy society and a prosperous and sustainable economy."[31]

Perhaps the time has come to expand the mandate of school transportation policies to better serve the actual needs of students and their families. Focusing more on preserving and protecting walkable school communities would be a great place to start. With such a policy in place, school guidelines and school curricula would be helpful in exposing students to the full range of viable transportation options. Making healthy choices more feasible and viable would render provincial wellness initiatives such as Nova Scotia's recent "Thrive!" much more effective. Then students and families would begin to really see the advantages of making choices that truly enhance a healthy society while promoting a prosperous and sustainable economy.

The EAC's child/youth active transportation programs are actually part of a nation-wide movement. The Canadian Active and Safe Routes to School Partnership is a national group working to increase the use of active, sustainable, and safe modes of transportation among school-aged children who travel to and from school. Its aim is to foster community cohesion and produce safer, calmer streets and neighbour-hoods for active transportation; to reduce greenhouse gas emissions and air pollution from motor vehicles; to increase physical activity; and to improve traffic safety.[32] School Travel Planning, Making Tracks, the Walking School Bus, and a few other branded national programs are being implemented in schools across Canada.

The Nova Scotia version is Safe Routes Nova Scotia, a series of child/youth active transportation programs led by the EAC. Working with school-based groups such as school administration, Parent-Teacher Associations, School Advisory Councils, student groups, and school staff – as well as outside of schools with youth and community organizations and stakeholders from education, health, safety, recre-ation, trails, environment, law enforcement, local government, and transportation and planning sectors – the EAC takes a comprehensive approach to increasing the adoption of active transportation habits by children and youth, making it easier and safer for them to choose for themselves.

The Nova Scotia project neatly summarizes the broad vision: "Active transportation means any non-motorized mode such as walking, cycling, in-line skating, skateboarding, scootering, wheel-chairing, cross-country skiing, canoeing, etc. Our vision is a Nova Scotia where walking, cycling or using other forms of active transportation is a popular and safe choice made by children, youth and their families for the trip to and from school and other places kids go."[33]

Schools in Nova Scotia, like those across Canada, are showing more sustained interest in child/youth active transportation. Since 2001, participation in the Ecology Action Centre's Walk to School Week/Month has grown among the province's 400 public and 25 private/independent schools. Starting with nine schools in 2001, the program expanded to reach 98 schools in 2010. Over 300 schools/groups are reported to have participated in at least one aspect of the EAC's child/youth programming between 2001 and 2010. All initiatives are coor-dinated by the EAC in partnership with the Nova Scotia Department of Health and Wellness as part of an Active Kids Healthy Kids Initiative. Safe Routes Nova Scotia supporters in 2014–15 included the Nova Scotia Department of Transportation and Infrastructure

Renewal, the Department of Health and Wellness, the Department of Energy, Mountain Equipment Co-op, and the Public Health Agency of Canada.[34] The long-term goal is for such initiatives to be more self-sustaining and less dependent upon provincial grant support.

Student transportation departments are being urged to move beyond busing schoolchildren and to embrace an expanded mission by supporting Safe Routes to School, walking and bicycling, and community well-being. In the light of education budget constraints, rising busing costs, and concerns regarding childhood obesity, Safe Routes to School proponents and student transportation officers would benefit from working together to help schools save money, decrease traffic, increase community safety, and improve the health of children.[35] Building smaller schools more centrally located in communities would seem to be a sensible alternative to more centralization, bigger schools, and longer bus rides compromising the long-term health of students. Sadly, however, few signs have appeared of the needed changes in school facilities planning and siting.

THE IMPACT OF STUDENT BUSING
ON THE SYSTEM

School districts today rely heavily upon their student transportation systems. Yellow buses take a bigger and bigger bite out of regional school district budgets and a sizeable proportion of students depend upon buses to get to and from school. Closing smaller schools and building regional elementary education centres or bigger high schools produces incremental increases in busing costs. Student transportation contracts are almost invariably awarded to one of the international student transportation corporations. School managers find themselves dealing with the Canadian branches of these transportation corporations. Technological advances such as route management software may increase efficiencies, but they can – and do – tend to remove the service providers from the actual clients, students, parents, and families.

A recent student transportation crisis in Atlantic Canada's largest school system demonstrates what can go wrong and the impact of irregularities in operations and disruptions in service. After awarding a second ten-year, $200 million system-wide contract to Stock Transportation in 2015, the Halifax Regional School Board daily transportation service (serving 23,000 students a day) began to experience a succession of problems. With a monopoly on HRSB transportation services, Stock management began to exemplify the tell-tale signs of service provider capture.[36] Two Stock bus drivers who blew the whistle on unsafe driving practices were fired, and a November 2017 Nova Scotia Utility and Review Board decision citing a litany of license violations raised serious questions about the safety of buses and the effectiveness of management. News of senior HRSB staff attending a PEI summer lobster party hosted by Stock's regional manager surfaced and smacked of collusion between the board and the vendor.[37] The final straw came in September 2018 when Stock and the HRSB bungled the introduction of *BusPlanner* software, completely disrupting the first week of school and creating chaos in Bedford-area schools.[38]

Nova Scotia's Education Minister Zach Churchill came up with $2 million for 37 more buses to defuse the parent uprising, and launched an investigation into the whole Stock Transportation fiasco.[39] Since a 2002 takeover by National Express Company, Stock has been a small piece of a massive international operation with $1 billion in revenues. In Nova Scotia, it operated 426 buses and employed some 600 drivers, mostly in the Halifax region. Nova Scotia Education was not the first to have issues with the company. Four years earlier, the Ottawa Student Transportation Authority had cancelled its contract with Stock, assigning 193 of their routes to three smaller firms: Campeau, Roxborough, and Direct Transportation Logistics. In early June 2019, Minister Churchill followed suit, announcing that the government had terminated the contract, subject to a one-year period of notice.[40] Concerned Nova Scotia parents were mostly placated by the decision, but provincial school authorities continued to resist public calls for a complete audit of student transportation services to ensure that the next contract rectified the identified problems.[41] While Stock lost its monopoly, the whole flap made this much clear: yellow buses do make the school system go around.

6

Public Choice in the System

Catholic Separate Schools, Linguistic Boards, and Diversity

The long-standing controversy erupted again in the midsummer dog days of 2018. A news commentary, written by Western University professors Samuel Tosow and Bill Irwin, ripped the scab off of a politically sensitive Ontario issue by proposing that the Catholic separate schools be merged into the Ontario public school system.[1] Seizing upon the opportunity to pitch the idea to Doug Ford's newly elected Progressive Conservative government, the two Western professors claimed that between $1.269 and $1.594 billion would be saved by merging the systems and it might help threatened small rural schools to stay afloat. Following a highly publicized 2006 Forum Research poll and a public appeal from Ottawa-based One School System and other advocacy groups,[2] the article went viral on social media and was read by some 20,000 people in a few short days. Then Education Minister Lisa Thompson rejected the proposal and reaffirmed the government's long-standing commitment to supporting Catholic separate schools, and both opposition parties were cool to the idea.[3] What the controversy revealed was that the continued existence of publicly funded Catholic schools alongside regular public schools remained a real bone of contention.

Public funding support for Catholic schools may have been in place in Ontario since Confederation, but it has always been a hotly contested matter. The struggle by Roman Catholic communities across Ontario to achieve equal status actually stretches back more than two hundred years. Since the occupation and settlement of Upper Canada in the eighteenth century, English Protestants, initially associated with the Church of England, had claimed territory and governance over Catholics, Indigenous peoples, and a whole range of minority groups.[4] The Roman Catholic minority established their own schools, and gradually, with the aid of French Catholics in the united Province of Canada, managed to secure recognition of the right to manage their own schools and a share of subsidies through the Common School Fund.[5] By the time of Confederation, Catholic school communities had carved out rights and privileges comparable to the Protestant public or common school system. The *British North America* (BNA) *Act* of 1867 constitutionally recognized Roman Catholic schools as separate but parallel public institutions.[6] That did not settle the question, however, and the twentieth century was marked by a succession of very noisy public debates over the legitimacy and validity of supporting a separate Roman Catholic system.

GROWTH AND EXPANSION OF ONTARIO SEPARATE SCHOOLS

The Roman Catholic school system expanded with the Baby Boom and encouraged Ontario's Catholic educational leaders to seek funding support to the end of high school. Saskatchewan had funded separate schools to Grade 10 ever since its creation in 1905. In 1965, that province passed *An Act to Amend the Secondary Education Act*, which authorized separate boards to offer grant- and tax-supported programs to the end of secondary school. That development brought Saskatchewan into line with five other educational jurisdictions providing public support for a complete denominational school system: Quebec, Alberta, Newfoundland, the Northwest Territories, and the Yukon.[7] The Ontario Foundation Tax Plan of 1963 improved grant support, and the implementation of regionalization in 1969 reduced the number of small local boards and solidified the Catholic system, strengthening its financial position.

Ontario's public school system responded to the increasingly diverse student population by becoming more secular from the 1960s onward. Elimination of the daily Christian prayer from secondary schools was part of a movement to remove the trappings of religious routine. In March 1969, the Mackay Committee published its report on *Religious Information and Moral Development*, recommending a complete halt to religious education in all primary and secondary public schools, except for the retention of a daily prayer in elementary schools.[8] Religious presentation at the secondary level was left to the discretion of principals. Such changes inadvertently aided Catholic separate

Figure 6.1 Catholic High School Funding Protest, Windsor, 1971

Ontario Premier Bill Davis was greeted by a Catholic High School Funding protest in Windsor during his 1971 visit.

schools, which continued to provide Christian instruction and offer
high school religion classes.

Shortly after becoming the Progressive Conservative leader, on
31 August 1971, William Davis closed the door on extending funding
to Ontario Catholic schools. Adopting the line drawn by his predeces-
sor, John P. Robarts, Davis maintained that such a move would open
a Pandora's Box and be too costly for the province. The establishment
of an equally funded denominational high school system would "frag-
ment the present system beyond recognition and repair, and do so to
the disadvantage of all." He was particularly concerned that the government would be "obliged" to do the same for other Protestant
students, Jewish students, and possibly others representing various
denominations.[9] Following his decisive 1971 election victory, Premier
Davis softened his position, giving Catholic school boards the option
of establishing schools beyond junior grades, albeit with limited financial support.

Changing demographics tilted the balance in favour of extending
tax support to Ontario Catholic high schools. The proportion of the
Ontario population that identified as Catholic rose by 5 percent from

1961 (30 percent) to 1981 (35 percent). New immigration broadened the Roman Catholic separate school population to include those practicing other forms of Catholicism. Between 1960 and 1980, Catholic school enrolment grew from one-third of the public school population to over half of that population. While there were twenty-three separate boards and fifty-seven high schools in 1971, forty-one new ones were established by 1984, twenty-five offering Grades 9 to 13 and sixteen offering Grades 9 and 10.[10] This growth would prove to be a factor weighing on the mind of Premier Davis.

Public pressure was also building around Davis and his cabinet. In 1977, Dr Henry B. Mayo suggested in his *Report of the Ottawa Carleton Review Commission*, "If a thing is right, it should be done, and the tradition should be broken (when prudential judgment allows, as St. Thomas Aquinas might say)." His report encouraged extension as a means to necessarily recognize both parental and religious rights, while appreciating a desirable diversity in Ontario schools.[11] The R.W.B. Jackson Commission on Declining Enrolment, a year later, also recommended a re-examination of extended funding.[12] Then in 1982, sparked by the 1981 Secondary Education Review Project Report, the Ontario Separate School Trustees Association (OSSTA) Board of Directors prepared a position paper that recommended the establishment of Roman Catholic boards of education, including elementary and secondary (Grades 9 and 10) panels, and suggested that grants be provided to equally fund the Roman Catholic secondary panel with partial subsidies going toward private Roman Catholic high schools (Grades 11–13).[13] The federal *Charter of Rights and Freedoms*, adopted in 1982, also re-affirmed the rights and privileges guaranteed in Section 29 of the Constitution with respect to "denominational, separate or dissentient schools."[14]

ONTARIO SEPARATE SCHOOL FUNDING DECISION AND ITS IMPACT

Rapid increases in Roman Catholic high school enrolment in Ontario's larger cities kept the issue alive in the 1980s. Overcrowding and the lack of space to accommodate the increased numbers added urgency to the appeal to address the shortfall in funding for Catholic high schools. Up until that point, the denominational system was dependent for its existence on private funding sources such as archdioceses, local parishes, and contributions from religious and lay teaching staff.

Facing a serious financial crisis in 1984, the Ontario Catholic bishops produced a joint statement for Premier Davis with a formal request for equal funding. Drawing upon historical claims and legal precedent, the bishops summarized their case:

> Children must be educated somewhere at public expense and since it is visibly not possible to adapt public schools to satisfy the legitimate philosophical and religious views of a respectable segment of the population, it seems unfair that those who work to provide acceptable education for their children in alternative ways should be deprived of reasonable support for public funds.[15]

Ontario Catholic teachers and students then rallied to the cause. In the spring of 1984, the Ontario Elementary Catholic Teachers' Association (OECTA) utilized its Task Force on Education Policy to strongly re-affirm its support for extended separate school funding. The OECTA also actively supported Ottawa Catholic high school student Rick Chiarelli and his provincial student advocacy group, the Ontario Students Association for Fair Funding (OSAFF), planning to take the government to court with the financial help of Catholic school boards and principals.[16] With Davis's term as premier winding down, the timing proved to be right for a more definitive policy.

Premier Davis eventually reversed his long-standing position on Catholic high school funding. Shortly after the 1981 provincial election, he signalled to Education Minister Bette Stephenson and her Deputy Minister Harry Fisher that "I want to do it." Over the next three years, he consulted with the Catholic bishops and began to prepare the ground for a turnaround in policy. The OSAFF campaign exerted some pressure by staging Catholic student protests and preparing to launch a court case to argue for the constitutional right of separate school boards to operate high schools with tax monies and grants. Two weeks before the announcement, Davis visited Cardinal Emmett Carter at his home, where the Catholic theologian expressed some apprehension over the potential for the OSAFF case to create sufficient turbulence to scuttle the plan. Davis's next-door neighbour in Brampton, Archbishop Philip Procock, may have exerted greater influence on the premier. On 12 June 1984, in what was staged like a surprise announcement, Davis unveiled Bill 30 extending funding to Grade 13 for all separate boards in Ontario.[17]

Premier Davis's official statement gives what stands as the most cogent explanation for his decision. His press release provided seven reasons:

- the absence of provincial grants and of the power to tax for the support of separate schools beyond Grade 10 was, in the minds of Roman Catholics, "arbitrary and inequitable";
- separate school completion would strengthen the social fabric of Ontario;
- this new education policy would honour the Confederation contract of 1867;
- a basic education in 1867 consisted of graduation from elementary school; a basic education in 1984 meant attaining a secondary school diploma;
- times had changed: in 1971 completion would have involved building many new high schools; in 1984 there was abundant excess classroom space;
- completion would not cripple the viability of the public high school system; one third of Ontario's pupils were in separate schools, yet the public elementary school system was still viable; and
- the letter of the old law cannot substitute for common sense.[18]

The announcement sparked much public speculation over the premier's motives in reversing his position. Testifying before a Legislative Standing Committee in September 1985, Davis saw it as a case of difficult unfinished business that required attention.[19] Demographics were a factor, according to Education Minister Stephenson, because close to 500,000 students were enrolled in separate schools. An imminent visit to Toronto by Pope John Paul II may well have been a consideration in the timing. Close observers and political confidantes, including TVO host Steve Paikin and Hugh Segal, claim that Davis had been troubled for years by the funding inequities and had finally resolved to make things right.[20]

The decision did not settle the matter; as public debate raged on, Davis stepped down as premier, and his successor Frank Miller was swept out of office, but a 1987 Supreme Court of Canada ruling upheld the constitutional right to publicly funded separate schools.[21] It led to a rapid expansion of the number of Catholic high schools in Ontario.[22] By the year 2001, there were 172 English-language and

51 French-language Catholic high schools. Some 104 English high schools and 47 French high schools had been added since Davis rejected funding back in 1971. All but a few Catholic separate boards had extended their operations to the end of high school.

THE QUEBEC TRANSFORMATION –
FROM DENOMINATIONAL TO LINGUISTIC BOARDS

Canada's primarily French-speaking province, Quebec, faced similar educational challenges, but took a decidedly different approach. Since Confederation, Section 93 of the BNA *Act* was assumed to prohibit legislation prejudicial to those denominational rights of Catholics and Protestants that were recognized by law in 1867. Because Section 93 incorporated rights by reference to pre-Confederation law, it was a matter of debate and controversy as to which rights were actually protected. Contrary to popular belief, Quebec did not in fact have a province-wide dual denominational school system in 1867, because that arrangement was enacted in 1869, following Confederation.[23] Had that legislation been enacted before the federal union, as originally intended, all denominational boards would have been protected under Section 93. The only constitutional protection afforded in Quebec to Catholics and Protestants in Montreal and Quebec City and to Catholic and Protestant minorities elsewhere was the right to dissent from participating in the majority system. In short: a public choice between two distinct forms of education.

For nearly a hundred years, the two denominational systems, with their Catholic and Protestant school boards, functioned in what McGill Education professor William Smith aptly termed "splendid isolation" from each other and from state education authorities.[24] That state of peaceful Catholic and Protestant coexistence ended abruptly with the arrival of the Quiet Revolution of the 1960s, and the onset of the initial wave of education reform in the province. The creation of the Ministry of Education of Quebec (MEQ), the regionalization of existing boards, and the beginnings to school-level parent participation proceeded as planned, but the quest for neutral "unified boards" was abandoned after encountering resistance.[25] Over time, however, Quebec society became increasingly secular and more multicultural and – as a result – maintaining denominational boundaries faded in importance. Bill 101, the Quebec Language Charter, passed in 1977, was designed to protect French language and culture, but it also reinforced the primacy of language over religion in the shaping of collective identities. In 1992, the Quebec Task Force on English Language Education identified the primary concerns of anglophone Quebeckers and attempted to address the contentious question of broadening access to education in English.[26] That report spawned a number of initiatives aimed at addressing issues vital to the welfare of English schools, including the establishment of an Advisory Council on English Education and the appointment of an Assistant Deputy Minister for the English-speaking community. All of these changes recognized the distinctiveness of the linguistic communities and seeded the idea of complete structural reform.

THE CREATION OF LINGUISTIC BOARDS – AND THE PRESERVATION OF ENGLISH SCHOOLS

The government of Quebec finally plunged into the challenge of educational restructuring. In 1995, a major "grassroots" consultation on the state of education was announced, to be undertaken by the Commission for the Estates General on Education. The Commission's final report (1996) recommended ten structural changes, including the creation of a non-denominational system and a decentralization of governance to increase local decision-making.[27] Most significantly, the Estates General maintained that such a restructuring should proceed unfettered by the constitutional framework of Section 93. Quebec's Minister of Education Pauline Marois accepted the Estates General recommendations, and in 1997 the MEQ embarked on a bold plan of action.[28] It led, in turn, to three fundamental policy initiatives: a constitutional amendment; the implementation of linguistic school boards; and a redistribution of powers among lay stakeholders in the Quebec system.

The earth-shaking structural change took effect on 1 July 1998. On that date, a school board system based on language replaced the denominational (Catholic and Protestant) school board structures that had existed since 1875 in Quebec. The total number of school boards was reduced from 156 to 72, and that meant an expansion of their territories. Sixty French-language boards were established to serve the one million francophone and immigrant students in the province, and nine English boards were set up to accommodate some 100,000 students who were eligible for English schooling under Bill 101 and who attended English schools.[29] Three special-status school boards, Cree, Kativik, and du Littoral, were unaffected by the restructuring.

Public reaction to the establishment of linguistic boards was muted, but the old tensions resurfaced during the first round of school board elections. An initial plan to restrict English voting rights to those parents whose children qualified for English schooling under Bill 101 sparked resistance, especially in the territory governed by the English Montreal School Board (EMSB) and in largely anglophone areas of the West Island and western Quebec. After intense debate, Quebec authorities finally agreed to allow voters to register and cast a ballot for the board of their choice. Parents of schoolchildren were required to register to vote in the language sector which their children attended, but anyone else was free to designate which system they preferred.[30] The intense controversy over voting rights had an unintended effect. While voter turnout in Quebec school board elections was traditionally low, hovering around 11 percent, the June 1998 English community turnout hit record numbers, reaching as high as 54 percent in some of the English boards. Much of the motivation was driven by the knowledge that voting in the English-sector election directed one's taxes to an English school board; failing to vote meant one's tax monies went, by default, to the coterminous French linguistic board. Once registered, Quebec school board voters returned to their former habits, and subsequent elections saw a return to low turnouts.

Establishing linguistic school boards in the 1990s recognized the realities of modern Quebec and the post–Quiet Revolution secularism of its major cities. School board elections in the francophone sector utterly failed to generate increased voter participation rates and in 2007 forced the postponement of regular elections. The 2014 Quebec school board elections were billed as crucial to the future of the boards, which together spend more than $11 billion in tax monies to serve the province's children.[31] Only a reported 5.5 percent of the 5.2 million eligible Quebeckers voted for the board chairs and commissioners on their linguistic boards. Nearly half of the chairs and commissioners ran unopposed and were acclaimed to office. Supporters of school boards in anglophone Quebec see these institutions as guardians of the English language at the community level. In the English Montreal School Board district, the 2014 participation rate was 21 percent, four percent higher than the province-wide English board average.[32] Twenty years after the transition from religious to linguistic boards, a new Coalition Avenir Québec (CAQ) government was planning to abolish school boards and elected commissioners and to replace them with educational service centres and school-based governing councils.[33]

THE RESILIENCE OF CATHOLIC SEPARATE SCHOOLS

Six provinces supported faith-based school boards until the arrangement began to come under fire twenty-five years ago. Confronting the realities of a more secular society and seeking school board consolidation, Newfoundland and Labrador, like Quebec, secured constitutional amendments to replace their faith-based school boards with secular, linguistic boards, and Manitoba followed suit in the 1990s. The provinces of British Columbia, Nova Scotia, New Brunswick, and Prince Edward Island have never had an education system that included separate schools. Separate publicly funded schools for Catholic children continue to exist in three provinces: Ontario, Saskatchewan, and Alberta. Under the original constitutional framework, only parents of children with Catholic backgrounds were accorded the right to choose between public and separate schools.[34] That provision has gradually been relaxed since the pivotal Ontario decision in 1984 to fund its Catholic schools to high school graduation. In a quid pro quo arrangement, Catholic bishops and principals in the mid-1980s began accommodating non-Catholics in their schools.

Public demand for school choice gradually grew, and Catholic separate school boards responded by starting to admit increased numbers of students of non-Catholic backgrounds.[35] With both public and separate Catholic boards facing shrinking enrolment, the competition for students intensified, especially in rural and small-town communities. Enrolling non-Catholic children in faith-based schools provided parents with another option and spared Catholic boards the necessity of closing underutilized schools or laying off teachers. Public perceptions of educational quality are an underlying factor, especially in Ontario where comparative school rankings tend to demonstrate that the Catholic schools may have higher student performance standards. Both factors explain, in large part, why Ontario Catholic boards have relaxed their Catholic-only admission policies and have also exempted students from formerly required catechism classes. In spite of overall declining provincial enrolments, some 650,000 Ontario students are still emolled in English-language and French-language Catholic elementary schools, accounting for about thirty percent of total enrolment in publicly funded schools.[36]

Ontario Catholic schools tend to outshine regular public schools when it comes to student achievement. Out of the top twenty-nine elementary schools in Ontario, ranked in 2012 by the C.D. Howe Institute, seventeen, or nearly two-thirds, were Catholic, even though the public system was twice as large. Across the Greater Toronto Area, nine of the top twenty schools were Catholic. That study, conducted by Wilfrid Laurier University economics professor David Johnson, utilized Grade 3 and 6 test scores from Ontario's 4,000 public and Catholic schools, and adjusted for demographic factors that tend to give students a boost, including having educated parents, length of time in Canada, and proportion of girl students. When asked to explain the results, Johnson told *The Toronto Star*: "Maybe they are more selective, or maybe Catholic schools just try harder because they know parents can always switch to the public school system – but somehow, and some way, Catholic schools seem to do better."[37] Such studies also lend credence to the claim that competition for Catholic students between the public and Catholic systems leads to slightly better student outcomes than if only one system were in place.[38]

Seeking alternatives to the one-size-fits-all public school in the Catholic system is now common, as recently demonstrated in Ontario and Saskatchewan. A February 2018 investigation by Toronto *Globe and Mail* reporter Caroline Alphonso documented the trend of Catholic school boards increasingly enrolling non-Catholic children and siphoning elementary students from the public stream. During 2016–17, the number of documented non-Catholic students reached almost 11,000, an 18 percent increase over the previous four years. As a percentage of the total student population in the separate system, non-Catholics accounted for more than 8 percent in 2016–17. The province's three largest boards in the Greater Toronto Area (Toronto, York, and Dufferin-Peel) stood alone among the twenty-nine English Catholic school boards as the only ones with policies that denied enrolment to students without a Catholic baptismal certificate. In some boards, upwards of a quarter of elementary school students and their parents or guardians did not have a baptismal certificate.[39] Ardent promoters of one unified school system claimed that Catholic boards facing shrinking enrolment were simply siphoning off public school students. More objective education observers, such as Toronto columnist Konrad Yakabuski, wondered why single-system proponents tended to overlook the appeal of Catholic schools based upon research that their students tend to perform better on provincial standardized tests.[40]

PROTECTING CATHOLIC SCHOOLS –
THE SASKATCHEWAN TEST CASE

A controversial Saskatchewan court ruling in April 2017 brought the question of school choice once again to the fore. Since Saskatchewan and Alberta joined the Dominion in 1905, their school districts have been required to provide public funding for secular public schools, as well as Catholic or Protestant separate schools whenever parents belonging to either group are a minority in a school district and request it. Public and separate schools must respect regulations pertaining to curriculum, inspections, and textbooks, but can run independently, and receive equal amounts per student in government funding.

A tiny local dispute, as is often the case, erupted into a raging Catholic schools controversy. It was sparked by the decision of forty-two multidenominational parents in the rural village of Theodore, fifteen years ago, to resist a public school closure, create a Catholic School Division, and then open their own publicly funded Catholic school. The court decision to end funding for non-Catholics to attend such schools had great potential for massive disruption. Some 10,000 students and their parents province-wide were left in limbo, facing the prospect of being forced out of their Catholic schools.[41]

Faced with such an educational disruption, Saskatchewan Premier Brad Wall stepped in to invoke the "notwithstanding" clause of the *Charter of Rights and Freedoms* to override the ruling and uphold school choice for parents and students on the grounds that it should be a cornerstone of public education.[42] Saskatchewan, like Alberta and Ontario, has a robust system with viable alternatives to public schools. While Saskatchewan has fewer publicly funded options than Alberta, there remains considerable demand for alternatives to secular public schools: more than one-fifth of students in each of these provinces are enrolled in fully funded Catholic schools.

Universal public services are popular and highly valued right across Canada, particularly health care. When it comes to education, that national value comes smack up against the appeal of school choice and public attitudes favouring a diversity of programs. Many Canadians, including a sizable share of our Indigenous peoples and recent immigrants, support the existence of an educational system that reflects the full diversity of our pluralistic society. Our leading national education organization, the Canadian Education Association, puts it this way: "a single, mandated version of schooling is not neutral:

it reflects the mores and assumptions of the dominant anglophone (or, in Quebec, francophone) elite ... Equality demands the recognition of difference." An array of schooling options also ensures that families who lack the means to put their children into private school are able to access educational models that have ethical, philosophical, linguistic, or disciplinary traditions that accord with their views.[43]

The constitutional status quo was not ideal with respect to accessibility to publicly funded schools. Public school supporters, under the strict constitutional requirement, did not have the right to send their children to the nearest Catholic school, even if it was the best alternative. Only children of Catholic families had the option of moving between the secular and separate public systems. The April 2017 Saskatchewan court decision expressly denied non-Catholic Saskatchewan families this range of choice. While it is highly desirable for Catholic schools to have some religious component to their philosophy and curriculum to justify their separate existence, it was not clear why they should not be permitted to relax their denominational admission requirements or religious expectations for their students. The School Choice Protection Act, introduced 8 November 2017, confirmed the Saskatchewan government's intention to invoke the constitutional notwithstanding clause to provide "parents and students" with "the certainty that they can continue to attend Catholic separate schools."[44] Court challenges continued into 2019, and the Saskatchewan government, supported by the Saskatchewan Catholic School Boards Association, made the case that "keeping enrolment to Catholic education open to everyone" was "fundamentally about parental choice in education."[45]

PUBLIC CHOICE AND DIVERSITY IN THE SYSTEM

Seizing upon news reports in February 2018 that up to 11,000 non-Catholic students were attending Ontario Catholic schools, the Elementary Teachers' Federation of Ontario (EFTO) called for the elimination of the Catholic separate separate school system.[46] If such a policy were ever adopted, either those 11,000 non-Catholic students would be compelled to return to their local public school, or their families would be left with no choice but to pay tuition fees to attend a religious school of their choice. The EFTO public appeal and the One Public School movement, of which it was a part, actually run counter to the established norms across Canada.[47]

The funding of faith-based schools is not about to disappear from the System. Six provinces, from British Columbia to Quebec, have found a variety of ways to fund religious K–12 schools. Only in Atlantic Canada is the option of funding support to attend religious schools not part of the System. Under the various forms of support, funds also transfer without confirmation of a precise match between the students' religious beliefs and those professed by their chosen school. Eliminating such funding would, Deani Van-Pelt of Cardus Education Foundation points out, adversely affect thousands of families, especially in the Ottawa region, where most of Ontario's non-Catholics attending publicly funded Catholic schools live.[48]

In British Columbia, Manitoba, and Quebec, parents seeking a religiously oriented education for their children have the option of enrolling them in a subsidized independent school. In these provinces, independent schools meeting provincial standards receive from 30 to 60 percent of the per-student annual funding amount allocated for public school students. These faith-oriented independent schools are required to meet provincial curriculum standards, generally hire provincially certified teachers, and top up their funding gap with tuition fees or donations from the wider school community.[49] Government funding for these alternative school options is not contingent on whether the student's religious identity matches that of the school.

Today Alberta and Saskatchewan fund the widest variety of religious school options. They both offer fully funded Roman Catholic separate systems and, in addition, support qualifying religiously oriented independent schools at 50 to 70 percent of the provincial per-student rate for public schools.[50] Ontario only funds one type of religiously oriented school: fully funded Catholic separate schools. That explains, for the most part, why – given the structural barriers – Ontario parents desiring a more faith-based education for their children have turned in increasing numbers to the only option available, the Catholic system.[51]

7

The "One-Size-Fits-All" Model

Uniformity, Inclusion, and Marginalization

The vast majority of students in the System are still educated in the common, everyday, garden-variety, one-size-fits-all model school, especially those attending schools outside the major metropolitan centres. A June 2017 Fraser Institute student enrolment study, covering the 2000–01 to 2014–15 school years, found that the public schools continue to enroll the majority of students, but were gradually losing ground to alternative education program options, including independent schools and home education. Of the ten provinces, only New Brunswick, a jurisdiction with few school alternatives, recorded any increase in students attending an anglophone public school.[1] Major school systems, such as the Toronto District School Board and the Calgary Board of Education, have succeeded in stemming the outflow by offering public school alternative programs or specialized schools. French immersion programming, offered by anglophone school districts, continues to draw students with its cachet among affluent, upwardly mobile parents and families.[2] Without the French immersion option, those districts likely would have experienced more erosion in student enrolment over the past fifteen years.

Inclusive education has, until recently, been a sacred cow in the Canadian education world. Striving for the full inclusion of all students in the regular classroom may be a worthy goal, but it has significantly altered class composition, has made teaching far more challenging, and has not satisfactorily meet the needs of all children. A few Canadian provincial school systems, following the lead of New Brunswick, have elevated "inclusive education" to an exalted status.[3] For many children and teens with severe learning disabilities or complex needs, however, the regular classroom is not the most enabling learning environment. It's also rendering today's diverse classes, at certain times, nearly impossible for regular teachers to teach. Most ironic of all, the "inclusive classroom," in attempting to accommodate a myriad of student needs (without adequate learning supports), has come to exemplify the one-size-fits-all model because it effectively marginalizes those with severe learning or language difficulties.

Universal education has taken on a completely different form in contemporary Quebec. The Quiet Revolution of the 1960s had a profound influence with lasting effects on society and culture, and on the state school system. McMaster University history professor Michael Gauvreau identified the fundamental shift in his 2005 book *The Catholic Origins of Quebec's Quiet Revolution*.[4] "People stopped going to church," he claims, and it led to "a massive emptying out and loss of Catholic institutions." The 1964 creation of a Ministry of Education and the ushering in of state-managed education marked the shift away from Catholic church authority. Severing denominational schools from the publicly funded school system in the 1990s pointed the Quebec system in a new direction. Suspicious of Pierre E. Trudeau's "Canadian" brand of multiculturalism, a succession of Quebec governments espoused "interculturalism." That Quebec policy recognized French as the common language of cultural interaction, while embracing "pluralism" and claiming to be "highly sensitive to the protection of rights."[5]

Quebec's cultural distinctiveness, once based around Catholic identity, became more and more aligned with a francophone state religion – secularism. Collective rights embodied in the primacy of secular values made Quebec less hospitable to newcomers and religious practices out of sync with mainstream Québécois society,[6] That is how the Quebec school system once again became a major battleground in fierce public debates over "reasonable accommodation" and restrictions on religious symbols and attire.

UNIFORMITY AND THE SEARCH FOR SCHOOL ALTERNATIVES

Canada's school-attending population is declining with our aging population and the shrinking number of school-age children. Between 2000 and 2015, the number of Canadians aged 5 to 17 declined

6.6 percent, and every province, except for Alberta (showing a growth of 11.6 percent), recorded a decline over that period. The vast majority of families send their children to either English or French public schools. What is more surprising, however, is the fact that public schools are attracting, year after year, a slowly diminishing share of that school-age population. In 2000–01, no Canadian province had less than 90.6 percent of its students in a regular English or French public school. Fifteen years later, every province still showed at least 86.8 percent of all students attending some form of public school.[7]

Students and families are looking increasingly for alternatives to the mainstream public school system. While five provinces (in Atlantic Canada and Saskatchewan) still enroll more than 96 percent of their children in public schools, the proportion in public schools in 2014–15 had dropped significantly in British Columbia (to 86.8 percent) and Quebec (to 87.6 percent). A sizable number of Quebec students have traditionally attended independent, mainly French Catholic, colleges, and 12.3 percent of all students still do today. British Columbia surpassed Quebec in independent school enrolment in 2014–15, registering 12.9 percent. Over the past fifteen years, every province except New Brunswick recorded growth in the number of students attending independent schools, but the share choosing such schools rose in every case, particularly in Saskatchewan. Withdrawing students in favour of home education is still relatively rare, but homeschooling accounts for over 1 percent of total enrolment in Manitoba, Alberta, and Saskatchewan.[8] Attending the everyday, garden-variety public school is not what it once was in Canada.

THE ALLURE OF FRENCH IMMERSION

Getting one's children into French immersion programs continues to be the preferred route for families looking for something different. While French-English bilingualism rates may be waning in Canada, the public demand for French immersion places remains high and parents can be quite determined to get their children into the program, which has been aptly described as a "private school for the upwardly mobile middle class."[9] The initial vision of educating children for a unified, bilingual nation espoused in 1968 by Prime Minister Pierre Trudeau provided the initial incentive, but immersion soon became a mania of its own. In 1977, a decade after its inception, the program

Table 7.1
School Choices in Public Education, 2014–15

Province	Public Anglo- phone	Public Franco- phone	Separate Anglo- phone	Separate Franco- phone	Charter School	Total Public System	Indep- endent School	Home School
BC	89.5	0.9				86.8	12.9	0.4
AB	68.1	1.1	23.5		1.4	94.1	4.4	1.4
SK	73.3	0.9	22.1			96.3	2.4	1.2
MB	87.9	2.7				90.6	7.9	1.5
ON	62.6	1.3	26.3	3.4		93.6	6.1	0.3
QC	8.5	79.1				87.6	12.3	0.1
NB	69.7	28.8				98.5	0.8	0.7
NS	92.5	4.0				96.5	2.7	0.8
PEI	94.4	4.1				98.4	1.1	0.4
NL	97.9	0.5				98.4	1.4	0.2

The graph of Public-School Enrolment by Type of School, 2014–15, illustrates the range of school options across Canada.

Source: Fraser Institute

enrolled 45,000 students across the country; by 2011, the number had increased to more than 342,000.

Active and informed Canadian parents, especially in and around major urban centres, are well-versed in French immersion's benefits. Children learn another language without any detrimental effect on their English skills. Working memory, used in activities such as math, is improved, especially among those aged five to seven. Even reading scores in English are significantly higher for French immersion students than non-immersion students, according to a 2004 study, even after allowing for socio-economic factors. Speaking French as a second language does provide added work opportunities later in life, and potentially higher salaries. Outside Quebec, bilingual men earn on average 3.8 percent more than their unilingual counterparts, according to a 2010 University of Guelph study. Bilingual women earn 6.6 percent more on average. The advantage is even greater within Quebec.[10] Given those practical realities, it is easier to understand the mania surrounding immersion.

French immersion programs do accentuate and possibly deepen division along lines of social class, gender, and disability. A 2008 study from the Canadian Research Institute for Social Policy looking at French immersion in New Brunswick reached that conclusion.[11] Girls are more likely to be enrolled than boys, and the French immersion stream has fewer kids designated with special needs. If New Brunswick students with special needs were spread evenly throughout the system, every class – French or English – would have 3.4 students with special needs. But when a school offered French immersion, the average number of special needs students ending up in the English stream was 5.7. Given the challenges of providing special help in French immersion schools, the result has been larger numbers on average in the regular English- or French-only classes.

More affluent families have flocked to French immersion. The richer the family, the more likely their kids will be immersed in French, according to figures from a Toronto District School Board study. In 2009–10, 23 percent of all French immersion students came from families in the top 10 percent of income. Meanwhile, only 4 percent of French immersion students came from the bottom 10 percent of family income.[12] While the pattern is not uncommon for enriched alternative programs, it is clear that the majority of students in immersion are from more advantaged families.

The direct impact of French immersion is visible to classroom teachers. "What a program like French immersion does is it siphons off those kids who have engaged families who make sure the kids do all their homework," Andrew Campbell, a Grade 5 teacher in Brantford, Ontario, told *Maclean's*. "Because of that, the opportunities in the rest of the system are affected because the modelling and interaction those kids would provide for the other kids in the system aren't there anymore."[13]

THE ILLUSION OF INCLUSION

Integrating students with special needs has been a high priority for Canada's provincial school systems for the past two decades. It is now generally agreed that public schools should embrace an overall philosophy of inclusion which supports the right of all children to the best possible education. Full inclusion – the idea that all children, including those with severe disabilities, can and should learn in a regular classroom – has also taken root in many school systems, and most notably in the province of New Brunswick. Since the 2006 adoption of Halifax law professor Wayne MacKay's report on *Inclusive Education*, New Brunswick has aggressively pursued the "everyone must be educated in the mainstream classroom" model of inclusive education.[14] The prevailing model, at its best, provides a helpful bridge to full acceptance and integration, but, at its worst, carries the expectation that the learning–challenged should fit into the regular classroom with a minimum of resource supports.

A full Provincial Review of New Brunswick Inclusive Education was launched in 2011–12, co-headed by Dr Gordon L. Porter, a leading Canadian advocate and consultant on inclusive education. Five years after its official adoption, the review was definitely being undertaken by a commission stocked with "friendlies." Given growing public concerns over how the model was working to meet the needs of the most severely challenged, a few critical questions came to mind: Would the Provincial Review actually examine whether "mainstreaming" is "the most enabling environment" for all special needs children? Would the Review yield longitudinal, validated research demonstrating the superiority of "full inclusion" for students with all types of learning disabilities? And how were students with "complex and severe needs" actually faring under the current system?

Dr Porter's December 2011 commentary, featured on the Canadian Education Association's blog, suggested that none of those questions would be squarely addressed in the forthcoming review.[15] For an education consultant with such a mandate, he sounded more than a little biased in favour of "full inclusion" for everyone. His main preoccupation, in his own words, was advancing his thirty-year struggle for "equity and quality" in "an inclusive education system." He expressed deep disappointment over the "back-sliding" over "the last ten years." Some of our largest Canadian school districts, Porter noted, "are not only maintaining the number of students in self-contained special education, they are actually increasing it."

The New Brunswick review was definitely tilted in the direction of sustaining inclusion for all. Professor MacKay and Gordon Porter were not only the leading proponents, but they had friends in high places. As head of the NB Human Rights Commission, Porter successfully enshrined inclusion in the provincial code. He was a key member of the Transition Team when David Alward and the Conservatives came to power, and Krista Carr, executive director of the NB Association for Community Living, was the spouse of Jody Carr, then the Minister of Education. The NBACL was, without a doubt, the most zealous organization promoting full inclusion for all kids.

Full inclusionists tended to be deeply committed to defending "human rights" but rather inclined to dismiss research and evidence contradicting their perceptions. The Learning Disabilities Association of Canada (LDAC) and one of its founders, Yude M. Henteleff, continued to claim that the "fully inclusive classroom" was "only one of the right ways to meet the best interest of the special needs child."[16] Such views were considered "off-side" in New Brunswick.

A November 2005 LDAC policy on Educational Inclusion confirmed their support for "the availability of a continuum of education services," from regular mainstreamed classes to "a small class setting" and "an even more intensive program such as those offered by a special school."[17] Four years later, an independent review of best practices research in Learning Disabilities Education, conducted in 2009 by Dr Anne Price of the Calgary Learning Centre for Nova Scotia Education, reaffirmed the wisdom of a more flexible approach offering a variety of service options suited to the needs of the child.[18]

Full inclusion remained controversial as a one-size-fits-all special education policy, even in New Brunswick. Over the previous decade, Fredericton lawyer Harold L. Doherty, had fought a determined fight for his son, Conor, and hundreds of other parents of kids and teens with Autism Spectrum Disorder. His blog, *Facing Autism in New Brunswick*, amplified their voices. It served as an invaluable source of information on the limits of New Brunswick policy and made a compelling case for a change in policy direction. After years of advocacy, Harold secured a "self-contained class" in Leo Hayes High School for his own son, but he's continued the struggle on behalf of autistic children, youth, and young adults.

The New Brunswick government, like a few other provincial authorities, was wrestling with the challenges of educating students with "complex special needs" and "youth-at-risk." A visionary 2008 report, *Connecting the Dots*, by former Youth Advocate Bernard Richard, pointed that province in a better direction.[19] His recommendation for a Centre for Excellence garnered most of the attention, but his report also made a strong plea for "children with complex needs who are no longer in the mainstream" and called for the creation of a new education authority to support children "marginalized" in the New Brunswick system.

RETHINKING INCLUSION IN NEW BRUNSWICK

The eventual June 2012 report on inclusion in New Brunswick, co-authored by Porter and Angela AuCoin, simply reaffirmed the province's inclusive education philosophy and policy. Minister of Education Jody Carr hailed the release of the report in his 5 June 2012 media statement and announced that New Brunswick was reversing its cost-cutting course and spending $62 million more on implementing inclusive education over the next three years. That amounted to a ringing endorsement of a report which recommended that the province forge ahead with its twenty-five-year struggle to "transform the thinking of school leaders" and continue to make the regular classroom the focus of student support services.[20]

The *Strengthening Inclusion, Strengthening Schools* report, produced by the two well known inclusion theorists, was not the final word on the subject. Striving for the full inclusion of all students in the publicly funded school system is a most worthy goal, but the report's findings revealed that it was still more of an illusion than a reality in New Brunswick schools, especially for those students with severe learning disabilities or complex needs.[21]

One in ten Canadians reportedly suffers from some kind of learning disability, and between 2 and 4 percent of New Brunswick's public school students, estimated to number from 2,100 to 4,200 in 2011–12, were struggling at school with serious learning challenges. The Porter-AuCoin report also acknowledged that a mixed bag of alternative school programs continued to exist across the districts, serving some 1,000 or so students with significant learning challenges. Serving growing numbers of children with Autism Spectrum Disorder further complicated the problem. Some 1,238 of New Brunswick's 74,579 anglophone public school students had been diagnosed with autism and many already required significant learning supports. Irrespective of the Porter-AuCoin report, this was fast becoming the biggest challenge facing the province's regular kindergarten to Grade 12 schools.

Since the adoption of MacKay's 2006 report on inclusive education, the province had pursued full inclusion in regular classrooms with dogged determination. The Education Department, working closely with Gordon Porter's Inclusive Education Initiative and the NBACL, had become the leading Canadian proponent of the one-size-fits-all regular classroom model. The Department was closely aligned with the NBACL, to the point where their websites virtually mirrored one another. Vocal critics of the existing model, such as Fredericton autism advocate Harold L. Doherty, charged that the province's current regime was "philosophy-based" and turned a blind eye to students with "complex needs" who were being marginalized and eventually left by the wayside.[22] Classroom teachers, lacking the necessary expertise and resource support, according to the NB Teachers' Association's Heather Smith, were gradually being overwhelmed by the growing numbers of "students in difficult situations."

New Brunswick's full adoption of inclusive education since 2006 had certainly tested the limits of the all-inclusive classroom as the answer for all K–8 students and the vast majority of high schoolers. Alberta, Ontario, and Nova Scotia had all responded to shifts in the composition of the student population by offering more self-contained classes and viable alternative school programs. The neighbouring province of Nova Scotia provided a stark contrast. There, a small number of private, independent Special Education (Grade 3–12) schools had emerged since the 1970s to fill the gap by providing a vitally important lifeline in the continuum of student support services.[23] Demand for such schooling grew after 2000 to the point where the Nova Scotia Education Department began looking at implementing a provincial tuition support program serving students with more acute learning difficulties.

The Nova Scotia Tuition Support Program (TSP), initiated in September 2004, provides an option for students with special needs who cannot be served at their local public school. It is explicitly intended for short-term purposes and works on the assumption that students can eventually be successfully transitioned back into the regular system. The TSP provides funding which covers most of the tuition costs to attend designated special education private schools (DSEPS) and any public alternative education centres that might eventually be established in Nova Scotia.

Critical special education student needs were not being met under the New Brunswick one-size-fits-all classroom model. My June 2012 AIMS research study, *Building a Bigger Tent*, provided a detailed cost-benefit analysis of New Brunswick's implementation of inclusion, identified a significant hole in the system, and examined the pent-up demand for a full continuum of service, from mainstreaming to self-contained classes to special needs schools. It rejected the findings of the Porter-AuCoin report and called for a truly independent, arm's-length review, seeking to assess the unmet demand for better alternative "lifeline" programs, meeting the needs of those who are simply unable to cope in a regular classroom.[24] The study also recommended that New Brunswick authorities take a closer look at Nova Scotia's service delivery model, including Special Education schools and the ground-breaking Tuition Support Program (TSP) that renders them more accessible to families with severely learning challenged children. While the Porter-AuCoin report produced more funding for student supports, it lacked "lifeline school programs" with the potential for achieving significantly improved outcomes for severely learning-disabled kids.

BUILDING A BIGGER TENT – FOR FULLY INCLUSIVE EDUCATION

Severely learning-challenged students continue to be marginalized in the New Brunswick school system. During the 2012–13 school year, Korey Breen's son was struggling in elementary school and suffering from three debilitating conditions: fear, anxiety, and loss of confidence. The clouds lifted when the Moncton mother of three found an educational lifeline in a tiny, home-like school established to serve kids with severe learning challenges. There her son finally felt safe, accepted, and at home. Finding a place like Riverbend Community School was a godsend, but only the beginning of that struggle to turn her son's life around. "Raising a child with special needs and severe learning disabilities and no financial support," she confessed, "has been extremely difficult and takes everything we have."

Struggling students in Moncton, New Brunswick, have very few options outside the regular mainstream public school system.[25] For elementary students with severe learning challenges and their families, Riverbend Community School was really the only option, and, even then, only viable when they can scrape together the money to pay its hefty $11,500 tuition fees. For hundreds of families this is simply beyond reach. My May 2015 research report, published by the Atlantic Institute for Market Studies (AIMS), demonstrated that a gaping hole still existed in New Brunswick's Special Education safety net.[26] Without access to a Tuition Support Program, Korey's son and hundreds of others continue to struggle on the margins of the regular school system. Moncton's Riverbend Community School was a beacon of hope that could easily serve as a pilot school for a completely new approach embracing the full continuum of special education support services.[27]

The Nova Scotia Tuition Support Program (TSP), initiated in September 2004, provides the bridge for many families without the financial means to pay much in the way of tuition fees. system. TSP funding covers most of the tuition costs to attend designated special education private schools (DSEPS) in Nova Scotia. At a cost of $2.5 million a year, it currently serves some 225 students attending three designated schools in six locations across Nova Scotia.[28] Over the past few years, the TSP has been sustained and further improved in Nova Scotia, but a similar program has yet to appear in either New Brunswick or Prince Edward Island. Consistent and reliable support from the Nova Scotia Department of Education and Early Childhood Development has been of great help to families that are in – or near – crisis. Since February 2012, it's been easier to qualify, and parents now have more secure support, a blessing for those desperately in need of financial assistance to pay the tuition fees. Providing access to specialized program schools not only helps to reduce potential long-term social and economic costs, but in Nova Scotia is already helping to producing happier families and more productive young citizens.

ADDRESSING INCLUSION – THE ELEPHANT IN THE SCHOOLROOM

Teachers are beginning to speak out of class about their biggest concern – inclusion and its impact upon class composition. One veteran Cape Breton teacher, Sally Capstick, drew widespread attention in December 2016 when she broke her silence to address what she described as the "elephant in the room."[29] "I've never seen teachers so upset," she told CBC Radio's *Information Morning Cape Breton*. Capstick claimed that inclusion is something people don't want to mention as a problem, adding that the idea behind it sounds wonderful in principle. "But it's gotten to a point that the diversity in the classroom is unbelievable," she said. Over her thirty-year teaching career, Capstick had witnessed a significant increase in the demands placed on teachers. While class sizes were once much larger, teachers then never faced the complex challenges they face in today's classrooms. More recently, she reported teaching a Grade 8 class where the ability levels of students ranged from pre-primary to Grade 9. More and more students are now on individual program plans (IPPS), she noted, requiring an array of accommodations and specialized supports. Speaking up was difficult, since no one wants to be painted as insensitive to special-needs children. The fundamental problem, Capstick revealed, is that when "teachers try to be all things to all people" then "no one gets what they need."

Teacher surveys across Canada support Capstick's claims in identifying class management as a fundamental problem and "class composition" as the biggest obstacle to professional satisfaction. Building upon Canadian school research, it is clear that special needs policy, designed by theorists, is not working and needs rethinking to achieve a better educational environment for teachers and students alike.[30] Back in September 2013, Gordon Thomas of the Alberta Teachers Association (ATA) used a class of 37 students as an example of the challenges facing stressed-out high school teachers. In his worst-case scenario, out of the 37 students, four had learning disabilities, five were in transition from other provinces, one exhibited serious behavioural issues, three were repeating the course, seven were functioning below grade level, and one was chronically absent because of a dysfunctional home life. In such overcrowded classes, Thomas asked, how can we expect teachers to provide constructive and rewarding learning experiences, let alone introduce innovative practices? Coping in such diverse classrooms goes far beyond class size, and dealing with them requires confronting the oft-hidden issue of class composition.[31] Most Special Education researchers concur that "smaller classes have the greatest positive impact on students with the greatest educational needs." It is now clear that both *class size* and *diversity* matter.

Today teachers try to adapt their teaching to address the individual needs of the learners in their regular classrooms. Class size reductions from kindergarten to Grade 3 and possibly beyond can produce improved student achievement, provided that the total context is conducive to such improvement.[32] Class sizes actually dropped in all Canadian provinces except British Columbia over the decade from 2001 to 2011. At the macro-economic level, from 2001–02 to 2010–11, student enrolment has dropped 6.5 percent, the number of educators rose 7.5 percent, the student-teacher ratio declined by 12.9 percent, and spending per pupil rose by 61.4 percent. Class size reductions and caps from kindergarten to Grade 3 or Grade 6 explained the overall smaller class sizes. As the classroom becomes larger and more diverse, however, the task of teaching becomes increasingly onerous. All of this has obvious implications for inclusive education. The success of inclusion is, in large measure, determined by the extent to which teachers have the necessary supports and services to be able to effectively integrate students with special educational needs into their classrooms and schools.

In the Spring of 2011, the Canadian Teacher's Federation (CTF) conducted a national teacher survey on the theme of "The Teacher Voice on Teaching and Learning" to seek input from across Canada on teacher concerns.[33] The CTF survey provided a snapshot of what class size and composition looked like across the country. The survey secured responses from nearly 3,800 teachers representing 9,894 classes in English and French schools, drawn from twelve participating CTF member organizations.[34]

Class Size Analysis: Average class size was 21.3 students, ranging from 22.1 students for Grades 4–8 to 19 students for junior kindergarten or kindergarten (JK–K). English schools (including French immersion) had an average class size of nearly 22 students, while French as a first language schools had a slightly smaller average class size of just over 19 students.

Class Size by Grade Level: Over a third of the classes for all grade levels combined contained 25 students or more (8.3 percent contained 30 students or more). For Grades 4–8, nearly 39 percent of classes contained 25 students or more (6.5 percent contained 30 or more); for Grades 9 and over, 40.3 percent of classes contained 25 students or more (13.5 percent – over 1 in 7 classrooms – contained 30 or more students); for Grades 1–3, just over 14 percent of classes contained 25 students or more; for JK–K, nearly 12 percent of classes contained 25 students or more.

Average Number of Special Needs Students: This category comprises students with identified exceptionalities (i.e., designated behavioural problems or mental or physical disabilities, as well as other special needs students, including gifted students), and English Language Learners and French Language Learners (defined as students whose first language differs from the school's primary language of instruction and who require supports). The average number of students with identified exceptionalities per class was 3.5, ranging from 3.8 students for Grades 4–8 to 1.9 students for JK–K.

Class Composition: Students with identified exceptionalities accounted for 16.3 percent of total students in the surveyed classrooms, ranging from respective shares of 17.1 percent for Grades 4–8 to 10 percent of students for JK–K. Of classes surveyed, over 81 percent had at least one student with formally identified exceptionalities, and 27.7 percent contained 5 or more students with identified exceptionalities. In Grades 4 and over, not only were class sizes generally larger, but almost 1 in 3 (30.6 percent) classes contained 5 or more students with identified exceptionalities.

Students with Language Learning Challenges: The average number of English Language Learners and French Language Learners (ELL/ FLL students) per class was 2.6. The prevalence was higher the lower the grade, ranging from 4.7 students for JK–K to 1.7 students for Grades 9 and over. ELL/FLL students accounted for an average 12.2 percent of total students in the classroom, ranging from respective shares of 24.7 percent for JK–K to 8.2 percent for Grades 9 and over.

The CTF survey was most revealing, but it had some limitations. It looked at students "identified" as Special Needs but did not include students who were undiagnosed or those with other glaring needs such as students from low-income families (with poverty-related issues of hunger, illness, and/or instability), students with mental health problems, or immigrant and refugee students.

Recent studies of the state of inclusive education in New Brunswick and British Columbia, conducted for researchED Canada, exposed the extent of a looming crisis affecting classroom teachers.[35] In the case of New Brunswick, a province honoured in February 2016 by Zero Project for its "legally-binding policy of inclusion," Guy Arsenault and the New Brunswick Teachers' Association started demanding a full Special Education review to secure "positive learning environments" and come to the aid of teachers forced to "don Kevlar clothing in the classrooms."[36] Out west, in British Columbia, a protracted, bitter five-week 2015 BCTF teachers' strike produced only meagre gains in containing class sizes, while more and more classes have from four or more to seven or more special needs students.[37]

The first real breakthrough on containing class size and composition came through a landmark 2016 Supreme Court decision. The British Columbia Teachers' Federation scored a court victory in November 2016 restoring teaching contract protections governing class size and composition removed in 2002 by the former Liberal government of Gordon Campbell.[38] That decision effectively restored previous provisions limiting class size, the number of special needs students in each class, and the number of specialist teachers required in schools. Before

2002, the number of special needs students could not exceed three without additional supports, such as an additional adult teaching assistant. At the time of the ruling, the BCTF reported that 16,516 classes had four or more special needs children, and some 4,163 had seven or more such children.[39]

Fixing the fractured BC inclusive education system would not come easily. Restoring class sizes and composition to pre-2002 levels would cost some $250 million to $300 million more each year and, in all likelihood, meant the restoration of some 3,500 full-time positions lost over the previous fifteen years. Despite the dramatic decision, special education experts forecast it would take time to gear up the system to train teachers and fully meet the needs of students with diverse learning needs. One BC mother of a Grade 3 special needs child, Erica Cedillo, spoke for many: "It's a hard journey and the experience still hurts," she told *CBC News*, "but I definitely feel hopeful."[40]

Stresses and pressures faced by classroom teachers have approached the breaking point. An April 2018 Nova Scotia Inclusive Education report, *Students First*, confirmed the prevalence of "student behaviour challenges" that "disrupt[] the teaching and learning of students at all grade levels." After a six-month-long study of classroom conditions from Primary to Grade 12, Chair Sarah Shea and her commission recommended setting aside the conventional inclusive classroom education model in favour of a new three-tiered system of supports along the continuum from full inclusion to small-group support to individualized programs and alternative schools.[41] One of the report's top priorities was to address unmet special education needs, particularly among children in distress "exhibiting challenging behaviour," and to help students "fearful of attending school" because of their peers' violent and aggressive behaviour which "seriously undermined" public education.

Confronted by mounting pressures for change, schools were beginning to adapt and education policy-makers coming to recognize the necessity of providing education that better fits the child. The real-life classroom had become not only far more diverse, but increasingly challenging to manage, let alone teach anything substantive in. Class size based upon student-teacher ratios had long been accepted and used in staffing schools, but its utility was now being questioned by front-line teachers. Student diversity, driven by inclusion and the growing numbers of severely learning-challenged and disadvantaged kids, was the new normal. The rise of "coddled kids" and "helicopter parents" compounded the challenges. Tackling class composition was fast emerging as the top priority in teacher-led school reform.

SECULARISM AND QUEBEC EDUCATION

One education issue which illustrates how Quebec is distinct from the rest of Canada is the matter of secularism, *laïcité* (laicity), or the separation of religion from government. Over the past two decades, it has emerged and dominated political discourse and produced convulsions affecting recently arrived immigrant families and Anglo-Quebeckers accustomed to periodic surges of Quebec nationalist feeling.[42] The raging debate has also inflamed passions and aroused Islamophobia, intensely felt by Muslim women and girls in the school system.[43] On 27 March 2019, in the most recent attempt to legislate a vision of secularism in the province, the Coalition Avenir Québec (CAQ) government tabled Bill 21 (2019), *An Act Respecting the Laicity of the State*. The legislation, passed on 16 June 2019, bans public servants in a list of jobs from wearing religious symbols at work. Its restrictions not only apply to schoolteachers and principals, but directly affect students in universities, colleges, and schools planning on seeking future employment in the public sector.[44]

The CAQ plan to affirm the secular character of the Quebec state is not really new, but a continuation of a project first initiated by a previous Parti Québécois government.[45] It originated as an offshoot of the "Charter of Values" unveiled in 2013 by Premier Pauline Marois and the PQ. That proposed charter aroused intense opposition because it was closely associated with an effort to ban religious symbols and regulate the hijabs and burkas worn by some Muslim women.[46] The PQ's Liberal successors, under Premier Philippe Couillard (2014–18), took up the cause and introduced a bill that barred Quebeckers from receiving and delivering public services, including boarding buses, with faces covered. It was passed into law, but suspended in 2017 by a Quebec court amid questions about how it would be implemented.[47]

THE DOCTRINE OF "REASONABLE ACCOMMODATION"

The recent debate over secularism in Quebec has its roots in the immediate aftermath of 9/11 and the War on Terror. An earlier controversy involving a Montreal school board decision to ban a twelve-year-old Sikh boy, Gurbaj Singh, from wearing his kirpan (ceremonial dagger) to school demonstrated the potential for social disruption.[48] Early in 2007, a small hamlet in the heart of French Quebec, Herouxville, introduced a "code of conduct" for immigrants and brought a simmering "cultural accommodation crisis" to a boil.[49] Talk radio shows, op-ed pages, and kitchen conversations were ignited by very public debates about whether a YMCA in Montreal's Mile End should frost its gym windows at the request of a next-door Hasidic synagogue or whether publicly funded daycares should serve halal meats.[50]

Confronting a raging culture war in January 2007, Quebec's Liberal government appointed a Consultative Commission on Accommodation Practices Related to Cultural Differences, co-chaired by prominent intellectuals Gérard Bouchard and Charles Taylor.[51] Their May 2008 report waded into the sensitive questions about how immigrants can or should integrate with Quebec society, and how to uphold the ideal of secularism while accommodating non-conforming religious practices. The Bouchard-Taylor report recommended removing a large crucifix from the Quebec National Assembly (QNA), abandoning prayers before municipal council meetings, and barring civil servants in positions of authority – such as judges, police officers and prosecutors – from wearing religious symbols at work. It also attempted to draw the line at the school system. Students and teachers, as well as nurses, should be allowed to wear religious attire such as the hijab and turban to school.[52]

SECULARISM, BILL 21, AND THE SCHOOLS

The CAQ's Bill 21 goes one step further in reaffirming and enforcing secularism in the public sector. Unlike previous legislation, it stipulates exactly which professions would be restricted from wearing religious symbols, including teachers and principals. It is also more court-proof – because it invokes the notwithstanding clause to protect it from being struck down by courts for violating the Canadian and Quebec Charters of Rights.[53] While Bill 21 does not target any one religion specifically, Charles Taylor has expressed grave reservations about its potential impact on visible religious minorities. In his April 2019 testimony during QNA hearings on the bill, he reversed his previous position. Since the horrific late January 2017 Quebec Islamic Cultural

Centre mass shooting, he claims any change must be considered in the context of a society "full of Islamophobia."[54] Fierce public debates over Bill 21 and mass protests by teachers, students, and affected public officials did not alter public opinion. According to a May 2019 public opinion poll, a majority of Quebeckers (63 percent) favoured the measure restricting religious symbols, and of that cohort, 88 percent showed signs of anti-Islamic sentiment. The only age group that broke with the trend was youth aged 18 to 25, consisting mostly of university/college students and recent graduates.[55]

Airing the divisive issue of "reasonable accommodation" and the introduction of Bill 21 flamed the embers of Islamophobia and upset a whole range of Quebec minorities, including the Jewish community and already aggrieved Anglo-Quebeckers. Quebec youth in the Muslim community were already struggling to maintain an Islamic lifestyle and religious identity in the face of the pressure to conform with the dominant culture. A 2001 ethnographic analysis identified some of the real-life challenges of Muslim teens, including racism, gender identity issues, and Islamophobia. School experiences reinforced their status as "minoritized youth" and feelings of marginalization.[56] While young Muslim women were clear targets of Quebeckers seeking to ban face-coverings, Muslim male youth report being on the receiving end of racism and intolerance ever since the 9/11 New York City terror attacks. Secondary-school Muslim teens, surveyed by McGill University researcher Naved Bakali, reported encountering bias from classmates and teachers triggered by racist and hostile attitudes toward their perceived religious faith. State policies such as the Charter of Values and secularism simply contributed to the secondary school atmosphere of intolerance toward the other, particularly visible minorities.[57]

The public fight against the CAQ secularism law reveals how far the Quebec government will go in imposing its neutral state agenda inside and outside the school system. The education debate over Bill 21 became news as far away as Europe and the Middle East. Quebec's Education Minister Jean-François Roberge faced a barrage of criticism in early July 2019 when he tweeted a picture of himself at a summit in France with Malala Yousafzai, an Afghan Nobel Peace Prize winner who was nearly killed by the Taliban for her activism championing education for girls. Asked on Twitter whether Yousafzai could teach in Quebec while wearing her head scarf, Mr Roberge said no – she'd

Figure 7.1 Montreal Protest against Bill 21, 2019

A close-up of young protestors demonstrating against Bill 21 in Montreal
after it was passed into law in June of 2019.

have to take it off – an assessment later backed up by Premier
Legault.[58] Not even world-renowned author and teacher Malala
would be permitted to circumvent the Quebec law barring religious
attire from the schools.

Passage of Bill 21 made Quebec the first jurisdiction in North
America to enact legislation enforcing a religion-free dress code.
Quebec's largest school board, the French-language Commission
scolaire de Montréal, lined up with the Quebec English school boards
in refusing to implement Bill 21 without consultation or modification.[59] The Quebec government of Premier François Legault sees this
law as the next stage in the evolution of the modern Quebec state,
exemplified in the state school system.[60] It is also a clear demonstra-
tion of the profound influence of the French intellectual culture,
privileging collective rights over individual rights and liberties. Severing
religion from the state is, in many ways, like defending the republic.
Any sign or kind of encroachment on laicity/secularism, including the
presence of religious symbols or the wearing of religious attire, is seen

as a threat to the state.[61] Democratic public institutions, from the CAQ and PQ perspective, exist to represent the will of the majority, which, at times, means overriding the interests of minorities. The Quebec state school system is considered a vital instrument in advancing secularism, another variation on one-size-fits-all schooling.

8

The "Success for All" Curriculum

The Downside of Universality

Progressive, student-centred learning was the new orthodoxy in the K–1 2 Canadian system of the 1980s and the vast majority of public schools embraced what amounted to a "success for all" curriculum. Coming face-to-face with that curriculum in local schools turned active, engaged parents into passionate and fiercely determined reformers. One of the best-known was Malkin Dare, a Waterloo mother who discovered, much to her chagrin, that her son Laurie was unable to read in Grade 2.[1] Glowing report cards disguised his reading difficulties and had lulled Dare into thinking her son was doing just fine. Talking with his teacher and school officials, she was assured that Laurie would probably pass his year. Shocked by this revelation, Dare, who had trained as a teacher, found a phonics workbook at a bookstore and began tutoring her son. Within six weeks, he was reading at grade level and one of Canada's best-known parent education advocates was born.

Dare quickly learned that she was not alone and that many of her Waterloo neighbours had kids who were also struggling while bringing home decent-looking reports. After doing some research, she was appalled at what she discovered about the form of child-centred learning that had taken root in most elementary schools. The dominant theory, seeded by American progressive education professor John Dewey and sanctioned by the 1968 Ontario Hall-Dennis report, was what Dare identified as the source of the problem. She volunteered in Laurie's school and tutored neighbourhood kids to see how the child-centred ideas translated into practice. Some children with innate abilities were thriving under the new system, but others, mostly boys, were floundering in the more open, progress-at-your-own-pace classroom. A widening gap could also be observed between the motivated academically able and the stragglers, making life much more difficult for regular classroom teachers.

Raising concerns about curriculum philosophy and reading instruction got Dare nowhere. When she took her concerns directly to the Waterloo school district, Chair of the Board Elizabeth Witmer brushed it all off, and Dare was treated to a lecture by a board consultant singing the praises of child-centred learning. Taking her story to the local paper elicited support from twenty concerned parents who joined with Dare in forming the Waterloo group Parents for Learning. Giving voice to their concerns sparked hardened school board resistance. Then, in 1991, Dare saw a television news report focusing on a similar group called Concerned Parents of Etobicoke. Together, the two groups created the Organization for Quality Education (OQE), and began producing a monthly newsletter, compiled and edited by Malkin Dare for more than two decades. Through her parent organization, later known as the Society for Quality Education, the soft underbelly of progressive education was exposed and forces of education reform unleashed that proved hard to contain.[2]

Dare's 1998 parent advocacy book, *How to Get the Right Education for Your Child*, provided a compelling explanation of what had gone wrong in Canada's elementary schools.[3] Schooling in what Dare dubbed "John Dewey Public School" was a real eye-opener for most parents. Teachers were expected to be guides who eschewed explicit instruction and tried to "facilitate" the "discovery of new learning," making it more "relevant" to each individual learner. She described, in graphic terms, how the backlash against a core curriculum and structured learning played out in the schools:

> Each teacher is expected to develop his or her own curriculum, custom-made for each child, fresh-minted every year. Teaching materials often have to be searched out, photo-copied, or made, since workbooks and textbooks are suspect. In an attempt to instill a love of learning, every effort is made to make school fun and easy. "Self-concept" is paramount, and thus students' work is rarely corrected and always passed, while report cards focus on the positive ... Even if students are not ready for the work of the next grade, they are promoted anyway, lest their self-esteem be damaged – usually with the result that at least a third of the class is in trouble.[4]

This picture of the Canadian progressive school and its constructivist or individualized curriculum may have been exaggerated, but it did pinpoint some of the glaring deficiencies of the new curriculum and pedagogy bequeathed by the child-centred learning movement. It also helps to explain why the pendulum began to swing back in the other direction from the mid-to-late 1990s onward with the advent of national and provincial testing and renewed emphasis on account-ability for improving student performance. In many places, touring the local elementary school, even today, one will see plenty of examples of the continuing influence of that form of romantic progressivism.[5]

Public elementary schools remain philosophically progressive and occupy the front lines of the quest for universality. Offering universal, accessible K–12 education has ushered in a fundamental change in the essential purpose of schools – from transmitting core knowledge and habits of industry to embracing "success for all" and preparing record numbers for university and college studies. Since the rise of educational progressivism in the late 1960s and early 1970s, the cur-riculum has expanded and become incredibly overcrowded. Teachers are stretched to the limit trying to master a curriculum meeting an ever-widening range of needs – from the fundamentals of literacy and numeracy to social justice, anti-racism, mental health, well-being, and service learning. Trying to please every interest has become ingrained in schools and stretched the curriculum as schools take on more and more responsibilities to ensure "success for all." Far too many schools attempting to be "good at everything" run the risk of "not being exceptionally good at anything."[6]

WHAT SHOULD SCHOOLS BE TEACHING?

Most Canadians, when asked this question, provide a relatively straightforward answer. Central to what most people expect schools to teach is a sound curriculum providing students with the requisite knowledge, skills, and values to function effectively and to contrib-ute meaningfully in contemporary society. Children come to school to be taught by teachers because they need to acquire knowledge, skills, and values to make their way in life. This basic purpose of schooling, delivered through the curriculum, is widely accepted, particularly by most university/college educators and employers. It is so ingrained that most informed observers consider it a matter of common sense.[7] That rather pragmatic conception is, oddly enough, contested by many occupying positions at all levels within the public school system.

Competing schools of thought over the purpose of schooling can be traced back centuries, and in Western society back to the Ancient Greek philosophers. Subject content, instruction, and expectations, including the centrality of liberal education and the place of arts and athletics, have been the focus of ongoing debates and disputes over the generations.[8] With the advent of compulsory attendance and the spread of universal schooling, the fundamental purpose was tested and standardized curriculum imposed in most educational jurisdictions, including Canada's evolving provincial school systems. Champions of competing curricula and pedagogies continued to fight it out well into the twentieth century, engaged in simmering disputes pitting traditional/essentialist curricula and pedagogical methods against progressive or child-centred approaches.[9] Such educational battles are often waged along various battle lines, most notably in proxy "reading wars" and "math wars."

Expanding public education to serve all children in their diversity has aggravated and perpetuated the schism now being battled out in the realm of education policy and school governance, leaving educators on the outside looking in on the debates. While progressive philosophy and attendant curricula held sway in the Canadian system, the revolving door of policy has been driven by curriculum reformers leaping from one fad to another, in which new initiatives are embraced, then discarded in disappointment, only to be resurrected in modified form. Front-line educators, observing this repeated cycle of changes, know only too well that reforms come and go, initiatives are compromised or die of poor implementation, and no one seems to confront the hard realities of universal education.[10]

Fierce debates about what students should learn, which children should learn it, and how it should be taught have continued throughout the ages. The Western Canon bequeathed by the academic curriculum of the Classical Greek city-states placed strong emphasis on reading, writing, arithmetic, and music, leavened by a focus on physicality and the military arts.[11] Grammar, logic, and rhetoric were essential to a Classical education, as explained in Plato's dialogues. The three subjects together formed what came to be known as the *trivium*.[12] The subjects of the trivium were the foundation for the *quadrivium*, the upper division of medieval education in the liberal arts, composed of arithmetic (number), geometry (number in space), music (number in time), and astronomy (number in space and time). Taken together, the trivium and the quadrivium became accepted as the building blocks of the Classical liberal education. Subject knowledge derived from the great works formed the core of this essentialist tradition, but – it must be noted – Plato also offered this pearl of wisdom: "Knowledge which is acquired under compulsion has no hold on the mind."[13] Today, in the age of universal education, this tradition is almost eclipsed by modern progressivism, which champions a child-centred vision focused far more on engaging the student than on teaching subject knowledge, particularly in the elementary grades.

Child-centred educators countered the essentialist tradition with their own philosophy of constructivism, founded on the belief that children are natural learners – and that great schooling is all about engaging children's interest and giving them the freedom to ask the big questions. Adopted as the cardinal principle of progressivism, the idea of constructivism found its origins in Jean-Jacques Rousseau's most famous work, *Emile*, a classic of the European Enlightenment. In Rousseau's worldview, man (humankind) is born naturally free and good and remains in that state unless corrupted by society and its institutions. "Let us lay down as an incontestable maxim," he wrote, "that the first movements of nature are always right: there is no original wickedness in the human heart."[14] For Rousseau and other leading naturalistic educators who followed, such as Johann Pestalozzi and Friedrich Froebel, the core mission of education was to help children find their natural selves and stave off corruption, and to resist the imposition of society's deadening discipline.[15]

JOHN DEWEY AND THE NEW ORTHODOXY OF PROGRESSIVISM

Constructivism was championed most influentially in North America by John Dewey, the founder and director of the Laboratory School at the University of Chicago (1896–1904). For Dewey, educational philosophy was a practical exercise to be worked out through testing his "working hypotheses" of both teaching practice and curriculum development. He attempted to "find out by trying, by doing – not by discussion and theorizing – whether ... [curriculum] problems may be worked out, and how they may be worked out." In his view, the first three years of the traditional curriculum were deficient because they were spent "on the form – not the substance – of learning," and he found "not much positive nutriment in this." His goal was to enable the child to appreciate and understand "the world around him" and to find a "capacity to express himself in a variety of artistic forms."[16]

Dewey's progressive theory and experiments spread widely in education circles. In the 1920s, the American educationist William H. Kilpatrick adapted Dewey's ideas for integrating curricula and developed the project method aimed at teaching students to "plan, direct and execute their own learning."[17] A Canadian version of it was pioneered in Alberta in the 1930s by an influential Calgary educator, Donalda Dickie, who called it the "enterprise method."[18] The two progressive educators, Kilpatrick and Dickie, both urged teachers to organize their curricula not on the basis of subjects, but around topics or problems that were appealing to students and taken from the world around them. Defenders of teaching subjects were appalled and saw these new approaches as opening the way to a lowering of standards, a dumbing-down of the curriculum, and even a potential threat to human civilization.[19] The ensuing debate degenerated into a familiar pattern – an exchange of slogans and stereotypes with little relation to the real world of the classroom. It erupted once again into a fierce public debate from 1968 to the mid-1970s, following the release of the infamous Ontario Hall-Dennis report, *Living and Learning*, a modern siren call for the new progressivism of child-centred learning and schools where students not only "did their own thing" but proceeded at their own pace.[20]

The progressive disdain for a knowledge-based curriculum proved to be anathema to traditional educators of the liberal education persuasion and to cognitive psychologists who continued to see value in teaching domain-specific subject knowledge. One of the first to challenge the new progressivism was E.D. Hirsch, Jr, former University of Virginia professor and leading proponent of a core knowledge curriculum. After founding the Core Knowledge Foundation in 1986, Hirsch developed a content-rich curriculum and presented it in his 1987 education bestseller, *Cultural Literacy: What Every American Needs to Know*.[21] Contending that children thrive when challenged to master essential facts, dates, events, and concepts, he proposed a core curriculum that provides them with a prescribed body of classic texts and stories, imparting essential historical, literary, and scientific subject content. Mastering the core content knowledge, Hirsch claimed, should be first in priority. "The how-to elements of creativity, problem-solving, language comprehension, and critical thinking" were, in his words, "far, far less important than domain specific knowledge."[22] His critique found sympathy among conservative reformers, including Chester Finn Jr of the Thomas B. Fordham Institute and Diane Ravitch, then a New York University education professor. Breaking with the progressive consensus in Canada was Mark Holmes, an Ontario Institute for Studies in Education (OISE) professor and chief advisor to Dare's Organization for Quality Education.[23] Essentialists such as Hirsch and Holmes challenged the dominant "progressive mind-set" which failed to recognize the fact that children need to master key subject content before acquiring and employing higher-order skills.

Educational progressives continue to hold sway in the Canadian educational establishment and are safely ensconced at Toronto's OISE and most faculties of education. For the most part, the education debate is framed by progressive educators as a contest between new and modern student-centred approaches and traditional back-to-basics thinking. Since the advent of international and provincial testing in the early 2000s, it is often depicted as an ideological battle between "success for all" education and "global education reform." Whatever the framing, the assumptions and ideas of progressives and constructivists still exert considerable influence, particularly in the preparation of teachers. Popular education speakers and writers, such as Alfie Kohn and Sir Ken Robinson, are perennial favourites on the education conference speaking circuit. As a very persuasive speaker and writer, Kohn enjoys a wide following among Canadian educators sympathetic to his critique of standards and testing, his resistance to testing and graded schools, and his dismissal of the value of homework.[24] One of Kohn's most vocal Canadian advocates, the late Red Deer teacher Joe Bower, established a popular blog, *For the Love of Learning*, and it served from 2004 until late 2015 as a popular platform for constructivist educators and progressives favouring student-centred class activities, the dismantling of standardized testing, ungraded schools, and the abolition of homework.[25]

One Canadian province that tacked in a different direction was Quebec, an educational bastion of teacher-guided learning and didactic instruction. In the late 1990s, the Quebec Ministry of Education attempted to deviate from that approach by embracing what was termed the "Reform," a plan of "pedagogical renewal" aimed at introducing student-centred pedagogy in the form of "Project-Based

Learning." Inspired by the bold ideas of leading Quebec educator Paul Inchauspé and his 1997 report, the Reform set out to achieve two seemingly contradictory objectives: teaching the core subjects of French and math, while reforming pedagogical methods and seeding "cross-curricular competencies."[26] The Quebec plan stands out as one of those progressive educational ventures that simply failed to stick in the System.

Implementation of the Quebec Reform encountered stiff resistance from classroom teachers. Fifteen years on, one of those close observers, former Université de Montréal professor Claude Lessard, identified the sources of resistance.[27] Three main sticking points proved to be its undoing: the threat to teachers' collective professionalism posed by a "state as pedagogue" initiative; the adoption of constructivism and self-regulated learning at odds with didactic instruction, mastery learning, and objective-referenced assessment; and the impossibility of marrying the new cross-curricular competencies with their preferred forms of assessment, namely graded report cards and secondary school examinations. In the case of mathematics, Quebec math teachers continued to set high expectations and adhere to didactic instruction and mastery learning, and produced students who repeatedly led the country in their performance on national and international student achievement tests.[28] Successive governments gradually distanced themselves from key elements of the Reform, including the implementation and evaluation of cross-curricular competencies. Defenders of the Reform claimed the challenges were the result of rushed and poor implementation, but front-line teachers saw its disappearance as a small victory for teacher autonomy and educational common sense.[29]

CURRICULUM FADS AND PASSING FANCIES

For the past fifty years, Canadians have debated, taken pride in, and fretted about the quality of education in their schools. Prominent education reformers have charged that students are not learning enough or that the system is in decline, while educators and experts have complained that the schools were not adapting to changing society or were behind the forefront of social progress.[30] Larger political and social goals, such as expanding the reach of the K–12 system, embracing diversity and inclusion, and raising graduation rates, have been major drivers, even when they may compromise the schools' capacity to produce a quality education for students. Generations of reform-minded education policy-makers have embraced one panacea after another, from ability streaming and "special classes" to vocational programs to differentiated curricula and instruction. Misconceptions abound, such as the capacity of schools to solve any social problem, the notion that content knowledge is not important, or the idea that only a certain proportion of students are capable of benefiting from a high-quality education. Curriculum initiatives come and go in cycles, setting off waves of change, but either doing harm or making no discernable difference for teaching and learning in the classroom.

Much of the curriculum controversy over the condition of public education centres on the so-called reading wars. The recent phase dates back to 1955 and the storm of public criticism aroused by Rudolf Flesch's provocative book *Why Johnny Can't Read*. Serialized in many newspapers, the book hit a nerve, especially among parents skeptical about newer ways of teaching basic skills.[31] Progressive educators responded to the onslaught by attempting to prove the superiority of student-centred classrooms without basal readers, textbooks, lesson plans, or homework, but they were unable to allay the public's concerns. Flesch claimed that the neglect of phonics had caused a national crisis in literacy, and the resulting wave of concern reverberated through Canadian education. The popular Look-Say storybooks, such as the widely used *Dick and Jane* series, were targeted as texts based upon flawed theory that required students to memorize words and guess at some words instead of sounding them out using decoding strategies. Flesch also charged that the Look-Say or whole-word method had swept the textbook market despite the fact that it had little or no support in the research. His claim that "reading isn't taught at all" because books were "just put in front of children" drew the ire of elementary school educators.[32]

Flesch made a dent in the new reading methods. While his book was praised in the media and popular magazines, it was almost universally panned in education journals by reviewers who dismissed the author as irresponsible, unqualified, and off the mark. An authoritative review of the research from 1912 to 1965, conducted in the 1960s by Jeanne S. Chall of the Harvard School of Graduate Education, lent some support to Flesch's claim that phonics programs helped with early decoding, produced better word recognition and spelling, and were more effective, especially with children from families of lower socio-economic status.[33] It did surprisingly little, however, to dissuade teachers trained and committed to whole-word programs.

Figure 8.1 Rudolf Flesch's *Why Johnny Can't Read* (1955)

A popular best-seller, Rudolf Flesch's *Why Johnny Can't Read* (1955) was serialized in newspapers and became a handbook for the "back to basics" movement.

The whole debate flared up again in the 1980s and 1990s with the appearance of the whole language (WL) approach to reading. The resurrected movement began with the writings of a Canadian professor, Frank Smith of the University of Victoria in British Columbia, and his American colleague, Kenneth Goodman of the University of Arizona. Influenced by constructivist thinking, Smith and Goodman believed that learning to read should be as easy as learning to speak. Both WL advocates were critical of instruction that emphasized phonics, phonemic awareness, or decoding skills. "The effort to read through decoding," Smith wrote, "is largely futile and unnecessary" and most children learn to read "despite exposure to phonics."[34] Much like the whole-word methods of the 1920s, the whole language approach proposed that children be exposed to literature that matched their personal interests. Students in such elementary classes were encouraged to read for meaning and pleasure rather than study grammar or the mechanics of language.[35] Whole language was another example of the rebellion against drill, workbooks, and textbooks, this time aimed at phonics, which, overdone, could deaden students' interest in reading.

Whole language dominated reading programs throughout the 1980s, driven largely by Smith and his disciples in education faculties across Canada. While Jeanne Chall had urged that schools go easy on teaching phonics, limiting it to the first two grades, WL crusaders sought to stamp the structured method out altogether. The results were disastrous, as demonstrated by the American National Assessment of Educational Progress (NAEP), which reported that nearly 40 percent of pupils were "below basic" in the 1990s. Students in the Black and Hispanic communities did worse, with 60 to 64 percent performing at the lowest level in Grade 4, compared to 27 percent of white students. In Ontario, provincial tests revealed that only 60 percent of Grade 3 students read well enough to cope with reading in the next grade.[36] Finally, reading experts reached a consensus that a balanced approach worked best, giving emphasis to both phonemic awareness and reading comprehension.

The revised approach known as Balanced Literacy calmed the waters, but did not really resolve the rumbling among proponents of systematic phonics. Thousands of parents in the 1990s were "hooked on phonics," judging from the record commercial sales of such programs. "Forced to do something but unwilling to abandon their beloved Whole Language," Malkin Dare wrote, "education leaders added a few bells and whistles, and renamed the approach 'Balanced Literacy.'" "The added features," she claimed, "mean that kids tend to do slightly better than they did under Whole Language, but the 'new' Balanced Literacy approach is still miles from enough."[37] Dare's prediction proved remarkably accurate.

A new antidote, known as Reading Recovery (RR), emerged as a convenient band-aid. Developed by Marie Clay in New Zealand in 1985, it attracted a loyal following as a means of responding to the alarmingly high incidence of reading failure in early elementary grades. With Dare and her allies campaigning for the restoration of phonics, Reading Recovery programs popped up all over North America as the answer.[38] The RR program was seized by education departments and boards as the latest panacea. By 2000, RR had spread to 10,000 American Grade 1 classrooms and had made inroads in Canada, particularly in Ontario and Nova Scotia. Between 1986 and 2011, Nova Scotia poured millions into RR, training some 600 teachers and running 33,000 kids through the twelve-week, intensive, one-on-one program.[39] Throughout the 2000s, it was rare to find a school that did not claim to be offering a balanced program paying lip service to structured literacy, but whole language programs supplemented with Reading Recovery remained prevalent. Most elementary schools professed to be offering a balanced program, but reading levels either remained static or declined on Grade 3 and Grade 6 provincial tests.[40]

THE NEVER-ENDING MATH WARS

The teaching of mathematics proved to be another contested curricular battleground. Much like the domain of early reading, mathematics has been beset by wave upon wave of curriculum reforms over the past fifty years. A "new math" curriculum developed by American mathematics professors in the 1960s sought to dislodge traditional methods and was promoted widely by the National Council of Teachers of Mathematics (NCTM) in collaboration with the National Science Foundation. The new curriculum stressed the conceptual nature of mathematics, integrated the various math disciplines, introduced real-world problems, and de-emphasized mental computation skills. The high tide of the new math was reached in 1967–68 when progressive methods were dominant and no textbooks were approved that did not conform to the new order. The new math met its downfall, however, when student test results raised serious questions about its effectiveness.[41] The final blow came in 1973 when mathematician Morris Kline's book *Why Johnny Can't Add: The Failure of the New Math* fuelled an all-out parent and teacher rebellion against the conceptual methods. The public reaction led to a "back-to-basics" movement that attempted to restore computational skills – adding, subtracting, multiplying, and dividing – and to ensure standard algorithms remained at the core of early mathematics instruction.[42]

The revised NCTM standards, released in 1989, failed to patch up the rift between new math advocates and back-to-basics campaigners. Developed by educational constructivists, the NCTM curriculum put a heavy emphasis on "hands-on" learning activities, mathematical games, working with plastic manipulatives and computers, and group learning. Drilling students was out, and so was emphasizing getting the correct answer.[43] Public and parental concern over so-called "fuzzy math" registered when it was revealed that the NCTM standards had not been field-tested and little evidence existed of their effectiveness. Claims that basic skills had been rendered obsolete by calculators only added to the backlash. While the vast majority of mathematics education professors and district consultants favoured the new "discovery math" in a 1993 survey, only two in five American PTA members and one in four high school principals accepted the underlying philosophy.[44]

Signs of dissent appeared in the early 1990s, but a full-scale counterrevolution against the NCTM standards broke out in 1995 in the state of California. Launched on the internet, a math reform advocacy group known as Mathematically Correct took direct aim at "the new new math." One of the most effective critics, Marianne M. Jennings, an Arizona State University mathematician, produced a widely circulated critique of her daughter's richly illustrated high school textbook and its "rainforest algebra" approach.[45] In 1997, the resistance hit the American national press in a series of critical articles exposing what was labelled "fuzzy math" because it seemed to belittle math based on getting the right answers. The critics claimed, based on cognitive research, that students could not master higher-order skills if they lacked the basic foundational skills, and, in addition, that knowing the right answers was critical in fields such as science, engineering, and medicine.[46]

The new approach survived the onslaught because mathematics educators closed ranks and held their ground. Adopting a new line of defense, the NCTM forces countered with the claim that their holistic

Weapons of Math Destruction ™

Figure 8.2 Constructivism in the Math Classroom (Weapons of Math Destruction)

Secondary school mathematics teachers tend to be critical of constructivist approaches, much preferring to teach the foundations, then proceed to higher-level problem solving. This satirical cartoon accurately conveys their skepticism.

approach was, at heart, a pedagogy or way of teaching rather than a prescriptive curriculum. A new generation of mathematics educators, including British research professor Jo Boaler and Canadian educator Marian Small, emerged in the 2000s to sustain the NCTM reform agenda. Boaler's initial research 1997 study in England, *Experiencing*

School Mathematics: Teaching Styles, Sex, and Setting, won accolades and was republished in 2002 in the United States. Students who were actively engaged in mathematics learning using problem-solving and reasoning, she claimed, achieved at higher levels and enjoyed math more than those who engaged passively by practising methods demonstrated by the teacher in class. After moving to the Stanford Graduate School of Education, she became a champion of math reform based upon "inquiry-based learning," addressing gender inequities, and establishing a link between testing and math anxiety. As the leading Canadian disciple, Small has co-authored mathematics textbooks and given hundreds of workshops demonstrating the constructivist approach to K–12 mathematics instruction.

The Math Wars continue today and are very much alive in Canadian K–12 education. Constructivist math curriculum consultants, heavily influenced by Boaler and Small, continue to ensure that textbooks, learning materials, and conferences reflect that still-dominant curriculum philosophy, focusing more and more on student-centred approaches to closing the gender and equity gaps in mathematics education. Since September 2011, Manitoba mathematicians, led by Anna Stokke and Robert Craigen, have exposed the continuing decline in student scores and challenged the dominance of discovery math approaches with a math education advocacy group known as WISE Math, the Western Initiative for Strengthening Education in Math.[47] University of Winnipeg math professor Stokke spotted "a huge problem" when she discovered Manitoba grade school students not being taught how to do vertical addition, to carry or borrow numbers, or to recite their times tables. The WISE Math advocates identified the source of the problem – new math and inquiry-based teaching approaches that guide students to estimate answers and use multiple strategies in basic calculations, effectively complicating the process of arriving at the right answer. Such approaches were integral to the Western and Northern Canadian Protocol (WNCP), a common framework, initiated in 1995 and revised in 2006, used to develop curricula right across Canada.

After quickly gathering 1,000 names on a petition and two years of advocacy, Stokke and Craigen achieved a small breakthrough in September 2012 when Manitoba's Education Minister revised the provincial curriculum for kindergarten to Grade 8, explicitly requiring students to learn times tables, to demonstrate standard algorithms for key math operations – and to perform them without using a calculator.[48] It was a small step forward, but did little to fundamentally alter the dominant ideology or to help parents outside of Manitoba looking for help in building their children's essential math skills. In 2011–12, for example, Ontario's student testing reported a five-year decline in Grade 3 and 6 students' math skills and growing numbers of students registering a drop in their achievement between Grade 3 and Grade 6. The Executive Director of the Society for Quality Education, Doretta Wilson, noted that the SQE website math worksheets were their highest-demand resource, and added, "it doesn't look like tutoring centres are going to go out of business any time soon in Ontario."[49]

RIDING THE TWENTY-FIRST-CENTURY LEARNING WAVE

Confronted with mounting concerns over early reading challenges and the decline in mathematics scores, leading public school advocates remain unfailingly optimistic and positive about the "next great thing" in education. The Internet and smart technology have changed the rules of engagement for teachers as well as students, bringing the latest research within a few keyboard clicks. One would think that providing a forum for asking deeper questions would be more widely accepted in assessing province-wide and school board–wide initiatives before they are rolled out every September in our K–12 school system. It can, however, be a little threatening to those promoting theory-based curriculum reform or pedagogical initiatives. Questioning such initiatives, most teachers sense – at least in some school systems – is not always conducive to career advancement.

A recent book on Canadian education, *Pushing the Limits*, written by Kelly Gallagher-Mackay and Nancy Steinhauer, is relentlessly upbeat and focuses almost exclusively on well-funded "lighthouse projects" in the Greater Toronto Area and a few other Canadian jurisdictions.[50] While the title is somewhat puzzling, the subtitle is far more indicative of the book's real intent, i.e., explaining *How Schools Can Prepare Our Children Today for the Challenges of Tomorrow*. It is, for the most part, a neat compendium of curriculum initiatives reflecting current policy directions in Ontario, the Canadian province that often sets the national education agenda.

Success stories abound in *Pushing the Limits* and they served to provide credence to provincial curriculum initiatives underway, particularly in Ontario, Alberta, and British Columbia. The overriding assumption is that schools exist to "prepare our students for the future" and to equip them with "21st century skills." Grade 7 teacher Aaron Warner at Regina's Douglas Park Elementary School, creator of the two-hour-per-week Genius Hour, repeats a very familiar claim: "Sixty per cent of the jobs of the future haven't been invented yet." That buttresses the overall thesis that lies at the heart of the book.

The popular claim can be traced back to a TED Talk by British education guru Sir Ken Robinson. What's the problem with repeating Robinson's claim and citing a statistic to support that hypothesis? It is a classic example of transforming education or "building the future schoolhouse" on what Hack Education commentator Audrey Watters has termed a theory of mythical proportions, instead of evidence-based policy-making. Citing the statistic that "60% [or 65%] of future jobs have not been invented yet" is doubly problematic because no one can authenticate the research behind that oft-repeated number.[51] The entire claim has now been thoroughly discredited. One of those who popularized that statistic, Dr Cathy Davidson of The Graduate Center CUNY, was unable to validate the claim and no longer uses it in her research or lectures. Furthermore, two British researchers, Daisy Christodoulou and Andrew Old, reached similar conclusions and, on the BBC World News Service program *More or Less,* aired 29 May 2017, they shared their findings that it was essentially a bogus statistic.[52] One can only hope that Canadian educators, on the basis of the *Pushing the Limits* book, will not perpetuate that edu-myth in schools across Canada.

CONFRONTING THE CROWDED CURRICULUM

Even the most ardent public school promoters concede that today's schools are expected to do far too much. Provincial ministries of education continue to embrace transformative visions that further embed the whole-system commitment to progressive reform and universal student progress. Yet children who enter kindergarten flush with curiosity and anticipation see their enthusiasm declining through the grades until boredom sets in around Grade 8 in most classrooms. Too many students find little intellectual engagement in high school and see the experience as a social experience where the greatest value lies in forging relationships with friends.[53] In larger urban and rural high schools, the course menu has expanded and students sail though from one grade to another aided by the widespread phenomenon of "social promotion."[54] While struggling students fade out in their graduating year, the vast majority of high school seniors, well over 80 percent in most provinces, graduate and move on to the next stage, in most cases university or college.

The school curriculum is, according to most education analysts, a problem, for one reason or another. Public education critics across North America are fond of depicting today's curriculum in rather unflattering terms using descriptors such as the dumbed-down curriculum or the feel-good curriculum.[55] One of Canada's leading education authorities, former British Columbia Deputy Education Minister Charles Ungerleider, offered this thumbnail assessment: "The curriculum of the public school has become bloated, fragmented, mired in trivia, and short on ideas," he wrote in his 2003 book *Failing Our Kids.* "It does not demand that students connect what they learn with anything else. It does not challenge them to reach beyond the limits. The curriculum stifles curiosity. Although it demands effort, it does not reward deep thought."[56]

Public school curricula are always expected to accommodate and to absorb expanded mandates, usually in response to information overload and a parade of burning social issues. A new Ontario vision for education, *Achieving Excellence and Equity*, announced in April 2014, exemplified the grandiose plans that promise to achieve academic excellence, while ensuring educational equity and ensuring student well-being.[57] Enveloped by the internet and inundated with social media, students and teachers are drowning in information but starving for wisdom. Our schools are society's last meeting place where children of all origins, capabilities, and inclinations come to be educated and outfitted for life and the workplace. The primary legacy of progressive education reform is the creation of the near-universal public-school experience. Teachers can become overwhelmed by what American education researcher Rick Hess aptly describes as an "overflowing bucket" of well-intended directives.[58] When the public is roused by a wave of sexual abuse cases or teen suicides, perplexed by teen cyberbullying, or swept up in fears about a looming teen mental health crisis, education policy-makers and senior administrators are conditioned to respond based upon the assumption that all such issues need to be addressed in the schools. That is why, when

Figure 8.3 Jumbled and Overcrowded Curriculum: Ontario
Curriculum Integration, 2014

Ontario's *Achieving Excellence and Equity* guideline, released
in April 2014, attempted to marry academic excellence, educational equity, and student well-being. A Ministry of Education
wordle demonstrated the complexity of the task of integrating
the curriculum.

problems such as junk food consumption, eating disorders, homopho-
bia, racist graffiti, and teen suicide reach unacceptable levels, these
concerns inevitably spawn programs in public schools.

One traditional core academic subject that is being squeezed out
of the contemporary curriculum is history and social studies. From
the 1960s to the mid-1990s, history as a discrete subject moved from
the centre to the periphery of the school curriculum, and was reduced,
in most provinces, to a single required history course (focusing on
Canada and contemporary issues). While classroom teachers debated
what a revitalized history would look like in the 1980s, veteran
Toronto teacher Bob Davis once noted, "the subject was disappearing
under our feet." Curriculum trends such as the rise of Canadian Studies
with its sociological emphasis, the dissolution of national history,
inquiry-centred approaches, and "skills-mania" all contributed to the
subject's gradual disappearance.[59] While the teaching of Canadian
history then experienced a revival, fuelled from 1997 to 2010 by the
Dominion Institute and Historica Canada, it proved short-lived.[60]
Leading history teachers, alarmed by the withering of their subject,
object to the erosion of historical-mindedness and bemoan the inability
of today's students to see trends such as the removal of bronze statues
or the renaming of historic buildings in any kind of broader or deeper
historical context. Recognizing the neglected past of Indigenous

peoples is long overdue, but curriculum changes are essentially burying the political memory of youth and eroding democratic citizenship.
"It's difficult to fit everything into four years of high school," Historica
Canada's education manager Bronwyn Graves commented recently,
"but I don't think history should be sacrificed or rolled into social
studies in order to check all those boxes."[61]

The school curriculum, defined broadly as what is taught and
offered inside and outside of class, is normally assumed to be expand-
able. Floundering student discipline and unattended behaviour issues
in the early years create problems in the higher grades. Career education, life skills, media studies, and mental health literacy have earned
a place among the more familiar subjects of language, literature,
mathematics, science, and social studies in the public school curriculum. The fundamental problem with this so-called "additive function"
is that while initiatives and subjects are added, little or nothing is
removed, and there is no corresponding increase in the school day or
the school year.[62] It may be time to ask how much of the expanding
mandate of schools is the result of institutional failures elsewhere.

Today's schools are stretched to the limit, attempting to be all things
to all people. If schools are to be the place where social and public
health issues are addressed, then changes are required to integrate
those specialized services and to allocate space for them.[63] Teacher
union leaders such as Ontario Secondary School Teachers' Federation
President Henry Bischof are beginning to speak up against top-down
initiatives and "the influence of self-appointed gurus, ideologues and
advocates who promote unproven trends and fads."[64] Hard questions
need to be asked about the capacity of teachers overburdened with
new responsibilities, and about the need to re-engineer the whole
educational service model to either focus on teaching children or
continue to respond to an ever-increasing range of children's needs.

9

Student Assessment Experiments

Soft Skills and Hard Realities

Systems thinkers in K–12 education now recognize that assessment drives curriculum. Changes underway in provincial student assessment, presented as educational advances, demonstrate that systems management remains so ingrained that it can be adapted to new purposes. Concerns over the increasing emphasis on preparing students for provincial, national, and international tests sparked a counterreaction from 2013 to 2018, driven largely by an Ontario student assessment coalition committed to finding ways of systematically assessing social and emotional learning. This movement, known in Ontario as Measuring What Matters (MWM), emerged in 2013 and attempted to "broaden the measures of success," but actually sought to either soften student achievement standards or banish standardized testing all together.[1] It all came to a halt in June 2018 with the earth-shaking election of Doug Ford's Progressive Conservative government at Queen's Park and the return, for a time, of a "back-to-basics" education reform agenda.

The Ontario "Broader Success" project was part of a global assessment reform movement. Initiated by Toronto parent advocate Annie Kidder and her People for Education organization, it was in the vanguard of the nationwide educational effort after 2010 to counter the influence of student achievement testing by incorporating softer cross-curricular competencies and socially progressive attitudes. Supporters of the MWM movement took their cue from North American education gadfly Alfie Kohn and international achievement test opponents objecting to "the negative consequences of the PISA rankings" and claiming that "measuring a great diversity of educational traditions and cultures using a single, narrow, biased yardstick could, in the end, do irreparable harm to our schools and our students."[2] It was also clear that

Kidder and her coterie of MWM soft-skills assessment researchers had the ear of Liberal Premier Kathleen Wynne and exerted extraordinary influence over educational policy-making within the Ontario Ministry of Education. Among the group assembled to produce white papers covering various social and emotional learning domains were York University mindfulness/self-regulation advocate Stuart Shanker, McMaster University clinical psychiatrist Jean Clinton, Queen's University creativity specialist Rena Upitis, and University of New Brunswick citizenship researcher Alan Sears.[3]

A fall 2017 Ontario student assessment initiative, *A Learning Province*, provided a clearer indication of where it was all heading and the potential adverse impact on front-line teachers.[4] Heavily influenced by the Ontario People for Education project, the province was actively preparing to plunge ahead with Social and Emotional Learning (SEL) assessment, embracing what Dr Ben Williamson aptly describes as "stealth assessment" – a set of contested personality criteria utilizing SEL "datafication" to measure "student well-being." Proceeding to integrate SEL into student reports and province-wide assessments was contentious because American experts in the field were warning that the "generic skills" are ill-defined and possibly unmeasurable.[5] With the Kathleen Wynne Liberal government in power at Queen's Park it also looked unstoppable.

The final Ontario student assessment report, released by the premier's education advisors in April 2018, confirmed that provincial education policy-makers in the Wynne government were intent upon re-engineering provincial testing and "broadening the range of qualitative feedback" to students and parents. While provincial testing survived the review, proposals were tabled to phase out large-scale Grade 3 assessments to reduce test anxiety and to rule out any use of them for either student diagnostic purposes or the ranking of schools.[6] It all went down in flames in June 2018 when the Ford government proclaimed its "back-to-basics" agenda reaffirming support for provincial testing, reviewing the sex-education curriculum, and planning to improve student achievement levels, particularly in mathematics.[7]

ORIGINS OF THE STUDENT ASSESSMENT REFORM INITIATIVE

Assessing students' social and emotional competencies was the driving force behind the latest educational trend with a distinctly "New Age" orientation. Over the previous five years, educational talk was thick about the supposed key to student achievement in schools known as "grit" – being passionate about long-term goals and showing the determination to see them through.[8] While American and British school authorities buzzed about grit and the possibility of creating a "grit index," the movement gained surprisingly little traction in the somewhat insular world of Canadian education. Teaching and measuring social-emotional skills surfaced on the emerging policy agenda, but the whole orientation tilted more in the direction of developing and measuring students' soft skills instead of sharpening their competitive instincts.

Grit was all the buzz in American K–12 education from 2007 until 2013, and school systems were scrambling to get on board the latest trend. A 2007 academic article, researched and written by Angela Duckworth, made a compelling case that grit plays a critical role in success. Author Paul Tough introduced grit to a broad audience in his 2013 book *How Children Succeed: Grit, Curiosity, and the Hidden Power of Character*, which went on to spend a year on the *New York Times* bestseller list.[9] The same year, Duckworth herself gave a TED talk that was viewed more than 8 million times online. Since then, grit initiatives have flourished in United States school systems. Some schools were trying to teach grit, and some districts were attempting to measure children's grit, with the outcome contributing to assessments of school effectiveness. Angela Duckworth's 2016 book, *Grit: The Power of Passion and Perseverance*, was one of the hottest North American non-fiction titles that year.[10] In spite of the flurry of public interest, however, grit did not really register in the Canadian educational domain.

The Ontario student assessment initiative sprang, almost fully formed, from a different place. Over the twenty years of its existence, the Ontario-based People for Education advocacy organization had been a thorn in the side of Ontario's student testing agency and a tenacious critic of its provincial achievement testing, focusing almost exclusively on literacy and mathematics. Originally a parent advocacy group lobbying for increased education funding, it had evolved by the 2000s into more of a policy advisory organization with close links to the Ontario Liberal governments of Dalton McGuinty and Kathleen Wynne.[11] With the accession of Wynne to the premiership in January 2013, Kidder seized the opportunity to pursue the goal of broadening the existing measures of student success to embrace social-emotional skills or competencies.[12] Making an explicit commitment to "move beyond the '3R's'" and redefine the established testing/accountability framework, Kidder and her well-funded Toronto-centred research

Figure 9.1 Annie Kidder and Ontario Education Minister Mitzie Hunter, 2017

Founder of People for Education Annie Kidder succeeded in promoting a new approach to student assessment, Measuring What Matters, consistent with her long-standing resistance to standardized testing. She reached the height of her influence from 2013 to 2018 and became a close confidante of successive Liberal Ministers of Education.

team began creating a "broad set of foundational skills" and developing a method of "measuring schools' progress toward those goals."[13]

The Ontario MWM advocates proposed a draft set of "Competencies and Skills" identified as Creativity, Citizenship, Social-Emotional Learning, and Health – all to be embedded in what were termed "quality learning environments" in both schools and the community.[14] The proposed Ontario model made no reference whatsoever to cognitive learning and subject knowledge, nor to the social-emotional aspects of grit, perseverance, or work ethic. While it professed to be research-informed, the whole enterprise was driven by a team of Canadian education researchers with their own well-known hobby-horses.[15] The co-chair of the MWM initiative, former BC Deputy Minister of Education Charles Ungerleider, assembled a group of academics with impeccable "progressive education" (anti-testing) credentials, including OISE teacher workload researcher Nina Bascia, Clinton, Shanker, Upitis, and Sears.

Two years into the project, the MWM student success framework had hardened into what began to sound more and more like a new catechism. The research director, David Hagen Cameron, a PhD in Education from the University of London, hired from the Ontario Ministry of Education, began to focus on *how* to implement the model with what he termed "MWM change theory."[16] His mandate was crystal clear – to take the theory and transform it into Ontario school practice in four years, then take it national in 2017–18. Five education researchers were recruited to write papers making the case for including each of the domains, some 78 educators were appointed to advisory committees, and the proposed measures were field-tested in 26 different public and Catholic separate schools (20 elementary, 6 secondary), representing a cross-section of urban and rural Ontario.

As an educational sociologist who cut his research teeth studying the British New Labour educational "interventionist machine," Dr Cameron was acutely aware that educational initiatives usually flounder because of poorly executed implementation. Much of his focus, in project briefings and academic papers from 2014 onward, was on how to "find congruence" between MWM priorities and Ministry mandates, and how to tackle the tricky business of winning the concurrence of teachers – particularly how to overcome their instinctive resistance to district "education consultants" who arrive promising support but end up extending more "institutional control over teachers in their classrooms."[17]

Stumbling blocks emerged when the MWM theory met up with the everyday reality of teaching and learning in the schools. Translating the proposed SEL domains into a set of student competencies and ensuring supportive conditions posed immediate difficulties. The MWM reform promoters came foursquare up against the challenges of achieving "system coherence" with the existing EQAO assessment system and bridging gaps between the system and local levels. Dr Cameron and his MWM team were unable to effectively answer concerns about increased teacher workload, the misuse of collected data, the mandate creep of schools, and the public's desire for simple, easy-to-understand reports.[18]

The 2015 MWM progress report claimed that the initiative was moving from theory to practice with field trials in Ontario public schools. It simply reaffirmed the proposed social-emotional domains and made no mention of Duckworth's research or her Grit Scale for assessing student performance on that benchmark. While Duckworth was cited in the report, it was for a point unrelated to her key research findings. The paper also assumed that Ontario was a "medium stakes" testing environment in need of softer, non-cognitive measures of student progress, an implicit criticism of the well-established Ontario Quality and Accountability Office system of provincial achievement testing.[19]

Whether grit or any other social-emotional skills could be taught – or reliably measured – remained very much in question. Leading American cognitive learning researcher Daniel Willingham's 2016 *American Educator* essay addressed the whole matter squarely and punched holes in the argument that grit can be easily taught, let alone assessed in schools.[20] Although Willingham is a well-known critic of "pseudoscience" in education, he does favour utilizing "personality characteristics" for the purpose of "cultivating" in students such attributes as conscientiousness, self-control, kindness, honesty, optimism, courage, and empathy, among others.

The movement to assess students for social-emotional skills also raised alarms, even among the biggest proponents of teaching them. American education researchers, including Angela Duckworth, were leery that the terms used were unclear and the first battery of tests faulty as assessment measures. She eventually resigned from the advisory board of a California SEL project, claiming the proposed social-emotional tests were not suitable for measuring school performance. "I don't think we should be doing this; it is a bad idea," she told *The New York Times*. Proceeding to integrate SEL into student reports and province-wide assessments hit another snag when Duckworth and a research associate David Scott Yeager produced a research study warning that the "generic skills" are ill-defined and possibly unmeasurable.[21]

BIG DATA, PERSONALITY PROFILING, AND STUDENT ASSESSMENT

Big Data and its perils are no longer a total mystery in the world of education. Millions of Facebook users were profiled by Cambridge Analytica without their knowledge, and that public disclosure in March 2018 heightened everyone's awareness of not only the trend toward data analysis–based personality profiling, but the potential for massive invasion of privacy. These controversial actions exposed the scope of Big Data and the wider aspirations of the data analytics industry to probe into the "hidden depths of people." It also, as UK expert Ben Williamson commented, tipped us off about the growing trend toward personality measurement in K–12 and post-secondary education.[22]

Williamson's ground-breaking 2017 book *Big Data in Education* sounded the alert that the collection and analysis of more personal information from schoolchildren would be a defining feature of education in coming years.[23] And just as the Facebook debacle raised public concerns about the use of personal data, a new international test of ten- and fifteen-year-olds was being developed by the Organization for Economic Cooperation and Development (OECD) – a powerful influence on national education policies at a global scale. Almost without being detected, it also emerged as a key component of Ontario's Student Well-Being Assessment, initially piloted from 2014 to 2016 by Ontario People for Education as the core objective of its MWM project.[24]

Most data collected about students since the 1990s has come from conventional international, national, and provincial examinations of knowledge and cognitive skills. Preparing students for success in the twenty-first-century workplace has been a major driver of most initiatives in testing and accountability. International test results such as the OECD's Program of International Student Assessment (PISA) have also become surrogate measures of the future economic potential of nations, feeding a global education race among national education systems.[25]

The advent of Big Data is gradually transforming the nature of student assessment. While the initial phase was focused on stimulating competitive instincts and striving for excellence, more recent initiatives are seeking to "broaden the focus of student assessment" to include SEL. Much of the motivation is to secure some economic advantage, but that is now being more broadly defined to help mold students committed to more than individual competitiveness. With the capacity to collect more intimate data about social and emotional skills to measure personality, education policy-makers are devising curriculum and assessment programs to improve personality scores. Despite the March 2018 Cambridge Analytica controversy, personality data is well on the way to being used in education to achieve a variety of competing political objectives.[26]

The science of psychographic profiling is a contested terrain where advocates and critics debate not only its validity, but its potential misuse in the field of assessment.[27] It is, however, based on psychological methods that have a long history of measuring and categorizing people by personality. At its core is a psychological model called the "five factor model of personality" or the "Big Five." These include "openness," "conscientiousness," "extroversion," "agreeableness," and "neuroticism" (OCEAN). Personality theorists believe these categories

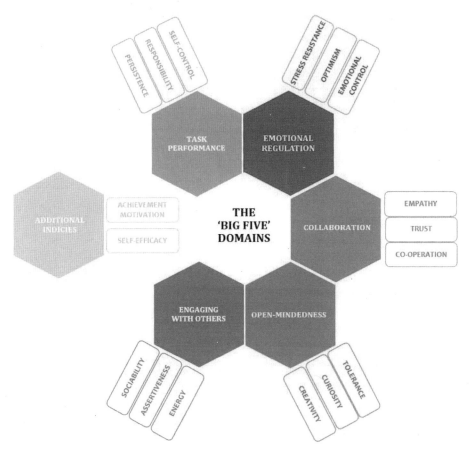

Figure 9.2 The OECD "Five Domains"

The preferred OECD Education SEL assessment model is based upon a psychological model called the five-factor model of personality – or the "Big Five." These include "openness," "conscientiousness," "extroversion," "agreeableness," and "neuroticism" (OCEAN). The Ontario version reflected a different set of value preferences.

are suitable for classifying the full range of human personalities. Psychologists have invented instruments such as the so-called "Big Five Inventory" to capture OCEAN data for personality modelling.[28]

ADVENT OF STEALTH STUDENT ASSESSMENT

The mining and use of personal student data are commonplace in the data analytics industry and have surfaced as a new branch of student assessment. The term "stealth assessment" is applied when the process involves collecting and analyzing personal data without explicit consent, utilizing the latest technology and algorithms. It was initially coined by leading researcher Dr Valerie Shute, a professor at Florida State University and formerly principal research scientist at Educational Testing Service.[29] Widely used by Facebook, Scholastic, Dreambox, and the non-profit Khan Academy, it is being introduced into student assessment by Pearson PLC, the world's dominant learning corporation and the firm contracted to develop and manage global testing for the OECD's Education Office. Today, commercial software programs register every single answer a student gives and aggregate data on the student's knowledge, primarily in mathematics and reading. Leading University of Chicago economist James Heckman co-authored a 2014 OECD report on measuring "non-cognitive skills" and has urged education policy-makers to make "personality investments" in young people, claiming that it leads to high returns in labour market outcomes.[30] Plans are underway at the international, national, and state/provincial levels to expand that function to aggregate personal data and to map it against personality models.

The 2018 OECD PISA test included, for the first time, a battery of questions aimed at assessing "global competencies" with a distinct SEL orientation. In 2019, the OECD also launched its international Study of Social and Emotional Learning. Designed as a computer-based self-completion questionnaire, at its core the test is a modified version of the Big Five Inventory. The OECD version mapped exactly onto the five factor personality categories with "emotional stability" substituted in place of "neuroticism."[31] When fully implemented, the social and emotional skills test results will assess students against each of the Big Five categories.

The OECD Education Skills experts, working in collaboration with Pearson Learning International, firmly believe that social and emotional skills are important predictors of educational progress and future workplace performance. Large-scale personality data is seen by OECD Education to be predictive of a country's potential social and economic progress. Although the OECD and Ontario Student Well-Being advocates both claim that it is strictly a test of social and emotional skills, Williamson claims such projects employ the same family of methods used in the Cambridge Analytica personality quiz. Upon closer examination, the same psychological assumptions and personality assessment methods underpin most of the latest education ventures.

The OECD is already a powerful influence on the molding of national education policies. Its PISA testing has reshaped school curricula, assessments, and whole systems in the global education race. It is increasingly likely that its emphasis on personality testing will once again reshape education policy and school practices.[32] Just as PISA has influenced a global market in products to support the core skills of literacy, numeracy, and science tested by the assessment, the same is now occurring around SEL and personality development. Canada's provincial and territorial ministers of education, working under the auspices of the Council of Ministers of Education, Canada (CMEC), have not only endorsed the OECD's proposed "global competencies," but proposed a variation of their own to guide assessment policy.[33]

The 2017–18 Ontario Student Assessment initiative deserves closer scrutiny through the lens of datafication and personality profiling. Its overarching goal bears repeating: "Update provincial assessment and reporting practices, including EQAO, to make sure they are culturally relevant, measure a wider range of learning, and better reflect student well-being and equity." Founder of People for Education Annie Kidder hailed the plan for "embedding" the "transferable skills" and positioning Ontario to take "a leading role in the global movement toward broader goals for education and broader measures of success in our schools."[34]

Critics of large-scale student assessments are quick to identify the underlying influence of globalization and the oft-stated goal of preparing students for the highly competitive twenty-first-century workplace. It can be harder to spot currents moving in the opposite direction and heavily influenced by what Kathryn Ecclestone and Denis Hayes aptly termed the "therapeutic education ethos." Ten years ago, they flagged the rise of a "therapeutic education" movement exemplified by classroom activities and programs, often branded as promoting "mindfulness," which pave the way for "coaching appropriate emotions" and transform education into a disguised form of "social engineering" aimed at producing "emotionally literate citizens" who are notably "happy" and experience "emotional well-being."[35]

Preparing students to be highly competitive human beings or to be creative and cooperative individuals is risking reframing public education in terms of personality modification, driven by ideological motivations, rather than the pursuit of meaningful knowledge and understanding. It treats children as guinea pigs for experimenters

engaged in either market competition preparation or social engineering, and may well stand in the way of classroom teachers pursuing their own evidence-based, knowledge-centred curriculum aims.
The appropriation and misuse of personality data by Facebook and
Cambridge Analytica led to a significant worldwide public backlash.
In education, however, tests and technologies to measure student
personality, according to Williamson, have proceeded unchallenged.
Capturing and mining students' personality data with the goal of
shaping students to "fit into" the evolving global marketplace would
seem to be equally controversial.[36] Stealth assessment has arrived,
and forewarned is forearmed.

ONTARIO STUDENT ASSESSMENT – THE PLUNGE INTO SOFT SKILLS (SEL) ASSESSMENT

Ontario under Premier Wynne aspired to global education leadership
in the realm of student evaluation and reporting. The student assessment initiative *A Learning Province*, conducted from September 2017
until March 2018, cast a wide net and targeted the existing provincial
testing regime with a plan to broaden future assessments to capture
the totality of "students' experiences – their needs, learning, progress
and well-being."[37] The "Independent Review of Assessment and
Reporting" process was supervised by some familiar Ontario education policy advisors, including past and present OISE insiders, Michael
Fullan, Andy Hargreaves, and Carol Campbell; and the equally familiar four pillars, achieving excellence, ensuing equity, promoting well-
being, and enhancing public confidence were repeated as secular
articles of faith.[38]

The sheer scope of the whole project and its potential impact upon
teachers' marking loads proved to be its major stumbling blocks. A
pithy January 2017 statement by British teacher-researcher Daisy
Christodoulou was germane: "When government get their hands on
anything involving the word 'assessment', they want it to be about
high stakes monitoring and tracking, not about low-stakes diagnosis."[39] In the case of Ontario, the pursuit of the datafication of social-
emotional learning and the mining of data to produce personality
profiles came to take precedence over the creation of teacher-friendly
assessment policy and practices.

One of the reasons Ontario has been recognized as a leading
education system was because of its success over the past twenty

years in establishing an independent Education Quality and Accountability Office (EQAO) with an established and professionally-sound provincial testing program in Grades 3, 6, 9, and 10. [40] While the EQAO had its critics, most objective observers agreed that it had succeeded in establishing reliable benchmark standards for student performance in literacy and mathematics. An October 2015 study, *Closing the Numeracy Gap*, prepared by Graham Orpwood and Emily Sandford Brown, testified to the enduring value of the Ontario provincial tests. [41] It documented and analyzed the "real and growing gap between the numeracy abilities of Ontarians and their numeracy needs," which was only possible because of annual EQAO testing in mathematics. It was particularly odd that Premier Wynne announced the assessment review in the wake of the release of the most recent EQAO report on dismal math results. Only half of Grade 6 students met the provincial standard in math, down from 57 percent in 2012–13. Among Grade 3 students, 62 percent met the provincial standard in math, a decrease of 5 percent over the past five years. [42]

Social and emotional learning gradually emerged at the very core of the Wynne government's *Achieving Excellence and Equality* agenda and fully embraced "supporting all students" and enabling them to achieve "a positive sense of well-being – the sense of self, identity, and belonging in the world that will help them to learn, grow and thrive." The proposed Ontario model was based upon a psycho-social theory that "well-being" has "four interconnected elements" critical to student development, with self/spirit at the centre. It was also, judging from the Ontario Assessment discussion paper, a clear attempt to revamp the mandate of the provincial testing agency. [43] Sensing what was in the works, Norah Marsh, CEO of EQAO, proposed some concessions in a new plan to "modernize EQAO" to "better support student learning." Future plans were revamped to include a renewed emphasis on "equity and inclusion," including the screening of test items by a proposed EQAO "sensitivity committee." [44]

A proposed new set of student report cards, originally scheduled for 2018–19 implementation, encountered teacher resistance. Initial template designs were structured around a distinct SEL component with teacher evaluations on a set of "transferable skills," shifting the focus from organization and work habits to well-being and associated values, while retaining grades or marks for individual classes. The proposed "Big Six" Transferable Skills were critical thinking, innovation and creativity, self-directed learning, collaboration, communication, and citizenship. Curiously absent from the Ontario list of preferred skills were those commonly found in American variations on the formula: grit, growth mindset, and character.[45] A letter of concern from teachers' unions, including the Ontario Secondary School Teachers' Federation (OSSTF), derailed the plan to plunge ahead immediately with that report card reform.

The proposed Ontario student assessment strategy flew in the face of the latest research and best practice in Britain and elsewhere. Much of the Ontario model was home-grown and hothoused by the Ontario People for Education project team working in close collaboration with the Ministry of Education. The seminal work on student assessment remains the 1998 research synthesis published by British Education Research Association (BERA) lead researchers Paul Black and Dylan Wiliam.[46] Education policy, they argued, treated the classroom as a "black box" where assessment initiatives are made or broken by "what happens inside" and it's up to the teachers. Formative assessment, or "responsive teaching," according to Black and Wiliam, was "the heart of effective teaching." Following up on this initial work, the British Assessment Reform Group identified the need for Assessment for Learning to put formative assessment into practice. Best practice in assessment exhibits five characteristics: provides effective feedback to pupils; actively involves pupils in their own learning; adjusts teaching to take account of the results of assessment; recognizes the profound influence of assessment on the motivation and self-esteem of pupils, both of which are crucial to learning; and embraces pupil self-assessment to help them understand how to improve.[47]

Today Wiliam still contends that research supports formative assessment but considers the Assessment for Learning (AfL) initiative to be a failure. Wiliam and Daisy Christodoulou, author of the 2017 book *Making Good Progress? The Future of Assessment for Learning*, have demonstrated that formative assessment associated with AfL fails because its assessment instruments are turned into another tool for summative assessment seeking to demonstrate measurable outcomes. It has proven difficult, they point out, to gauge the success of assessment items or instruments which are improperly utilized in system-wide assessments.[48]

Viewed through the lens of Wiliam and Christodoulou's research, the proposed Ontario student assessment philosophy and practice fell short on a number of counts.[49]

1   **The Generic Skills Approach**: Adopting this approach reflects a fundamental misunderstanding about how students learn and acquire meaningful skills. Tackling problem-solving at the outset, utilizing Project-Based Learning to "solve-real life problems," is misguided because knowledge and skills are better acquired through other means. The "deliberate practice method" has proven more effective. Far more is learned when students break down skills into a "progression of understanding" – acquiring the knowledge and skill to progress to bigger problems.

2   **Generic Feedback**: Generic or transferable skills prove to be unsound when used as a basis for student reporting and feedback on student progress. Skills are not taught in the abstract, so feedback has little meaning for students. Reading a story and making inferences, for example, is not a discrete skill; it is dependent upon knowledge of vocabulary and background context to achieve reading comprehension.

3   **Hidden Bias of Teacher Assessment**: Teacher classroom assessments are highly desirable, but do not prove as reliable as standardized measures administered under fair and objective conditions. Disadvantaged students, based upon reliable, peer-reviewed research, do better on tests than on regular teacher assessments. "Teacher assessment is biased not because [it is] carried out by teachers," Christodoulou reminded us, "but because it is carried out by humans."

4   **Unhelpful Prose Descriptors**: Most verbal descriptors used in system-wide assessments and reports are unhelpful – they tend to be jargon-ridden, unintelligible to students and parents, and prove particularly inaccessible to students struggling in school. Second-generation descriptors are "pupil friendly" but still prove difficult to use in learning how to improve or correct errors.

5   **Work-Generating Assessments**: System-wide assessments, poorly constructed, generate unplanned and unexpected marking loads, particularly in the case of qualitative assessments with rubrics or longer marking time. In the UK, for example, the use of grade descriptors for feedback proved much more time-consuming than the normal grading of written work. Primary teachers who spent 5 hours a week on assessment in 2010 found that, by 2013, they were spending 10 hours a week.

The proposed Ontario Assessment plan failed to properly address these major concerns:

- Teaching generic skills (SEL) doesn't work and devalues domain-specific knowledge;
- Social and Emotional Learning (SEL) models carry inherent biases and are unmeasurable;
- Data mining and student surveys acquire personality data without consent; and
- Student SEL data generated by algorithms creates more record-keeping and more marking, and cuts into classroom time.

The best-laid plans of the Wynne government simply went awry, and it all ended with the election of Doug Ford's PC government.[50] Proceeding to adopt SEL system-wide and to recast student assessment in that mold was problematic, according to US National Public Radio education reporter Anya Kamenetz, because it was proving impossible to assess student outcomes that have yet to be properly defined.[51] Stanford School of Education expert Carol Dweck also raised a red flag when she expressed concerns about using her Growth Mindset research for other purposes, such as a system-wide SEL assessment plan.[52] Phasing out Grade 3 provincial testing in reading and mathematics, as proposed in the April 2018 final report, drew unexpected criticism from *The Toronto Star* and hit a brick wall with the populist forces of "Ford Nation," who focused more on improving student achievement.[53]

Ontario's move toward SEL assessment suffered a setback with the defeat of the Wynne government and the dramatic shift in education policy that accompanied the arrival of Ford at Queen's Park. Within a matter of weeks, new Education Minister Lisa Thompson was championing the Ford "back-to-basics" agenda, and the premier unveiled a six-point plan for education reform, including a firm commitment to strengthen "standardized testing" and improve "academic achievement."[54] Pursuing "student well-being" as a system-wide priority and "broadening the measures of student success" were among the first casualties of the change in government.

THE "FORD REVOLUTION" AND STUDENT ASSESSMENT

Premier Doug Ford's first year in power proved to be a whirlwind of tumultuous changes as his PC government moved with "lightning speed" on many different policy fronts.[55] His education budget reductions and rollback of McGuinty-Wynne-era curriculum reforms triggered political confrontations with Ontario teachers' unions, school boards, and high school students. Throughout the summer and fall of 2018, Ford's Education Minister Lisa Thompson attempted to repeal the 2015 Ontario sex education curriculum (returning to a 1998 version), weathered a barrage of opposition from educators, and eventually produced a compromise curriculum document, including sections on such hot topics as sexual consent, cyber safety, and gender identity. Announced plans to raise class sizes in March 2019 were presented with a commitment that "no jobs would be lost," but plans leaked out that internal research showed more than 3,400 teaching positions would disappear over four years. Thousands of teachers picketed the Legislative Assembly and a tremendous number of high school students walked out of class on 4 April 2019, mounting a mass protest at Queen's Park. Minister Thompson proved to be an easy target for aggrieved educators. She was demoted in a June 2019 cabinet shuffle, and a youthful, more politically nimble Greater Toronto Area MPP, Stephen Lecce, was given the Education portfolio.[56]

Student assessment changes after the release of the Education Advisors' *A Learning Province* report attracted relatively little public notice. In its final few months, the Wynne government was surprisingly non-committal when it came to acting upon its own Ontario assessment review report, especially a recommendation to phase out Grade 3 provincial testing. The EQAO, chaired by its real founder, former NDP Education Minister Dave Cooke, ran interference, issuing an April 2018 media release expressing concern over the potential loss of "data of early student learning" and calling for further discussion before proceeding with the recommendations.[57] Adopting the Student Well Being agenda and proceeding with soft skills assessment did not figure at all in the Ford government's education plans. The People for Education research coordinator, David Hagen Cameron, read the signals and left his full-time position in April 2018 to become Senior Research Manager at the Toronto District School Board. In December 2018, the EQAO welcomed the Ford government's new Public Consultation on Education and supported modernization on the grounds that it would "improve provincial standardized testing."[58]

The political ground in Ontario shifted dramatically during 2018–19 and that had a real impact upon student assessment policy. Guiding the implementation of EQAO reform would be a Ford government appointee, former University of Ottawa education professor Cameron

Montgomery. He was appointed in February 2019 as the first full-time Board Chair of EQAO with a mandate to ensure that any changes were aligned with the Ford reform agenda.[59] After only two years as CEO of EQAO, Norah Marsh resigned in November 2019 to become Associate Director of Academic Services for the Durham District School Board in the suburbs of Greater Toronto.[60] The chief promoters of Ontario SEL assessment, Kidder and her People for Education entourage attempted to retool their initiative, but found themselves on the outside looking in at Queen's Park. The latest iteration of the People for Education model, "The New Basics," challenged the Ford government's claim that students lacked the essential "basics" in reading and mathematics and continued to press for "concrete commitments and resource allocations" which would broaden the range of "learning opportunities" and provide "an equitable chance for long-term success."[61]

Any hope of salvaging the pan-Canadian MWM student assessment movement was dashed in early 2019 with the rise to power in Alberta of another staunch educational conservative, Jason Kenney, and his United Conservative Party (UCP). Much like "Ford Nation" in Ontario, Kenney and the UCP in Alberta promised to introduce a "back-to-basics" approach, do away with "discovery learning," prioritize teaching mathematics with standard algorithms, and restore mandatory provincial testing in the early grades.[62] The OECD Education soft skills assessment movement still had some traction at the end of 2019 in the province of British Columbia, among C21 Canada CEO Academy group of superintendents, and the national Council of Ministers of Education, Canada (CMEC).[63] It had, however, for the most part, stalled in Ontario and Alberta, two provinces with considerable clout in the System.

10

The Big Disconnect

High School Graduates and the Preparedness Problem

Speaking at the Canadian Club to a downtown Toronto business crowd on 8 May 2017, Ontario's then–Education Minister Mitzie Hunter announced that, once again, the province had recorded its highest ever high school graduation rates, with 86.5 percent of students securing a diploma within five years and close to 80 percent in four years. Interviewed afterward, the minister was full of praise for students, parents, and teachers – and brimming with optimism over the success of Ontario's student engagement strategy. Critical to that strategy was a "relentless" focus on supporting students through their high school years. "So, whether it's four years or five years," Hunter stated, "I think every student needs to be supported to complete [high school]."[1] Since 2003–04, high school completion rates had jumped more than 20 percentage points, from 68 and 56 percent, respectively. Not everyone, however, was convinced that this was a cause for celebration, judging from the subdued reactions of *Ottawa Citizen* reporter Joanne Laucius, university professors, and high school teachers.[2]

Could graduating more students possibly be a bad thing? A decade after the shift to a "success for all" strategy had sparked controversy, much of the public debate focused on whether it was a case of a school system doing a better job or a case of "passing everyone" to boost the numbers. "Bragging about graduation rates is meaningless unless you have the metrics to show for it," said Doretta Wilson, executive director of the Society for Quality Education, who also questioned why, years after eliminating Grade 13, Ontario still counted five-year as well as four-year graduation rates. University faculty members, on the receiving end of the high school system, have been reporting for a decade or more that students entering their universities lack the skills essential to academic success. The universities, two Western University researchers claimed back in 2007, were performing the "sorting, weeding and cooling functions" once the responsibility of secondary schools. A 2016 *Maclean's* survey of 1,300 faculty members strongly suggested that the situation had not improved, reporting that only 32 percent of students possessed adequate academic skills.[3]

Skyrocketing Ontario high school graduation rates were no accident. Back in 2004, Premier Dalton McGuinty pledged to raise the graduation rate to 85 percent by 2011. His government poured some $1.5 billion into a "student success strategy" which included measures to boost the numbers such as subject concentration, co-op options, and a "credit recovery" system. The government missed the mark, recording an 81 percent graduation rate for 2011, but the numbers were moving in the right direction. It was also moving Ontario more into line with other provinces such as Nova Scotia and New Brunswick, whose rates were at or above 80 percent.[4]

Putting students first should be the highest priority, and that means ensuring that high school graduates are reasonably well-prepared with the capabilities and skills to lead a full and productive life. With high school graduation rates topping 80 percent in most Canadian provinces and some American states, it seems reasonable to ask whether rising levels of diploma attainment are actually the best way of measuring achievement levels.[5] Back in April 2013, American education commentator John Merrow of *PBS News Hour* posed the question this way: "Can an increase in National High School Graduation rates be trusted?"[6] Educational surveys conducted by the Toronto branch of McKinsey & Company, provinces such as Nova Scotia, and business organizations such as local chambers of commerce, all consistently flag concerns over rising graduation rates, suspect high school standards, and poorly educated graduates entering college and the workforce. Tough questions are being posed centring on what can be done to improve not only student outcomes, but also preparedness for college and the workplace.

THE ATTAINMENT/ACHIEVEMENT GAP

Education authorities across North America have been crowing a great deal during the past decade about rising high school graduation rates. On 25 June 2013, the Council of Ministers of Education in Canada (CMEC), chaired by Nova Scotia's Ramona Jennex, claimed that the OECD report *Education at a Glance 2013* showed that Canada was "one of the most well-educated countries in the world" on the basis of its high school and post-secondary education completion rates. A US education report, *Building a Grad Nation*, released in February 2013, claimed that American graduation rates had risen to 80 percent, a gain of 6 percent since 2001, and were on target to reach 90 percent by 2020.[7]

The 2013 OECD report delivered good news on educational attainment levels for many countries, including the United States. The graduation rates for upper secondary level (A 2.1) in 2011 among first-time graduates were extraordinarily high, while the gender differences and ages at graduation varied considerably.[8] Canada registered an 84 percent graduation rate (82 percent for men, 88 percent for women) and the average age at graduation was 19 years. For the United States, the national figures reported were 77 percent (74 percent for men, 81 percent for women), but the average age at graduation was only 17 years. Rising graduation rates were reported throughout the OECD countries. Japan and Finland led the pack of top nations, tied with 96 percent graduation rates, but the average Finn at graduation was 22 years of age. Canada's rate of graduation, 84 percent, was just above the OECD average of 83 percent at 20 years of age. The United Kingdom and Australia, both with national student testing systems and so-called "league tables," reported graduation rates of 77 percent and 74 percent respectively. Young women are graduating at higher rates than men in virtually every country, to the point where it is becoming a sleeping public policy issue.

High school graduation rates are soaring and, in many countries, national dropout rates are declining. In Canada, the Canadian Council on Learning (CCL) was one of the few agencies not simply content to report trends and inclined to look deeper. Back in December 2005, the first comprehensive national report on School Dropout Rates documented the dramatic decline of 7 percent in high school dropout rates from 1990–91 to 2004–05, noting that Atlantic Canadian provinces such as Nova Scotia led the way. The slackening in demand in the labour market for high school graduates was identified as the key factor, outweighing school retention initiatives.[9]

Rising graduation rates and declining dropout rates are worth applauding, to a point. Over the twenty-year period from 1990–91 to 2019–20, the number of Canadian young people ages 20 to 24 without a high school diploma dropped from 340,000 (16.6 percent) to 191,000 (8.5 percent), again most dramatically evident in Atlantic Canada. That is a positive development because, as John Richards of the C.D. Howe Institute pointed out in January 2011, Canadians without a diploma have an average employment rate of under 40 percent, whereas graduates average about 25 percent higher. In short, dropping out of high school leads to a life marked by bouts of unemployment and, in many cases, by poverty.[10] A recent Canadian Labour Force Survey for 2017, produced by Statistics Canada, provided a different view reflecting the new realities of the so-called "gig economy" dominated by part-time and contract work. More than 12 percent of younger Canadians, ages 15 to 24, many with post-secondary diplomas, were unemployed and more than one quarter were underemployed, or holding degrees but working in jobs that do not require higher education. A university degree, Wilfrid Laurier University instructor Kimberley Ellis-Hale told CBC News, is "not a guarantee of a job" anymore.[11] It is also accurate to say that underemployed university grads are, in effect, squeezing early high school leavers right out of the workforce.

HIGHER EXPECTATIONS, LOWER EFFORT

Provincial student attainment levels, however, only tell part of the story. Graduation rates no longer provide a clear indication of the true student success rates or relative strengths of Canada's provincial school systems. Student graduation rates represent educational *attainment* levels; they often do not align at all with assessment data testifying to student *achievement* levels from province to province. This contemporary phenomenon might be termed the "Big Disconnect" in Canadian education.[12]

One of Canada's top-performing provinces on international tests, Alberta, tends to have among the lowest graduation rates and surprisingly high dropout rates. Alberta's Education Department long contended that the low graduation rate could be explained by Alberta's more carefully audited reporting system and the number of young Albertans moving in and out of the oil-rich province over the course of a school year. High school completion rates have also lagged among the province's disadvantaged communities. While graduation rates are gradually rising, only half of Alberta's First Nations, Inuit, and Métis students graduated from high school in three years in 2014–15. The official line has changed in Alberta.

Table 10.1
High School Graduation Rates, by Province, 2015–16

	On-time graduation rate percentages (2015/2016)	Extended-time graduation rate percentages (2015/2016)
Can.	79	88
N.L.	80	94
P.E.I.	78	90
N.B.	86	93
Que.	74	83
Ont.	81	92
Man.	82	89
Sask.	78	87
Alta	77	83
B.C.	79	89
N.W.T.	55	NA

Canada's Atlantic provinces tend to be tops when it comes to graduation rates. The pattern of graduation rates province-to-province does not align with student performance levels on national and international student assessments. Nova Scotia's unofficial graduation rate remained the highest, at 87 percent.

Notes: The on-time graduation rate (2015/2016) comprises students who entered Grade 10 ("Secondary 3" in Quebec) at the beginning of the 2013/2014 school year and graduated from Grade 12 ("Secondary 5") by the end of the 2015/2016 school year.

The extended-graduation rate (2015/2016) comprises students who entered Grade 10 ("Secondary 3" in Quebec) at the beginning of the 2011/2012 school year and graduated from Grade 12 ("Secondary 5") by the end of the 2015/2016 school year.

Nova Scotia, Yukon, and Nunavut did not participate in the second pilot data collection.

Source: Education Indicators in Canada: An International Perspective, 2018, Statistics Canada

"I was in Grade 12 in 2002 and I remember some of my classmates talk about leaving school and going to the oil-patch," Edmonton school trustee Michael Janz said. "It was such a hot economy that they felt like they didn't need a high school diploma to get a really good job. Now, a lot of Albertans are thinking of diversification of the economy and that a high school diploma will be the bare minimum requirement in tomorrow's workforce."[13]

Provinces with the highest high school completion rates are not known for being educational leaders when it comes to comparative student achievement levels on international or national tests. The three Maritime provinces, for example, have traditionally had extraordinarily high graduation rates and low dropout counts, but their students perform in a mediocre fashion at best on PISA and other standardized student assessments. In the case of Quebec, normally the country's top-performing province in mathematics, graduation rates languish, reportedly because of its more rigorous mathematics curriculum, Grade 10 and 11 provincial examinations, and the relatively high rural francophone dropout rate. Anglo-Quebeckers have much higher completion rates, but those who leave the province to complete high school or switch to private schools are also identified as "dropouts" from the state system.[14]

The variations in high school graduation rates can be an eye-opener. One recent Statistics Canada data set showing comparative senior secondary school completion rates, based upon 2015–16 figures, showed that graduation on-time rates ranged from a high in excess of 85 percent in Nova Scotia and New Brunswick to rates from 74 to 77 percent in Quebec and Alberta. (See Table 10.1.) Since the elimination of the last Nova Scotia Grade 12 exams in 2012, the province has no system-wide reliable measure of the achievement or competencies of graduates, nor are any results reported to the public. While reported student scores for Grades 9 and 10 students either languish or decline in Nova Scotia, reported graduation rates went through the roof, rising from 86.1 percent in 2009–10 to 92 percent in 2015–16.[15] That strongly suggests it is time to blow the whistle on the widening student attainment/achievement gap and to examine the buried "preparedness problem."

RELAXED STANDARDS – "NO-FAIL" POLICY AND THE CREDIT RECOVERY SYSTEM

Canadian high school students, particularly since the 1980s, have been awarded inflated high school grades, and this has been a major contributor to the soaring graduation rates. Some of the student success strategy policies aimed at boosting graduation rates to 85 percent sparked resistance, especially among secondary school teachers. The most contentious of these policies proved to be the credit recovery system introduced in Ontario and gradually adopted elsewhere across Canada. Teachers in Ontario objected because the initiative made it next-to-impossible to hold underperforming students to account, depriving classroom practitioners of their autonomy, essentially ruling out deducting marks for late assignments, and providing struggling students with "multiple opportunities" to secure course credits. Students were, in effect, given the right to retake missed classes, redo assignments, and complete "make-up tests." Many teachers complained that principals, under pressure from above, were changing failing marks into passing grades. In a hard-hitting 2011 book,

Lowering Higher Education, Western University sociology professors James Côté and Anton Allahar called it "a clear case of the tail wagging the dog."[16]

The whole issue of threatened standards and encroachment on teacher autonomy came to a head in Ontario in the spring of 2009. In May of 2009, the Ontario Ministry of Education simply posted a memo on its website and announced a major change in student assessment philosophy and policy that impacted every teacher in the province's 4,000 public schools. The Ministry policy announced that students' behaviour was to be separated from their achievement in the classroom and in student reporting.[17] From then on, teachers were expected to base their grading strictly upon how students performed on tests, assignments, and examinations. Holding students accountable for behaviour, including attendance, completing assignments, and showing up for exams, was to be treated separately and preferably reported with anecdotal descriptors, but not included in their marks. Common teacher practices were disrupted because it was no longer acceptable to deduct marks for being late or skipping class, and students were now entitled to write make-up tests when they were ready and prepared to do so. The capstone of the plan was a credit recovery program to rescue struggling students falling behind in their work. Students who were failing a course or missing assignments were permitted to quickly make up for missed classes, assignments, and examinations at the end of the term or school year. The whole philosophy was not new and had been percolating among board consultants for a decade; mandating it was a significant change for teachers.[18]

Introducing softer standards and enabling more students to graduate served the Ministry's purposes and, for the most part, appeased students and parents facing more competition to gain entry into universities and colleges. High school teachers were upset by the changes in student assessment policy, and the Ontario Secondary School Teachers' Federation (OSSTF) not only voiced their opposition but commissioned a study of the assessment changes. Later in the spring of 2009, the study was released, identifying the negative consequences of so-called "no fail" policies. A petition protesting the relaxed standards and detrimental effects of the "no fail" policies was circulated.[19] While the opposition was brewing, an April 2009 study of the views of Ontario university professors surfaced expressing concern about the declining quality and preparedness of incoming students, who exhibited a greater "expectation of success without the requisite effort."[20] Even though the national media covered these two visible expressions of dissatisfaction, the Ontario Ministry of Education ignored the concerns and plowed forward with the assessment reform. Teachers who resisted were painted as "tough" on kids or mischaracterized as seeking to maintain a quota of failures. Facing unpleasant encounters with school administrators, most secondary school teachers were forced to comply while mumbling under their breath and quietly complaining in the far corner of the staff room or in the school parking lot.[21]

The Ministry held its ground and resorted to invoking a common defense of educational change. In the 2009 memo, Ministry officials claimed that the assessment changes were introduced with the support of "top international experts," including some from Ontario. Foremost among those experts was Damian Cooper, an Ontario special needs education consultant and leading proponent of Assessment for Learning, who actively promoted both "no fail" and "do over" student evaluation practices. Defenders of such "soft, pass everyone" practices, like Cooper, saw testing and rigorous standards as harmful to the self-esteem of learning-challenged and disadvantaged students.[22] The Ministry policy memo endorsed that approach and contended that research showed giving students low grades or failing them was damaging and discouraged them from trying harder. Professors James Côté and Anton Allahar, and a sizable number of university professors, rejected such claims and considered the assessment changes to be a recipe for disaster. "Grades need to be used as accurate feedback," the two Western professors wrote, "not as a false reward to pump up self-esteem or feed narcissism."[23] In the coming years, their concerns would be borne out in university classes across Canada.

The "no fail" policy embedded in Canadian Assessment for Learning initiatives continued to be a major bone of contention for high school teachers, and the conflict was played out in underground battles over teachers' autonomy in the classroom. Giving students a second chance to pass tests, examinations, and other assignments gradually became accepted as student assessment policy promoting a unique twenty-first-century concept of "fairness." In Newfoundland's largest school board, the Eastern School District, the policy was changed in October 2011 so that students cheating or plagiarizing would no longer be assigned a mark of zero.[24] Eastern School Board Superintendent Ford Rice was quite accurate when he cited the work of Damian Cooper

Figure 10.1 Lynden Dorval and No Zeros Policy

The Alberta Physics teacher who challenged the No Zeros policy from 2012 to 2014, Lynden Dorval, was publicly hailed as a hero and eventually vindicated.

and claimed that the policy was "consistent in philosophy" with policies in other boards across Canada. When Lily Cole, president of the Newfoundland and Labrador Teachers' Association, condemned a practice which took assessment "out of teachers' hands," the school board backed off and left it to educators to resolve. The argument flared up again in Alberta in May 2012 when Edmonton physics teacher Lynden Dorval, a thirty-three-year veteran with an unblemished teaching record, was suspended, then fired, for continuing to award zeros, refusing to comply with a change in school assessment policy.[25] It all came to a head when the school board's computer-generated reports substituted blanks for zeros. An Alberta tribunal found that Dorval gave students fair warning, and that his methods worked because he had "the best record in the school and perhaps the province for completion rates." Two years later, he was exonerated, but the damage was done; he now worked part-time in an Edmonton independent school.[26]

GRADE INFLATION AND STUDENT
DISENGAGEMENT

Grade inflation provided another indication of the disconnect between attainment and actual achievement. Largely buried in official accounts of the state of education, grade inflation surfaces when high school teachers speak out, every once in awhile. It happened in late January 2017, again in Alberta, once the provincial bastion of higher graduation standards. Addressing the Edmonton Public Schools board in his three-minute slot, high school science teacher Mike Tachynski spoke out and amply demonstrated how Alberta was not immune to the disease of grade inflation.[27] Moving away from weighing final exams at 50 percent of the final Grade 12 subject mark was already contributing to grade inflation, leading to irregularities in grades that unfairly favoured some students over others. "Inflated grades create a lose-lose situation," Tachynski told the board. Students whose teachers are presenting more rigorous challenges may understand the material better but have a lower grade on their transcript. On the other hand, he said, students with "artificially high grades" may flounder when admitted to college or university programs.

The provincial data for June 2016, published in the *Edmonton Journal*, supported Tachynski's claim. Some 96 percent of students were awarded a passing grade in Math 30-1 by their teachers, but only 71 percent of those who took the diploma exam passed the test – a gap of 25 percentage points. For Chemistry 30, it was 15 percentage points. Going back to 2008, the gaps in pass rates between teachers' marks and diploma exam results had grown in five of twelve subjects over the span of nine years.

What's shocking about Alberta's slide in standards is that, as recently as November 2011, *Maclean's* had hailed that province as having Canada's best education system based upon the standards of its graduating students.[28] Based upon a 2011 University of Saskatchewan admission study of 12,000 first-year university students' grades, Alberta high school graduates dropped only 6.4 points, compared to as much as 19.6 points for students from other provinces. It was attributed at the time to Alberta's policy of basing 50 percent of the final grades on diploma exam marks.

Grade inflation has been identified as a major concern since the early 1980s in most school systems in the English-speaking world. In 2009, Durham University in the UK studied the phenomenon and

Table 10.2
Grade Inflation: Average Alberta Grades, 2009 to 2016

SUBJECT	2009 Class Grade	2009 Exam Grade	Difference in Grades	2016 Class Grade	2016 Exam Grade	Difference in Grades
Biology 30	72.9	67.0	5.9 %	75.9	69.1	6.8 %
Chemistry 30	73.5	64.9	8.6 %	76.6	68.4	8.2 %
English 30-1	72.0	64.0	8.0 %	72.8	63.7	9.1 %
English 30-2	63.9	64.0	-0.1	66.5	65.5	1.0 %
Social Studies 30-1* (2010)	73,4	64.6	8.8 %	75.2	64.1	11.1 %
Social Studies 30-2* (2010)	64.5	64.3	0.2	67.3	63.0	4.3 %
French Language Arts 30-1	72.3	71.6	0.7	78.3	65.5	12.8 %
Science 30	68.3	66.4	1.9	72.9	67.7	5.2 %

MATHEMATICS (New Curriculum)	2013 Class Grade	2013 Exam Grade	Difference in Grades	2016 Class Grade	2016 Exam Grade	Difference in Grades
Math 30-1	74.9	69.1	5.8 %	77.0	62.2	14.8 %
Math 30-2	66.6	57.7	8.9 %	69.2	61.6	7.6 %

Alberta provincial data provided concrete evidence of grade inflation from 2009 to 2016, comparing teacher-assigned grades with examination marks.

Source: *Edmonton Journal*

concluded that *an "A" grade was now roughly equivalent to a "C" grade in 1980.* Ten years ago, forty percent of Ontario high school graduates were leaving with an "A" average, eight times as many as in the more conventional British system. In Alberta at that time, it was only 20 percent, in large part because of compulsory exams in the core subjects. The internal battle inside the Alberta school system to contain grade inflation was essentially lost in the 2000s. "Superintendents were loath to undertake any action to ameliorate the problem," former Alberta senior administrator Jim Dueck wrote in his 2014 book, *Education Flashpoints*.[29] "Large-scale testing was contentious and acknowledging the significantly different results was thought to be inflammatory and likely lead to a backlash among union members, which at the time included principals."

Co-author of the much-discussed 2007 book *Ivory Tower Blues* James Côté insists that grade inflation ultimately hurts students. "It starts in high school. Giving higher grades is one way to reward kids fairly easily, boost their self-esteem and stop them from dropping out," Côté said. "That's the mandate our high schools are facing: lowering the dropout rate." That's why, he added, 60 percent of students applying to university had an A average by 2008 and the mark ranges were compressed so much that it had "reached a point of crisis."[30]

High school grade inflation is now rampant in school systems right across Canada. Out east, the problem was first flagged in a a May 2007 AIMS study focusing on the enormous gaps in New Brunswick and Newfoundland and Labrador between assigned class marks and diploma exam marks. In November of 2011, the University of Calgary's Dean of Arts blew the whistle on the alarming extent of Ontario grade inflation. "There's an arm's race of A's going on," he told the *Calgary Herald*. Since Nova Scotia moved its provincial exams from Grade 12 to Grade 10 in June 2012, that province's graduation rates have skyrocketed from 88.6 percent to 92.5 percent in 2014–15.[31] Students are well aware of the impact of high school grade inflation, especially when they take a real hit in their first set of university grades. In March 2013, the former president of the Ontario Student Trustees' Association, Zane Schwartz, described the artificially high grades as "a balloon that's ready to pop."[32] Over the past five years, little has been done to act upon that level-headed student comment. Highly selective university colleges and professional programs, such as University of Waterloo Engineering, have resorted to assessing student applicants by their high schools, not just their marks. Out of 74 high schools ranked by Waterloo Engineering in 2017–18, the average Ontario student dropped 16 percent, comparing graduation marks with end-of-first-year grades.[33]

THE PREPAREDNESS PROBLEM

Too many high school graduates are simply unprepared for the academic demands of university and expectations in the workplace. A 2009 Canadian Millennium Scholarship Foundation report, entitled *Persistence in Post-Secondary Education in Canada*, and conducted from 2006 to 2009, found that about 14 percent of university students dropped out in their first year. Among the most common identified causes were failure to meet deadlines, poor academic performance, and inadequate study habits.[34] That study carried considerable weight because it was based upon a survey of almost one million students and was, in all likelihood, representative of the general population. It also squared with the personal experience and analysis of well-known Manitoba teacher and education policy analyst Michael

Zwaagstra, who clamed that the schools were essentially setting students up for failure in university and college.[35]

Frontier Centre policy researcher Zwaagstra connected the dots between high school education and the first-year dropout problem. After high school, university provided a real jolt, and he was adamant that deteriorating standards right through the school system were the root cause of poor preparation. "The problem begins in the early grades where social promotion – the practice of passing students to the next grade regardless of their academic achievement, is commonplace across the country," Zwaagstra insisted. "Personal self-esteem receives a higher priority in many schools than actual performance." His view, common among high school teachers, was that, while failure was not impossible, "teachers are encouraged to do everything possible to ensure students graduate." It led, he added, to "watering down the content" in a curriculum increasingly devaluing subject teaching in favour of the fuzzy approach typified by the term "holistic learning." Eliminating Grade 12 graduation exams and resisting provincial testing only compounded the problem.[36]

University professors tend to share the serious concerns about the sad state of preparedness among "Wikipedia kids." In the 2009 survey conducted by the Ontario Confederation of University Faculty Associations (OCUFA), professors made it clear that they did not believe high schools were doing enough to prepare students for university. More than half of professors surveyed stated that students were less prepared now than students from just three years earlier. Among their litany of concerns, professors cited lower maturity levels, poor research skills, and expectations of success without the requisite effort as areas of concern. "It is very troubling that a majority of respondents are witnessing a decline in student preparedness," stated Brian Brown, president of OCUFA. "Study after study shows that success in university is linked to the preparedness of students for the rigours of the university curriculum."[37]

An April 2019 Ontario study assessing the academic skills of recent high school graduates sent further shock waves through the Canadian K–12 school system. That study, spearheaded by two leading sociologists, York University's J. Paul Grayson and Western University's James Côté, shone fresh light on the long-identified problem – growing evidence that secondary schools feeding universities are falling well short in addressing students' skills deficiencies.[38] First-year university and college professors who have long complained about the quality of students entering their institutions found confirmation in this study. Conducted at four Ontario universities – York, Western, Waterloo, and Toronto, which together enrolled 41 *percent* of Ontario undergraduates – the study simply added to the accumulating evidence. The researchers found that "only about 44 per cent of students felt they had the generic skills needed to do well in their academic studies, 41 per cent could be classified as at risk in academic settings because of limited levels of basic skills, and 16 per cent lacked almost all the skills needed for higher learning."[39] Dramatically rising graduation rates had clearly not translated into improvements in students' academic skills.

Education surveys seeking opinions outside the System also suggest that the public is simply not satisfied with the quality of recent graduates. One such survey, conducted in Nova Scotia for the October 2014 Myra Freeman Education Review, is a case in point. A majority of the 19,000 Nova Scotian respondents (53–54 percent), for example, claimed that students were neither "well prepared for the next grade," nor "well prepared for post secondary studies." The phenomenon of "social promotion" was also identified in the Freeman report as a factor in compromising student competencies and achievement levels.[40] Much of the push to drive up graduation rates has been driven by universities and colleges, particularly in Atlantic Canada. In the case of Nova Scotia, the province with more universities per person than any other, raising high school graduation rates has a strategic objective – churning out enough graduates to meet admission targets and fill seats in provincial universities and colleges. While high school graduation rates now exceed 90 percent, it is clear that sizable proportions of both employers and independent community members question the basic skills and competencies of the current crop of graduates.

SCHOOL TO WORKPLACE TRANSITIONS

School, college, and the workplace are far too often islands separated by hard-to-traverse expanses of water. Building bridges for high school leavers involves far more than simply clearing a path and creating easier off-ramps. It should involve paying far more attention to the cardinal principle of bridge-building science – sound foundations matter. A Nova Scotia Transition Task Force report, *From School to Success: Clearing the Path*, released in June 2016, looked well-intended, but appears to have missed the most critical piece – shoring up the foundations on both sides of the bridge.[41] With youth unemployment hovering above the Canadian national average, the task force focused mostly on repairing the bridges, providing more program supports, and offering better career counselling. It even proposed that high school graduates take a "gap year" on their own, presumably to acquire the requisite job-ready skills and work ethic.

How well-prepared students were for success in college and the workplace was not really addressed in the Task Force report. When pressed to explain what employers were looking for, the notable silence was filled by one Task Force member, Andrea Marsman of the Nova Scotia Black Educators Association. "There are issues around deadlines and attendance and work ethic," she told CBC *Nova Scotia News*.[42] "They were saying that over the past several years they've seen a decline of respect for those particular principles of work ethic." Boring into the report, the problem with the educational foundation of the K–12–level pillar came into sharper relief. While high school graduation rates soar above 85 percent, only four in ten university students complete their degree within four years. Some 30 percent never complete their university studies at all. At the community college level, 32 percent don't come back after their first year of study.

Raising graduation rates has been the priority in Nova Scotia, Ontario, and elsewhere for the past decade or so. School promotion policies and "no fail" student assessment practices have significantly raised retention levels. In spite of this, about five percent of Nova Scotia students drop out in Grade 11, unable to collect a diploma. Those who do leave before graduation, it is clear, are totally unprepared for the daily discipline/grind and rigours of the workplace. The Nova Scotia Task Force report simply accepted the current status quo – trying to help high school dropouts to graduate. While it is true that dropouts are twice as likely to be unemployed, and college dropouts have a 3 percent higher unemployment rate, the report did not really confront the quality and preparedness of students leaving the system. Instead, the Task Force recommended making it easier to graduate and funding more school-to-workplace bridge programs.

The Nova Scotia Transitions report completely flew in the face of the most recent evidence on employer satisfaction with Nova Scotia student graduates. In the Nova Scotia Education Review survey, released in October 2014, only 38 percent of the 2,309 community members surveyed felt that students were "well prepared" for college or university, and fewer still, some 18 percent, felt they were well

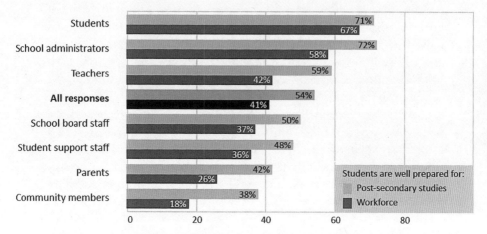

Figure 10.2 Student Preparedness for the Next Stage, Nova Scotia, 2014

A Nova Scotia Education Review report, released in October 2014, found great variations, among education stakeholders, on the question of how well-prepared students were upon graduation. The graph shows responses to two provincial survey questions: What percentage of students are well prepared for post-secondary studies (college or university)? And what percentage of students are well prepared for entry into the workforce (employability)?

Source: Minister's Panel on Education, *Disrupting the Status Quo* (Halifax: October 2014), figure 13, p. 35.

prepared for the workforce. Only one of three of the community respondents found students ".well prepared" to move onto the next grade, so that is hardly an earthshaking revelation.[43] A Canadian Council of Chief Executives 2015 report, *Career Ready*, suggested that too many poorly prepared or ill-suited students were going to university and that the university system would be better with 30 percent fewer students.[44]

A pertinent American study, based upon the PreparedU Millennial Preparedness Survey and produced in January 2014 by Bentley University researchers, provided some clearer answers.[45] It directly addressed the preparedness problem and found a surprising consensus around the source of the problem – a lack of focus on developing strong character, determination, resilience, and work ethic. It also found students' self-perceptions, fostered in schools, to be out of line with those of employers. Most alarming of all, businesses surveyed found many students unprepared or unemployable, but seemingly confident in their own abilities.

Compared to their American counterparts, Canadian education providers put much less emphasis on the need for students to develop "grit" and demonstrate a work ethic. Yet there is evidence that employers give it a much higher priority when assessing school leavers as potential employees. One April 2015 study, conducted for McKinsey & Company's Toronto office, surveyed 1,500 youth, 300 employers, and 100 education providers to assess the state of youth in transition from school to employment.[46] Two-thirds of the school leavers have post-secondary degrees or diplomas, one of the highest rates in the world. Having said that, the survey revealed the extent of the "perception gap" with respect to student preparedness. While 83 percent of the education providers felt that youth were "prepared for the workforce," only one in three employers (34 percent) and less than half of the youth (44 percent) agreed with that assessment. Employers were also seeking a different set of skills than the schools, universities, and colleges were providing.

The McKinsey & Company report identified and underlined the so-called "competencies gap." The top four skills employers seek are interpersonal and communications skills, such as work ethic, English proficiency, teamwork, and spoken communication, but educators said youth are only moderately competent in those areas. Youth believed that they learn best from practical or on-the-job experience, but only 16 percent reported that this was a major focus in school. One out of five Canadian employers does not interact or coordinate with education providers, and only 10 percent communicate frequently. In countries such as Canada, where school-workplace communication is less common, a higher proportion of employers report "disappointing outcomes" and particularly that a lack of skills is hurting their business.[47] It all adds up to a preparedness problem that begs for attention in the System.

11

The School Closure Wars

Resistance to Consolidation

Out of the mouths of children's storytellers comes the truth about kids, schools, and communities. Sheree Fitch is not only one of Canada's best-known children's book authors, she's also passionate about her chosen village, River John, Nova Scotia, and about preserving small rural schools. In September 2013, motivated by the struggle to save River John Consolidated School, she turned a familiar tale on end with a short poetic piece pointing out that "It Takes a Child to Raise a Village," and without a school, there are no children.[1] Her recent book, the whimsical 2017 folk tale, *Polly MacCauley's Finest, Divinest, Wooliest Gift of All*, is ostensibly about what a prized little lamb comes to mean to Polly and the village folk. Saving River John School from closure is very much a part of the story as the community fights to keep the lamb from falling into greedy hands.[2]

For Sheree Fitch, it all started on 28 February 2013, when the Chignecto-Central Regional School Board (CCRSB) held its obligatory school closure public meeting at River John Consolidated School. A crowd numbering exactly 287 residents packed the gymnasium in the small village nestled on the Northumberland Shore, drawn mostly from the 2,399 souls scattered throughout this northwest corner of Pictou County, Nova Scotia. Caught up in the exhilaration of the moment, Fitch rose from her seat, joined the speakers' lineup, and gave one of the evening's most impassioned pleas to save her local school.[3] Seeing the community gathered together sparked something inside her and she was completely hooked. With the school's future now in question, Fitch took to her personal blog in September 2013 with one of her more memorable posts, entitled "Maybe It Takes a Child to Raise a Village." It was written, from the heart, in her familiar poetic fashion and closed with these lines: "I want the school to stay open so the heartbeat of this village continues and the children do not have to travel miles out of their community, spend hours on a school bus, when the solution is here."[4] For the next two and a half years, Sheree and most of the village folk were totally consumed by the David-and-Goliath struggle to keep children in the local public school.

THE RISE AND FALL
OF THE RIVER JOHN HUB SCHOOL PLAN

Sheree Fitch was completely swept up in the battle to save River John Consolidated School. Outraged by an Internal Assessment Report plan to close the school and bus 76 students in different directions, parent council chair Abby Taylor had already rallied her entire besieged community and set in motion a plan to develop a Community Hub model to utilize the excess space in the building by leasing it to potential community partners, including the RCMP, a local film-maker, and an after-school program. The community spirit generated by the River John project caught Fitch's imagination and was hailed in March 2013 as a visible sign of rural regeneration on the Northumberland Shore.[5] In April 2013, the Chignecto-Central board of elected trustees, with the lukewarm support of Superintendent Gary Clarke, relented and agreed to give parents from River John and similar groups from two other threatened schools, Maitland District School and Wentworth Elementary School, the first opportunity in Nova Scotia to develop Hub proposals encompassing a new model for rural education.

The Nova Scotia government initially seemed more sympathetic to supporting the conversion of emptying schools into so-called community hub schools. The *Education Act* was amended in June 2014 to sanction Hub Schools, but the subsequent regulations presented another hurdle for River John and the other communities fighting to keep their schools.[6] Under brand new Hub School regulations, the community groups, consisting entirely of volunteers, found themselves tied up in administrative knots and forced to prepare a "business case" to cover all the costs of school operations, now in compliance with strict provincial regulations.[7] Upon hearing of the River John school struggle, renowned Canadian writer Margaret Atwood wrote a heartfelt letter in April 2015 to the local school board in support of their Hub plan. "I know that if the River John hub plan gets the go-ahead," she wrote, "it will be supported, not only from within Nova Scotia, but from people outside it as well. Me included."[8] Faced with a new and totally unexpected CCRSB report requiring the River John Hub Committee to provide ways of generating a next-to-impossible $173,123 annually and finding an additional $560,000 to replace the roof, Fitch and her allies pressed on against all odds, promoting an ingenious plan to transform the operating school into a school-based centre of creativity to be known as the North Shore Scholar Ship Centre. While defending the rural school plan at a critical 15 April 2015 meeting held in suburban Truro, Fitch levelled with the assembled board. Asked what the two-year struggle had been like, Fitch offered a graphic explanation: "It's like doing hard labour while on death row."[9]

The axe fell on River John Consolidated School in June of 2015. After two years, community rallies, picnics, and countless planning meetings, the River John Hub School plan was crushed like a bug at a fateful CCRSB board meeting by an 8-8 tie vote and the other two hub plans were summarily dismissed by the elected board. One of Fitch's staunchest allies on the River John Hub Committee, Marilyn Heighton, captured well their collective response: "It feels like we jumped through all their hoops and they slammed the door on us."[10] Direct appeals to Education Minister Karen Casey were to no avail.[11] The River John Hub School group refused to disband and carried on for much of the next year, offering a preschool program and trying to salvage their plan, before running out of energy and volunteer resources.[12] Eventually, the River Johners gave up and the school was demolished.

BUREAUCRATIC MANAGERIALISM AND THE CULT OF EFFICIENCY

Small rural schools remain as the last vestige of a radically different form of public education provided in local communities rather than regional education centres. Peering at public education through the lens of small schools brings into much sharper relief the problem of bureaucratic overreach in what Acadia University education professor Michael Corbett terms "the management of schooling in rural geographies."[13] While only about one in five Canadians live in rural communities today, most schools are still located in smaller places in the countryside, considered "rural," with fewer than 5,000 inhabitants. Despite the steady decline of that rural population as a percentage of the Canadian total since 1920, the raw population of rural Canada has actually risen slightly over the years. Some regions of Canada remain decidedly rural, including the Maritimes, the Prairie West, northern Ontario and BC, and most of the Canadian North. In Atlantic Canada, more than two in five people still live in rural places.[14] That is why, perhaps more than any other factor, resistance to the incursions of the bureaucratic education state seem to run the deepest.

For more than a century, Corbett reminds us, small schools have been targeted as "places in need of modernization, reform, professionalization, specialization and greater efficiency." The "consolidator's mindset" was an outgrowth of the rise of the new science of school and facilities management. Leading American educator Elwood P. Cubberley was one of the first to identify the so-called "rural school problem" in the early 1920s, and to this day the administrative outlook seems fixated on what smaller schools lack in terms of "modern" curriculum and facilities.[15] Closing small schools and consolidating students in larger education centres farther and farther from home are now routinely justified on the basis of general, often unsubstantiated claims of greater cost or management efficiency. In June of 2015, when Nova Scotia Education Minister Karen Casey was called upon to justify supporting a regional board's decision to close the three schools in River John, Maitland, and Wentworth, she reverted to the familiar language of financial viability used to justify the centralization of school systems.[16] In spite of the fact that smaller schools in rural places generate far fewer demands for capital or technology upgrades, system managers continue to portray rural schools as wasteful and inefficient facilities.

Today Canadian school authorities almost everywhere, claiming to be facing tight budgets and fixated on space utilization rates, tend to favour costlier new consolidations over conventional rebuilds or more cost-effective renovations of existing facilities. The revised Ontario *Guide to Pupil Accommodation Reviews*, introduced in 2015, is a classic example of imposing the conventional operational efficiency model on the review of schools for closure and minimizing or eliminating community impact assessments from school board mandates.[17] In the case of Prince Edward Island, the School Change Policy, promulgated in September 2016, set out three criteria for assessing schools, focusing on "maximizing the use of available resources" while maintaining "healthy, safe and effective learning environments" and "ensuring access to quality educational programs." Nowhere in the policy is there

any mention of building community relationships or enhancing community development.[18] During the six-month struggle in 2016–17 to
preserve the historic Pictou Academy, founded in 1816, school board
facilities managers with the Chignecto-Central Regional School Board
persisted, right to the end, with plans in their "Technical Report"
aimed at the "optimization of facilities."[19] Closing the Academy and
busing Grade 9 to 12 students to a larger comprehensive high school
was only beaten back when defenders of the PA tradition uncovered a
legal claim to having a high school in the Town of Pictou in perpetu-
ity and the entire town rallied around Mayor Jim Ryan, a passionate
former principal of the Academy.[20]

   Much of current policy and practice in school finance and capital
planning can be traced back to the textbooks produced by one of the
pioneers of American educational finance administration, Edgar L.
Morphet (1895–1990). Not only did Morphet favour school consolidation, he also produced the textbooks that demonstrated how it
could be done in practice.[21] In applying educational finance principles,
he and his academic disciples did much to entrench a new bureaucratic
ideology based upon economies of scale, operational efficiency, optimal
school size, and the allocation of pupil places. School planning assumptions and practices still bear the unmistakable fingerprints of Morphet's
technocratic thinking, including proposed optimal school and class
sizes, the recommended pupil-teacher ratio, and building capacity
ratings of students per square foot or "pupil places."[22] That school
consolidation mindset lives on today enshrined in provincial and
school board guides and planning documents. In one notable 2007
British Columbia School Trustees Association study, former superintendent Dick Chambers, a veteran of fifteen school closures (2001–06),
reviewed BC school closure history and provided detailed financial
analysis showing how closing elementary schools of between one and
two hundred students would allegedly "save approximately $200,000
without consideration of any instructional staff efficiencies."[23]

   School planners' regular claims that larger schools are more cost-
effective are essentially unproven because of the paltry state of the
supporting research. One peer-reviewed American article written in
2008 by Craig B. Howley did examine the relationship of construction cost to high school size.[24] It found that the smallest half of Grade
9–12 schools (planned for 138 to 600 students) were, on average, no
more expensive per student to build than the larger half (666 to 999
students) and were far less costly per square foot ($96 to $110). Actual

enrolments for smaller schools also tended to be higher than forecast, and for larger schools tended to be lower or overestimated in the plans. Based upon that research study, it is entirely possible that planned smaller schools may be less expensive and planned larger schools more expensive per student, a key cost metric. Today conventional wisdom about school size continues to deform the school capital planning process in ways that guide school architects and construction planners to plan larger rather than smaller schools.[25]

Supporters of small rural schools look at educational quality from a point of view totally at odds with that of the school planners. A unique 2006 study, entitled *Education on a Human Scale* and conducted by rural education scholars Michael Corbett and Dennis Mulcahy, challenged directly the prevailing ideology that "bigger schools are necessarily better schools." Commissioned by the Municipality of Cumberland County in Nova Scotia, they tapped into the frustrations felt by rural Nova Scotians in two small communities, River Hebert and Wentworth, and produced research calling into question the assumption that "school consolidation was synonymous with school improvement." School effectiveness, they contended, mattered more than the usual short-term dollars-and-cents calculations.[26] Unlike most school board accommodation review documents, the Corbett and Mulcahy study clearly demonstrated that school administrators and rural dwellers inhabited different planets when it came to their understanding of quality school programs for children.

The very strengths of smaller schools, urban as well as rural, their embeddedness in community and deep, supportive educational relationships, stand in defiance of an expanding System. Fifteen years ago, Corbett and Mulcahy found little evidence to support the case that small schools are inferior in programs. Small schools have been associated with higher academic achievement and attainment, as measured by retention and graduation rates.[27] When one looks at the cost per student graduate, most studies put small schools ahead of larger schools. An American study found that high school costs for graduates at smaller schools ($49,553) were marginally less than at larger schools ($49,578). The main factor was retention rates, since fewer small school students drop out of high school.[28] Given the fact that many rural schools serve disadvantaged communities, a strong case can be made that they produce more successful graduates and better life outcomes.[29]

Two of Ontario's leading authorities, Bill Irwin of Huron University College and Mark Seasons at the Waterloo University School of Planning, challenge the basic financial efficiency assumptions behind school closures, essentially overlooking the social and educational costs. Since 2012, Irwin and Seasons have been aggregating research in support of small schools and urging school authorities to embrace best practices in community planning and public engagement. Building upon Canadian school closures research, including *Vanishing Schools, Threatened Communities* (2011) and Michael Corbett's Nova Scotia findings, they document the serious and lasting impacts of closures, beyond the damage to local control of schools, encompassing the depletion of local financial, social, and human capital.[30]

SCHOOL CLOSURE MADNESS – A HARDY PERENNIAL IN THE SCHOOL SYSTEM

The annual February and March "School Closure Madness" arrives, like clockwork, to generate considerable heat amid the winter deep freeze. School closures come to totally dominate the local educational world in many rural and inner-city school communities beset by declining student enrolments. The winter of 2016–17 was a particularly bad season. Surveying the Canadian scene, school closure wars raged in rural southern and central Ontario, northern British Columbia, the suburban GTA Region, and the villages of Prince Edward Island, where parents, families, and community members mounted organized popular movements resisting further centralization and consolidation or standing up for threatened towns, villages, and neighbourhoods.[31]

A province-wide protest group, the Ontario Alliance Against School Closures (OAASC), called on the Ministry of Education in October 2016 to immediately halt school closures and scrap the current wave of school consolidation. In its open letter to Education Minister Mitzie Hunter, the OAASC claimed that a recently revised PARG (Pupil Accommodation Review Guideline) was flawed and must be rewritten.[32] Under the leadership of Sarnia advocate Susan MacKenzie, the OAASC proposed a moratorium and provincial review to determine the effects of extensive school closures on the health of affected children and their communities. In British Columbia, Premier Christy Clark faced such fierce opposition to proposed closures in Northern BC that she appointed a Secretary of Rural Education to look at alternatives. After the abolition of Prince Edward Island school boards and the adoption of the revised PEI School Change policy in September 2016, all 56 schools on the Island were reviewed and the consolidation plan proposed to close five schools and rezone others affecting 2,500 students, 700 of whom were rural children and teens.[33]

THREATENED SMALL RURAL SCHOOLS – COAST TO COAST

The struggle to save Canada's rural community schools from 2015 to 2017 was essentially the story of River John writ large. From coast to coast, from Whitbourne, Newfoundland, to Yarker, Ontario, to Quesnel, British Columbia, small rural communities found themselves under threat of school closures in the latest wave in an unrelenting process of administrative centralization and school consolidation. Short reports from the front convey the tenacity and determination of the community resistance to the abandonment of local schools.

School Closure Battle on the Rock

The first day of school in September 2016 at Whitbourne Elementary School, in the village of Whitbourne, on the Avalon Peninsula, turned out to be the last one in that school's existence. Originally slated to close in June of 2016, the Help Whitbourne Elementary School group, headed by parent Wade Smith, fought back, taking the Newfoundland and Labrador English School District to the provincial Supreme Court over the issue. The plan to close Whitbourne and bus the 80 elementary students for over an hour to Woodland Elementary in Dildo was quashed in court in midsummer 2016.[34] Just ten days later, the NL school board was back with another resolution to shutter the school. Whitbourne Mayor Hilda Whelan was adamant about keeping students in her community. "The school is the heart of our community," she told *CBC News*. "We definitely have an increase in enrolment and ... the government and the school board hasn't spent the money it should have in the last 40 years. They should be ashamed that the school is in such a dilapidated state."[35] The school board was deluged with twenty-seven public presentations, eighty-seven online submissions, and three additional emails, almost universally opposed to the closures. It was all to no avail, because on 20 September 2016, those hopes were dashed when the board voted to close Whitbourne and bus all of the students down the road to Dildo.[36]

The Northern BC Frontier Battleground

Out west in northern BC, Christina Moffat and Michelle Syverson, two mothers of children at Kersley Elementary, south of Quesnel, waged a similar community school battle against BC School District 28, Quesnel. On 20 February 2016, they mobilized parents to boycott and picket the school in protest against plans to shutter the 61-student school in their rural community. "We are also trying to bring attention to our cause," Moffatt explained, "which is not only about saving our school but also showing that parents province-wide that they have to stand up for the public education system." She strongly objected to the BC government of Christy Clark treating the school system as a "business model" and, in effect, treating students like "products."[37]

Kersley and the neighbouring 10 Mile Lake School in Quesnel district were only two of nine rural BC schools facing imminent closure in the winter and spring of 2015–16. Those local school skirmishes raged on across rural BC and throughout the Okanagan Valley, generating huge Save Our School rallies in Penticton and Osoyoos. In late March 2016, rural school advocates picketed the School District 67 offices in Penticton and hundreds rallied outside the threatened Osoyoos Secondary School to demand that School District 53 look at other options. Parent and local business owner Jamie Elder told CBC News that if the Osoyoos secondary school closed, the town would be crippled: "[W]e are at risk of going back to being nothing more than a summer tourist destination and a senior citizen's town," she said, "The appeal for families will end."[38]

With the school year winding down in June 2016, Premier Clark finally intervened, throwing a lifeline to the threatened rural school communities. During a stop in Quesnel, she announced some $2.7 million in small school grants to keep the schools afloat and appointed Osoyoos-Similkameen MLA Brenda Larson as a new provincial Parliamentary Secretary for Rural Education. Larson was mandated to lead "public discussions" with school trustees and rural communities, as part of what the premier described as a "renewed focus" on rural education. With a provincial election expected in May 2017, Osoyoos secondary school parent Brenda Dorosz was understandably skeptical. "I'm a bit hesitant to jump to conclusions," she told the Vancouver Sun.[39] "We will wait and see," she added, mindful that not all government promises come to pass, particularly when it comes to stable, sustainable education funding.

The BC Liberal government was swept out of power after the 2017 provincial election and the resulting Rural Education report was buried by the incoming John Horgan NDP administration. Finally, in March 2018, under pressure from Northern BC parent Trudy Klassen and the chair of the Prince George School Board, the BC Ministry of Education released a "draft" previously withheld from public view. It proposed a few incremental changes but stopped short of articulating any new vision. "This isn't an isolated problem. It's not a small problem," Klassen said. "There has to be a coordinated cross-governmental strategy and policy changes in order for rural education to be able to thrive."[40]

The Rural Ontario Front – Turning Villages into Ghost Towns?

Deep in the heartland of eastern Ontario, the village of Yarker, west of Kingston, exemplified what was left of rural life over large swaths of Canada's most populous province. The student population of Yarker Family School had dwindled by 2016–17 to just 26 junior kindergarten to Grade 3 students, and the Limestone District School Board put the school under review as part of a larger plan to "optimize the utilization" rates in school buildings. With four children under five, Yarker parent Jill Kilgour went into full panic mode. "Where am I going to send them?" she wondered. "If Yarker school was to close, they would be going a minimum of half an hour, but probably more like an hour on the bus."[41] It was just one of hundreds of schools across Ontario – most in rural communities – at risk of closing.

While Yarker's school was the only one in Stone Mills Township under review in March 2017, the Limestone District School Board was already pitted against the Township over the fate of its rural schools. Armed with a Long-Term Pupil Accommodation Plan, senior Limestone staff proposed to review the other four schools – all reportedly under-enrolled – during 2017–18. Under the Ontario Pupil Accommodation Review Guidelines (PARG), Limestone staff identified the schools for possible review, and the elected trustees on the board, headquartered in the City of Kingston, were authorized to "trigger" the actual closure process, just as they had for the Yarker Family School. A consultant's report, commissioned by the Township, warned that closing the schools would result in a drain of $3.2 million a year from the local economy, an amount equal to more than half the township's annual budget. In response to the threat, Robin Hutcheon of the Village of Tamworth founded Rural Schools Matter, to fight to keep schools open and save the township's rural way of life. One mother of two children, Lindsay McDougall, who moved to Yarker from downtown Toronto in 2010, announced she was considering a family move to Kingston. "I think you'd be looking at a whole lot of ghost towns around here," she told CBC *News Ottawa*, "because you'd gradually see the population get older and older, because young families would not move out to these areas. Eventually they would just shut down."

Hundreds of small or under-enrolled schools, mostly in rural Ontario, were also facing the same fate.[42] In March 2017, the Upper Canada District School Board (UCDSB), located further east along Highway 401 in Brockville, voted to close to close a dozen schools in small communities scattered throughout eastern Ontario.[43] Facing an estimated 10,000 vacant pupil places across all of the UCDSB schools, an aging inventory of school facilities, and no access to longer-term transition funding, the board simply defaulted to its usual practice.[44] Since a February 2015 reform of the School Review policy, optimizing the use of school buildings takes clear precedence over any real consideration of community interests or development possibilities.[45] Creative local solutions are not always welcomed by school boards bent on rationalizing or offloading underutilized facilities. Enterprising parents in the Township of South Stormont managed in the winter of 2017 to find a corporate sponsorship worth $400,000 to help save their small rural secondary school, Rothwell-Osnabruck High School. In the end, the Upper Canada District School Board voted to close the school anyway.[46]

Engaged parents facing the loss of their school can – and do – generate viable options for school renewal and rural regeneration. When a leading Ontario dairy products company, Chapman's Ice Cream, vowed to resist a local school closure in Markdale, Ontario, and to invest in the school's future, the Bluewater District School Board seemed ill-equipped to respond to that community-generated proposal.[47] Provincial policy under the PARG requiring the school boards to identify a "preferred option" from the outset also tends to reinforce the popular perception that "the fix is in" and that public meetings are staged just to meet minimum legal requirements for consultation, for coming up with options has been left to the community members, who say they've had limited support from the board.[48] Retired teacher Wayne Goodyear, who led a fight to save the Yarker School back in

Figure 11.1 Yarker Rural School Protest

Robin Hutcheon, chair of Rural Schools Matter, pickets the Limestone District School Board office in November 2017 in protest over the threatened closure of her small community school in the village of Yarker in Stone Mills Township, west of Kingston, Ontario. It represented, in microcosm, the larger struggle to preserve schools at the heart of rural life.

the 1970s, saw it as symptomatic of the myopic Queen's Park vision of rural Ontario. "We're not cabbages," he told CBC News Ottawa. The whole process, according to Goodyear, was and is profoundly "anti-rural," conveying a subliminal message: If you don't like it, "why don't you people move to the city?"[49] Prevailing attitudes rooted in what is termed the "metrocentric" worldview tend to spell the end for the Yarker Family School and those like it in the rural heartland.

The PEI School Closure War – ## Triumph of the Rural Strong Movement

Nowhere in Canada is rural life more cherished than in the villages dotting Prince Edward Island, and for that reason, community resistance to school consolidation runs deep in the red soil. Under a new September 2016 School Change policy, PEI's one remaining English Public School Board set the wheels in motion with the release of a comprehensive set of School Assessment reports delineating, in conventional fashion, school space utilization rates.[50] Early in 2017, the three-person appointed School Board, chaired by Deputy Education Minister Susan Willis, released its draft recommendations and embarked upon an ambitious province-wide school review process.[51] The whole exercise was explicitly aimed at reorganizing the province's fifty-six public schools to rebalance uneven student enrolments and close any school with space utilization deemed below provincial standards. Out of the total student population of 21,000 students, some 700 of the 2,500 students affected by the proposed zoning changes were in rural schools. Over half of the province's schools were to be affected by zoning changes, and five small schools were recommended for immediate closure, in Georgetown, Belfast, Bloomfield, St. Louis, and the St. Jean neighbourhood of Charlottetown.[52]

The announcement of the proposed closures touched off a storm of rural protest, with the Town of Georgetown, host of two major Atlantic Canadian Rural Renewal Conferences (in October 2013 and June 2016), at its epicentre. After narrowly averting the closure of Georgetown Elementary School in the spring of 2009, Georgetowners were quick to reactivate their distinctive school-bus-yellow "Our School, Our Town, Our Future" placards. With only fifty students remaining in their school, the Georgetown Save Our School Committee was in a far more precarious position for this second fight in six years. Spearheaded by parents Mallory Peters and Melvin Ford, the Committee managed to mobilize an estimated 600 men, women, and children to form a human chain around the threatened school, captured in an aerial photograph that landed on the front page of *The Guardian*, the PEI daily newspaper with the motto "covers the Island like the dew."[53] Out of that protest emerged a "Rural Strong" movement, a loose coalition of community groups from the five threatened schools.[54] While the Georgetowners focused on organizing rallies and exerting political pressure, the Save Belfast Consolidation Committee, guided by Keir White and Marcella Ryan, focused on the need for a K–8 school on the highway to the Wood Islands ferry, a long bus ride from other schools.[55]

The PEI school closure battle of 2016–17 came to a head after a series of PSB school review public meetings in mid-February 2017 and proved to be a rollercoaster ride right to the end. On the Public School Board's night of decision, 3 April 2017, hundreds of Islanders packed the Bluefield High School gymnasium, chanting "We Are Rural! We Are Strong!" and heckling the presenters.[56] Deputy Minister Willis and her Board rendered their verdict, sparing three of the five schools, and condemning Georgetown and Charlottetown's St. Jean to immediate closure in June 2017.[57] After announcing the decision, the three board members were compelled to flee by the back door under the watchful eye of a security detail. A mere fifteen hours later, it was all over. Premier Wade MacLauchlan, flanked by Education Minister Doug Currie, announced that there would be "no school closures," pulling the plug on most of the proposed school consolidation plan.[58] One of the beleaguered board members, veteran politician Pat Mella, resigned the following day in protest, but the final decision left Georgetown kids "doing cartwheels in the hall" and local parents "floating" around town on what Mallory Peters described as "cloud nine."[59]

BUSTING INTO THE IRON CAGE — TURNING SMALL SCHOOLS INTO COMMUNITY HUBS

Schooling on a smaller, more human scale is still considered out of step with the advance of educational centralization. For school system planners and managers, immersed in a bureaucratic, technocratic, and managerial world, rural schools are a "problem" precisely because they cannot be as easily measured as the cost per student or cost per square foot of school facilities. They are deemed too small to be efficiently managed, suitably specialized, or comprehensive in their range of program options. Rural communities lack the critical mass of people necessary to sustain the conventional consolidated school model and are therefore classified as "underutilized" in terms of students per square foot. During school accommodation review meetings, the whole discussion is framed around where the child is going (to school) rather than where he or she lives (the home). Closing of smaller and underutilized schools aids and abets the "erasure" of the rural school problem as an obstacle to the hegemony of the System with all that it offers: full-service, inclusive, efficient schooling for all students within a school district.

The priorities of the System smack of "neo-liberal thinking" and represent a skewed approach to improving the educational prospects and life outcomes for rural children and youth. Providing for an equitable distribution of resources through the school delivery system in a symmetrical fashion is not really the answer for rural school communities. Truly addressing and ameliorating the inequalities and poverty confronting many rural communities, Australian sociologist Hernan Cuervo amply demonstrates, requires taking into account the vital importance of public voice, recognition, and association.[60] These include teachers' concerns for issues of power, respect, and participation in their work that extend to policy-making processes and implementation; students' post-school aspirations; and, finally, parents' hopes and fears for their children's futures and the sustainability of their community. In the case of rural Newfoundland, Memorial University education professor Barbara Barter has shown how a "single-minded" strategy of school consolidation, masquerading as education reform, amounts to little more than fiscal accountability, adversely affects rural teachers' work, and puts student learning at risk.[61]

The Iron Cage of education has a way of foreclosing on successive attempts to introduce community-based schools. Two leading Canadian education researchers, the late George Martell and David Clandfield, provided a very thoughtful critique of the school system's stubborn and persistent resistance since the 1980s to true "community schools." In their Summer 2010 Special Issue of *Our Schools/Our Selves*, Dr Clandfield saw the demand for Community Schools as a manifestation of popular, progressive impulses provided that they "stay true" to their essential democratic principles. True community schools, operating as genuine two-way community hubs, he argued, could advance "really useful" learning and community development.[62] That vision took root in Nova Scotia between 2012 and 2015, incited by Clandfield's advocacy and nurtured by a determined provincial parent advocacy group, the Nova Scotia Small Schools Initiative. Every step of the way, the Nova Scotia community school advocates were confronted by, and tangled with, the provincial and school board mutations of the Iron Cage.

SMALL VICTORIES – SIGNS OF HOPE AND OPTIMISM

Local citizens rallying in defense of smaller schools armed with innovative ideas for cost efficiencies or creative solutions find solace and hope in small victories. Five years ago, the Nova Scotia village of Petite Rivière was the point of origin for the Community Hub School

Figures 11.2 and 11.3 School Bags on Bridge, River John, NS, 2015

Small school supporters in River John in Nova Scotia's rural Pictou County used a number of ingenious methods to appeal for public support. Placing student school-bags on the bridge and erecting a road sign won public acclaim, but failed to sway the regional school board based in the regional centre of Truro.

movement. That initial and imaginative community revitalization plan, devised by Nova Scotia Community College/Bridgewater instructor Leif Helmer and known as "Petite Plus," was too much innovation for the South Shore Regional School Board (SSRSB) to swallow.[63] In March of 2013, the regional board faced a budget crunch and was in full school closure mode, ultimately voting to pass on the Hub Plan renovation costing $6 million and to shutter Petite Rivière Elementary School, along with three other targeted elementary schools. The proposed solution was to build a new combined Petite-Penz School at a projected cost of $11 million. Three times since then, in 2013, 2014, and 2016, the board was denied the provincial grant support to build the new school. The South Shore board's refusal to revisit the matter, even after a ministerial letter pledging $6 million for renovations, left the Petite Rivière community in limbo, and sparked much public criticism over the Byzantine nature of petty school board politics.[64] With the closing date of June 2018 approaching, Petite Rivière school was saved by divine intervention. The province announced the dissolution of the SSRSB along with six other English school boards in February 2018, and the lame-duck board of trustees finally gave up their six-year campaign to force a closure of the Petite Rivière and Penz schools.[65]

Public-spirited companies with local roots can also make a difference. One of Canada's best-known dairy products companies, Chapman's Ice Cream, had more success cracking the code to save the threatened local public school in the company's rural hometown of Markdale, Ontario. Over more than a year of negotiations, Vice-President Ashley Chapman managed to circumvent the Bluewater District School Board's PARG regulations and then secure approval for a Hub School renovation, after putting $2 million into the project to rebuild and repurpose part of Beavercrest Public School.[66]

The school closure wars provide many lessons for reform-minded citizens up against the System. The last word on school closures belongs to Sheree Fitch, seasoned veteran of the River John closure war. Looking back on her exhausting three-year-long struggle to save River John's only school, she asked: "What does putting our students first really mean? And how can a rural economy grow by closing down schools in places where school really is the lifeblood of the community?"[67] Without a school, students are bused away, and the village lingers on unable to educate its own children or attract new families. Take heart from the small victories as rural school communities, one after another, from Markdale, Ontario to Petite Rivière, Nova Scotia to Belfast, PEI, succeed in beating the odds and find a way to succeed with school-centred community renewal.

12

School Boards in Crisis

The Withering of Education Democracy

A public voice is critical to the vitality and health of a publicly funded school system. One of the sad realities of contemporary K–12 education is that elected school boards, once the anchor of local education democracy, are disappearing across Canada and nearly extinct in Canada's four Atlantic Provinces. The centralization of educational policy-making since the 1990s has gradually eroded the governance role and significance of school districts in relation to provincial education authorities.[1] Provincial government policies, driven by a metro-centric perspective and a management efficiency ethos, exemplified in the adoption of testing and accountability regimes, have further promoted centralization and school consolidation.[2] The trend toward larger and larger school districts runs counter to the core democratic mandate of elected school trustees and district-level governance everywhere. An influential Nova Scotia report, Avis Glaze's *Raise the Bar*, recommended the dissolution of boards which, as constituted, were distant from the governed, ineffective in ensuring accountability, and unresponsive to parents and communities.[3] Nova Scotia's subsequent January 2018 decision to dissolve its English regional school boards signalled, for a time, their total elimination in Atlantic Canada.

Today's elected school boards suffer from an identity crisis. Unlike municipal councils, which raise and control their own revenues, school boards have been stripped of their taxing powers and are funded almost entirely by provincial authorities. In major urban districts, such as the Toronto District School Board and the Vancouver School Board, elected trustees tend to flex their political muscles, but soon discover that their powers are narrowly circumscribed under the current governance model. Subscribing to a "corporate governance model" also muddies the waters. Outside of the big cities, most boards are trained to act like an arm's-length corporate board that takes a "balcony view" of operations and stays out of day-to-day school operations. Confusion over just how hands-on school trustees should be underlies many of the problems that plague boards. Misbehaviour, financial ineptitude, and internal rancour plague school boards and, where they exist, spark outcries that they are dysfunctional and periodic calls for their abolition right across Canada.[4] When a 2013 Canadian School Boards Association (CSBA) governance report warned that the remaining boards in Atlantic Canada were "sinking ships," it sparked a defensive reaction and went largely unheeded.[5] That imperiled their existence in the region.

EARLY SIGNS OF TROUBLE

Elected school boards came under fire for their inability to effectively represent local interests, and over two decades they gradually lost their democratic legitimacy, one province at a time. One of the early warnings that regional school boards were too big to be effective was issued in 2003 by Queen's University education professor T.R. Williams: "Given the present size of boards, the traditional concept of an elected part-time trustee who can fully represent the interests of individual constituents is no longer viable. The current elected district boards are simply too large."[6] Merging of school boards into "huge administrative units" has made them "so large and politicized," as Williams forecast, that they "resort to formulaic approaches to distribute resources." While regional boards can provide some corporate direction, they were "woefully inadequate as a democratic institution in whose trust resides the development of education of thousands of individual, different learners." A 2009 report on Canadian school boards dismissed Williams's critique and his appeal to embrace innovative school-based reform plans, including publicly funded, autonomous charter schools.[7] Turning a blind eye to such growing concerns about eroding democratic accountability would prove costly in the long run.

METROPOLITAN SCHOOL BOARDS IN CRISIS

Turmoil and internal conflict within the Toronto District School Board (TDSB) from 2013 to 2015 grew so serious that it sparked public calls to abolish boards right across Ontario. It was touched off in January

Weapons of Math Destruction™

Figure 12.1 School Board Accountability

A searing satirical cartoon captures the view from the Public Gallery at a typical
North American school board meeting. Most elected boards allow presentations
and, in far too many instances, elected trustees seem to tune out the speakers.

2013 when Director of Education Chris Spence was forced to resign
amidst an embarrassing plagiarism scandal where he was discovered to
have plagiarized sections of his TDSB blog posts, published works, and
OISE doctoral thesis. In filling the vacant position, the board made a
fateful decision, appointing senior TDSB administrator Donna Quan,

first as interim director, then, in October 2014, as Spence's successor. Quan's term as TDSB director proved to be tumultuous and marred by division, pitting elected trustees against senior administration.[8] The ensuing school governance chaos called into question the effectiveness of boards and the very existence of elected trustees.

During her three years as education director, Quan proved to be a polarizing force and the elected board teetered on the brink of chaos. The veteran educator, a highly successful second-generation Chinese-Canadian and a laser-focused administrator, demonstrated an incredible work ethic and a passion for addressing educational inequities in the system. Under her leadership, however, tension and distrust boiled over, and, in March 2014, TDSB Chair Chris Bolton requested a police presence at board meetings after senior staff complained about being intimidated and harassed by trustees. In June 2014, Chair Bolton resigned, five months before his term expired, while the board was embroiled in a public dispute over a secret partnership between the TDSB's Confucius Institute and the Chinese government. One veteran trustee, Howard Goodman, clashed regularly with Quan, and the director pressed charges for forcible confinement and criminal harassment, although the charges were later dropped. The board's governance became so dysfunctional that Ontario Education Minister Liz Sandals finally ordered an independent investigation in November 2014. Chief investigator Margaret Wilson responded in January 2015 with a scathing report that decried "a culture of fear" at the TDSB, slammed trustees for their misbehaviour, and chastised Quan for her secrecy in withholding access to her employment contract. When Wilson discovered that the board had authorized paying Quan above the provincial scale, the TDSB was forced to roll back Quan's salary from $289,000 to $272,000 so it complied with provincial salary freeze legislation. In the wake of the Wilson report, Quan weathered a second provincial review until the Education Ministry arranged her secondment to York University, providing the embattled director with a graceful way out of the governance mess.[9]

The dysfunction and disorder at the TDSB, identified in Wilson's November 2014 report, spelled bigger problems for school boards. *Toronto Star* columnist Martin Regg Cohn led the charge to rid the whole province of trustees and boards. "Now it's time to take the next step," he wrote, "by stamping out school trustees once and for all." Tired of the "perennial tale of trustees at war with themselves, and their staff," Cohn mounted his case. Electoral turnouts for trustees had dipped as low as 10 percent, the candidates were mostly unknowns, and the power struggle among senior staff was visible for all to see. "Trustees were long ago stripped of their taxing authority, which has undermined their spending power," he noted. "As for school boards, they are emasculated entities that have lost their right to negotiate with teachers." School boards had a legitimate role in a "bygone era," but Cohn contended that they were now virtually powerless: "Today the province calls the shots – setting taxes, cutting cheques, and drafting the curriculum."[10] Vocal critics, reacting to the Toronto governance crisis, also began to claim that Canada's mega–school boards such as the TDSB were "too big to succeed" and might function better if broken up into smaller units.[11] While the Ontario boards survived the onslaught, it was clear that they were losing ground in the court of public opinion.

Up next was the Vancouver School Board (VSB). That governance crisis came to a head in October 2016 when British Columbia Education Minister Mike Bernier fired all nine elected Vancouver trustees and put the school board under provincial trusteeship. It was not totally unexpected, because in June of 2016 the elected board had refused to comply with a provincial requirement to produce a balanced budget and was racked with internal divisions, including accusations of bullying and harassment involving staff. The VSB, chaired by Mike Lombardi and controlled by a Vision Vancouver team of left-leaning trustees, was continually at odds with the Liberal government of Christy Clark. The possible closure of up to eleven under-enrolled schools was a major bone of contention. Senior administration had also filed complaints with WorkSafe BC, alleging that aggressive tactics by certain trustees had created a toxic work environment. "What we have witnessed from the Vancouver School Board," Minister Bernier said, "is a misplaced focus on political tactics rather than responsible stewardship." Even though the VSB trustees caved in and passed a balanced budget at the eleventh hour, the die was cast and the whole board was summarily dismissed.[12]

A labour tribunal review of the Vancouver School Board provided a somewhat one-sided analysis of the source of the governance turmoil. The February 2017 external review, conducted by Vancouver lawyer Roslyn Goldner for WorkSafe BC, revealed that the board was deeply divided along municipal party lines, torn by factionalism, and inclined to interfere in operational matters.[13] Former Board Chair Patti Bacchus and her successor Lombardi were identified as two board members who took a hands-on approach, badgered senior staff, and overrode administration on critical issues. Senior staff were expected to participate in an excessive and burdensome number of committees and consultations. By September 2016, the entire six-person senior management team was on indefinite leave, including chief superintendent Scott Robinson. All of this, Goldner claimed, had created a "toxic work environment."

The Vision Vancouver team of trustees, spearheaded by Bacchus and Lombardi, saw the whole controversy differently. Refusing to accept the blame, they pointed the finger at "political interference in the democratic process" by the Clark government as "a way to deflect from its neglect of public education."[14] The open conflict subsided in October 2017 when a new school board was elected, consisting of five new trustees and four holdovers, but minus both Lombardi and Bacchus.[15] Former vsb Chair Bacchus resurfaced as a tenacious Vancouver education watchdog, churning out regular commentaries for two different local newspapers. She was critical of a few decisions made by the Liberal government's appointed one-person board trustee, Dianne Turner, a Superintendent of Schools on secondment from the Delta School Board.[16] From her current perch as *Georgia Straight* education columnist, she not only holds the vsb to account, but dispenses regular advice to bc's ndp Education Minister Rob Fleming.[17] With Bacchus on the beat, her former board has no chance to fall asleep at the wheel.

Charges of racism, Islamophobia, and excessive travel spending threw the York Region District School Board (yrdsb), north of Metropolitan Toronto, into complete disarray throughout much of the 2016–17 school year. It started when a Markham elementary school principal, Ghada Sadaka, was discovered to have posted anti-Islamic material on Facebook, including videos purportedly showing "Muslim takeovers" of European states and articles claiming refugees harboured "terrorist sympathies" here in Canada.[18] When a group of local parents exposed the incidents, they expected the school board to act forcefully, effectively, and transparently to rectify the problem. What they encountered was a chief superintendent, J. Philip Parapally, and senior staff who closed ranks and insisted it was a personnel issue best dealt with under the code of confidentiality. Irate parents saw it differently, as a sign of deeper issues touching on racism, equity, and discrimination. One veteran yrdsb trustee, Nancy Elgie, made matters worse by dismissing a black parent's concerns and uttering a

Figure 12.2 Vancouver School Board Crisis
Fired Vancouver School Board chair Mike Lombardi accuses the
BC education minister of a provincial takeover, October 2016.

racial slur – the N-word – in a heated private conversation. A circular letter proposing a draft plan of community consultations, issued in January 2017 by Parapally, was rejected by the concerned parents as "disappointing" and woefully inadequate to address what they saw as "systemic racism."[19]

School board meetings at the YRDSB in Aurora in January 2017 attracted protesting parents and overflow crowds demanding action to rid the senior administration and elected board of their allegedly racist tendencies. Ontario Education Minister Mitzie Hunter, a well-respected member of the Ontario black community, finally intervened and appointed two investigators to get to the bottom of the allegations of racism and financial accountability lapses, centring on unreported travel expenses. Minister Hunter instructed the investigators to examine allegations of "systemic racism," unresolved concerns over "the board's equity and inclusive education policies," lack of accountability for "spending on trustees' international travel," and "deteriorating relationships" between trustees, the education director, and senior board staff.[20] A newly elected YRDSB board chair, Loralea Carruthers, attempted to steer the system into calmer waters, but Parapally was eventually forced out, largely as a direct result of his initial intransigence and subsequent damage control strategy.

Media coverage of the York school board crisis inflicted incalculable damage to the already tarnished reputation of elected boards across Ontario. Once again, *Toronto Star* columnist Regg Cohn repeated his public call, now with more ferocity, to abolish boards and get rid of elected trustees.[21] The York debacle was not, he pointed out, an isolated case, but rather indicative of similar cases of dysfunction in the TDSB, infighting at the Toronto Catholic school board, and problems replicated in the Ottawa, Hamilton, and Dufferin-Peel board districts.[22] Every board's governance irregularities and abuses, he claimed, were different, but the picture was becoming clearer. "Our school boards," Cohn wrote, "share a common pattern: poor accountability, weak governance, excessive ambition." While conceding that most of Ontario's 700 trustees were likely "dedicated and hard-working," they held what amounted to "phantom jobs." "Too often," he added, "they use school boards as stepping stones in their political careers, leaving a mess in their wake. They are part-timers just passing through, emasculated to the point of irrelevancy as they pretend to preside over unwieldy and unaccountable boards with sizable budgets." It was time, in his view, to put an end to "the charade of perennial investigations" and provincial supervision of "rogue boards" that were "an embarrassment to the students they teach – and the parents they serve."

THE WITHERING AWAY OF QUEBEC SCHOOL BOARDS

Evaporating public participation in school board elections spelled trouble for Quebec's 72 boards in the wake of the November 2014 vote. Only some 5 percent of eligible voters turned out for the 60 francophone boards, and anglophone voter participation stood at 17.25 percent, lower than in previous elections. Declining voter turnout attracted Education Minister Yves Bolduc's attention and he began proposing structural reforms, such as eliminating boards or reducing their number across the province.[23] After series of missteps and public apologies, Bolduc quit politics in February 2015, leaving school governance reform in limbo.

Anglophone Quebeckers seized the opening to begin mounting a campaign to retain their own linguistic boards on constitutional grounds. Former Quebec Liberal MP Marlene Jennings produced a September 2015 report, under the auspices of an Election Systems Study Panel, representing the key partners in Quebec English-language education.[24] Over three months of intense study, the Jennings panel discovered, to no one's surprise, that English-speaking Quebeckers saw maintaining their own boards as critical to the "community's overall viability." Citing the advice of constitutional experts, she reminded the Quebec Liberal government of Philippe Couillard that "the English-speaking minority has the right to manage and control its education system." Having said that, the Jennings report fully recognized that "the voices of parents" needed to be strengthened on the boards. It endorsed elected school boards but recommended that significant steps be taken to increase voter participation, including making it easier to vote. She recommended that the number of parents on each board of commissioners be raised from 3–4 to 6 to engage more parents in the process.[25]

The Quebec Liberal government wavered back and forth on the question of eliminating school board elections. In December 2015, the new Education Minister, François Blais, tabled Bill 86, an education reform bill proposing to replace elected school boards with locally appointed school councils composed of up to sixteen members, including six parents and six community members.[26] Almost immediately, the Quebec English School Boards Association (QESBA) condemned the proposed legislation as "unconstitutional" and pledged to challenge it in court. Facing turbulent waters, Blais was replaced by Sebastien Proulx and in May 2016 he decided to scrap Bill 86, giving elected boards another reprieve. A consensus proved to be elusive and Proulx continued to wrestle with the question of how to encourage higher voter participation.[27]

While the Quebec boards remained, they were far from healthy. School commissioners elected in 2006 were allowed to remain in office for seven years (until 2013), while the government postponed elections and pondered how to cure the problem. With the next election approaching in November 2019, the minister was again considering a delay until November 2020, reportedly to put off having to spend $20 million to stage the election.[28] The threat of abolition re-emerged in October 2018 with the election of François Legault and his Coalition Avenir Québec (CAQ) party to power. It was a component of the CAQ's 2018 election platform, and, in December 2018, Education Minister Jean-François Roberge made it clear that he fully intended to transform Quebec's 72 school boards into regional "service centres" reporting to the Ministry of Education.[29] When Roberge intervened directly to facilitate the transfer of three English Montreal

School Board schools to the French board, CBC *News Montreal* reported the news with a headline speculating that the "handwriting [was] on the blackboard" for all of Quebec's school boards.[30]

DISAPPEARANCE OF ELECTED BOARDS IN ATLANTIC CANADA

Local school boards are more of an endangered species in Atlantic Canada and have almost disappeared over the past two decades. Elected school boards of trustees came under fire for their inability to effectively represent local interests and, since the late 1990s, have gradually lost their democratic legitimacy one province at a time in the region.[31]

New Brunswick – Abolition and Partial Restoration

The first province to discard regional school boards was New Brunswick. That structural reform was implemented, in steamroller fashion and with relentless determination, by Frank McKenna's Liberal government (1987–97). After sweeping every seat in the 1987 provincial election, McKenna's Liberals enjoyed rock-solid public support and took full advantage of that opportunity in the field of education.[32] In November 1990, he established a Commission on Excellence in Education, co-chaired by James Downey and Aldéa Landry. Over the following two years, the commission produced a series of generally well-received reports recommending various reforms. In February 1992, the province implemented school district consolidation, reducing 27 English language boards and 15 French language boards down to 18 in total (12 English, 6 French, 6 Combined) at a projected savings of $5 million. Even though provincial Auditor General Ralph Black reported in February 1995 and again in January 1996 that the savings in the $641 million budget were negligible, this finding did little to dampen the enthusiasm for major reform exhibited by successive ministers of Education. In February 1996, the province announced without consultation or any warning that all school boards would be eliminated and elected trustees removed from office, effective 1 March 1996.[33]

Abolishing school boards further centralized an already centralized system of education governance. Much less information on public education reached the public, and, since public input was channelled through school councils, the majority of citizens with no children in the system were effectively shut out from participation. This glaring weakness was partially corrected in 2001 with the restoration of District Education Councils (DECs) populated by well-meaning volunteers serving in elected positions. With all authority still centralized at the provincial level, the DECs faced an uphill battle to gain public support and confidence. In July 2009, three members of New Brunswick's District 2 District Education Council (Mary Laltoo, David Matthews, and Pat Crawford) resigned, decrying the DEC governance model as a sham, with few real decision-making powers. In a joint declaration, the three dissenters claimed that they refused to remain as "part of a farce that is sold to the public as local governance."[34] Since then, there have been repeated calls to revamp the DECs and rejuvenate local education democracy in New Brunswick.

Prince Edward Island – Consolidation, Dissolution, and Redemption

The latest wave of educational restructuring in PEI originated during the 2008–09 school year when then–Eastern District School Board Superintendent Sandy MacDonald recommended the closure of eleven of its 43 schools. The painful and bitter 2009 battle waged to close eight of those 11 rural Eastern District schools created such upheaval that it eventually led to the dismissal of the entire school board. The whole question came to a head following the appointment, in January 2010, of Doug Currie as the province's new Minister of Education, and, shortly thereafter, the elevation of MacDonald to Deputy Minister of Education. One year after Currie's appointment, and following a succession of standoffs over rezoning with Eastern District Board Chair Bob Clow and his fellow trustees, the Education Minister intervened and fired the entire Eastern District Board. Citing the "acrimony among trustees" as his rationale, Currie vowed to clear the way to "move important policy forward." He replaced it with a one-person board, Charlottetown consultant Patsy MacLean.[35]

With the dismissal of the Eastern District Board, the fix was in for regional school boards and locally elected school trustees. In April 2011, Minister Currie announced the appointment of an Education Governance Review Commission and dropped hints that he was now looking at establishing a single province-wide English school board. The single English Language School Board, composed of appointed province-wide trustees, regularly challenged the Education Department's priorities and questioned its policy directives. A new Liberal government, headed by Wade MacLauchlan and elected in May of 2015, came into office looking for educational changes.[36]

The MacLauchlan government simply absorbed the school board into the Department of Education, Early Learning and Culture, and the three new advisory bodies reported directly to the department. In February 2016, Education Minister Currie announced a new "made-in-P.E.I." model of education governance which eliminated the role of school board superintendent. In place of elected boards, the province set out to establish what was termed a "learning partnership" with the Learning Partners Advisory Council and the other two provincial advisory bodies. Guided by Island educator Bill Whelan and acting upon advice from Ontario education change consultant Michael Fullan, the province opted for organizational stability and a provincial advisory system focused on student achievement.[37]

Centralization was official PEI education policy from 2016 to 2018. In September 2016, the Public Schools Branch assumed control of the whole system and issued Policy 14, Board Governance Policy. It confirmed that English-language school governance was now vested in a three-person Public Schools Branch Board, chaired by the Deputy Minister of Education, Susan Willis. Confronted with a barrage of public resistance, spearheaded by a Rural Strong movement, MacLauchlan and Currie finally relented on 4 April 2017. A mere fifteen hours after the Public Schools Branch voted to close two schools in Georgetown and Charlottetown's St. Jean district, they pulled the plug on the whole exercise.[38] The unique PEI governance model, dubbed the "troika," survived, lingered on into 2019, but did not survive a change in government. A newly elected Progressive Conservative government, headed by Dennis King, proved to be far more in tune with public concerns, especially in the rural communities of the Eastern District. In December 2019, PC Education Minister Brad Trivers announced that the King government would be reinstating elected school boards for English-language schools.[39] A new governance model was promised for the fall of 2020, ending eight years without effective elected representation.

Newfoundland and Labrador – Dissolution and Centralization

School boards in Newfoundland and Labrador, like those in PEI, struggled for public legitimacy and become a regular whipping boy

Figure 12.3 Save Island Schools
The PEI Rural Strong movement rally to save Georgetown in February 2016 featured a human chain around Georgetown Elementary School.

for concerns about a myriad of educational issues. Regional boards, according to Memorial University's Gerald Galway, "bear the brunt of public dissatisfaction" for "a long list of sins," including underfunding of schools, busing regulations, and closing or consolidating schools. Many of those policies, Galway points out, actually originate with provincial education authorities and are then "enacted – sometimes reluctantly – by the formal decisions of school district trustees." Provincial governments claim that school boards are "quasi-autonomous agencies" that "make their own decisions" within their legislated mandate. Yet, from time to time, in Newfoundland, as elsewhere, provincial premiers and ministers intervene to overturn local decisions that run counter to Education Department directives or arouse intense local opposition.[40]

Governments in Newfoundland and Labrador have taken full advantage of the low profile and status accorded school boards – and the relative invisibility of elected trustees. Elected board members remain relatively unseen by the average local taxpayer, especially those without children in the schools. Voter turnout in school board elections is low, board meetings rarely get media coverage, and most citizens are simply not well-informed about the work of boards. The invisibility of school boards means that they can be eliminated without much in the way of political fallout. That explains why the

government of Newfoundland and Labrador has been able to implement radical centralization schemes. Within the space of twenty years,
the province has managed to radically downsize the local governance
system three times, reducing the 27 English school districts to 10 in
1997, down to four in 2004, and then to a single district in 2013.[41]
Much like in New Brunswick, this restructuring was executed without
any public consultation or public debate.

The Newfoundland and Labrador School Boards' Association
(NLSBA) took no firm policy position and proved to be complicit in
the radical plan of school district consolidation. While superintendents
and trustees were eliminated, the Education Department stressed that
senior executive staff and managers would still be located in satellite
offices in seven outlying communities: Labrador City, Lower Cove,
Stephenville, Grand Falls-Windsor, Burin, Clarenville, and Spaniard's
Bay.[42] Four regional superintendents jockeyed for the role of School
Board CEO and former Deputy Minister Education Darrin Pike
emerged on top in the job competition, ready and willing to make
the case for a single English Language School Board. Deposed trustees
in the Western, Central, and Labrador school districts voiced opposition to the elimination of locally elected boards, charging that centralized control "almost spelled the end of public education."[43] Eventually,
the government responded by reorganizing the one remaining provincial Newfoundland and Labrador English School Board (NLESB),
and it now has four sub-districts and an elected province-wide board
with 17 trustees representing 252 schools.[44]

Nova Scotia – The Decline and Fall of Local Board Governance

Nova Scotia's regional school board system remained essentially
unchanged in its structure and organization for over twenty years.
The Nova Scotia model was established as a result of structural reforms
initiated in 1996 by the Liberal government of Dr John Savage as a
critical piece in their education reform agenda.[45] Guided by Education
Minister John MacEachern, the *Education Horizons* restructuring
plan reduced the number of boards and introduced province-wide
School Advisory Councils (SACs). As part of the plan, the Halifax
Regional School Board (HRSB) was created as a component of munici-
pal amalgamation. The HRSB amalgamation process, spearheaded by
Superintendent Don Trider, was, in his own words, a challenging time

where his educational leadership was exercised in a "turbulent policy environment."[46] Once the reorganized school boards were up and running, the structural status quo prevailed for two decades, while waves of restructuring happened in neighbouring Atlantic provinces. Three elected school boards were fired, two in 2006 and one in 2012, but the existing school districts were preserved and protected.[47]

Regional school boards became more and more distant and disconnected from local school communities. School boards consolidated and retrenched, and superintendents gradually expanded their authority over not only elected boards, but the whole P–12 school system. Closing schools led to bigger elementary and secondary school plants, and administrators now routinely refer to their schools as "buildings."[48] In the 2014 report *Disrupting the Status Quo*, the Myra Freeman commission found half of Nova Scotians dissatisfied with school system performance and saw the potential for improved governance with "less duplication of services" and "more openness" to working across boundaries inside and outside the system.[49] The NSSBA and its member boards operated in a peculiar educational bubble. When the decision to dissolve all seven English school boards was announced, it hit the leading members of the NSSBA and most regional board chairs like a bolt out of the blue.[50] The Nova Scotia government of Stephen McNeil, acting upon Dr Avis Glaze's January 2018 report, abolished the English boards and, in their place, vowed to establish a fifteen-member Provincial Advisory Council on Education, and enhance the authority of School Advisory Councils across the province.

CAUSES OF DISAPPEARANCE

The dissolution of elected school boards did not happen overnight. School boards in Nova Scotia, like those elsewhere, demonstrated some glaring and disguised deficiencies:

1. Governance Philosophy and Practice:

Informal and flexible governance practices were gradually supplanted, over time, by more formal guidelines and policies, patterned after John Carver's strict policy governance model, effectively neutering the elected boards. School board members were trained to adopt a corporate governance philosophy that significantly weakened their representative role as the public voice in the school system.[51]

Table 12.1
Acclamation Disease, Nova Scotia School Board Elections, October 2016

School Board	No. of Elected Members	Number Acclaimed
Annapolis Valley RSB	10	9
Cape Breton-Victoria RSB	14	6
Chignecto-Central RSB	15	12
Halifax RSB	8	3
South Shore RSB	6	3
Strait RSB	10	8
Tri-County RSB	9	4
Acadian Provincial (CSAP)	18	11
African NS Members	7	5
Totals	97	61 (62.9 percent)

Nova Scotia School Board election results in October 2016 showed that almost
2 out of 3 positions were settled by acclamation.
Source: Avis Glaze, Raise the Bar, 11

2. Size and Scale Problem – Too Big to Be Responsive

School district consolidation, from the 1990s onward, resulted in larger and larger boards where decisions were made further and further away from the schools. One of the early warnings that regional school boards were too big to be effective, issued by Queen's University Education professor T.R. Williams, was borne out in Nova Scotia. Elected part-time trustees proved to be unable to oversee elected district boards which were simply too large."[52]

3. Resistance to School-Level Democratic Accountability

School boards, with the support of the Nova Scotia School Boards Association (NSSBA), since the mid-1990s, successfully beat back any proposals to significantly restructure Nova Scotia education governance. During the 2006–07 school year, following the firing of two school boards, Charles Cirtwill, then acting president of AIMS, mounted a determined effort to replace existing school boards with "school-based management." Inspired by the Edmonton Public Schools model and with the support of former Superintendent Angus McBeath, Cirtwill seized the opportunity to rid the province of what were termed "dysfunctional boards" and to devolve more decision-making authority to principals and local school councils.[53] That proposal and other representations fell on deaf ears.

4. Introduction of Strict Board Member Discipline Codes

Following the twin firings of the H R S B and the Strait Regional School Boards in 2006, senior superintendents, with the department's support, began to enforce stricter "Codes of Conduct" on elected board members and to rein in and effectively muzzle unruly "trustees," especially during intense periods of school reviews for closure.[54]

5. Public Disengagement and Spread of Acclamation Disease

Elected school boards also suffered from an advanced stage of what might be termed "acclamation disease." In the October 2012 municipal election, only three of the province's eight school boards remained democratically healthy, and two of them had been cleansed through previous firings. The problem persisted in October 2016 when 63 percent of the candidates were elected unopposed in spite of an N S S B A campaign to encourage more public participation in school board elections.[55]

6. Inability to Address Declining Student Performance

School boards proved incapable of tackling the problem of lagging student performance. Nova Scotia's Auditor General Michael Pickup, in his December 2014 review of the Tri-County Regional School Board (T C R S B) based in Yarmouth, N S, found that board oversight did not stand up under close scrutiny. While investigating record low scores on math and literacy tests, Pickup uncovered serious lapses in "management oversight" and found that the board did not "spend appropriate effort on the fundamental role of educating students."[56]

7. Failure to Exercise Effective Oversight over Senior Administration

The Auditor General was most critical of the lack of oversight exercised by the elected boards in their dealings with their one employee, the superintendent, and his/her senior staff. In the case of the Tri-County Regional School Board he found little or no evidence that the

elected board properly evaluated or held accountable its own superintendent. The next AG report in November 2015 confirmed that
three other governing boards were not effectively performing their
oversight functions.[57]

8. Rigid and Inflexible Responses to School Closures and Hub School Renewal Plans

Closing small schools was one responsibility entrusted by the
Education Department to the regional school boards. From 2006
onwards, elected school boards occupied the front lines in successive
waves of school consolidation, pitting elected members against communities throughout rural and small-town Nova Scotia. The Nova
Scotia Hub School movement gave small community schools some
reason to hope. The eventual Hub School guidelines, developed
entirely by provincial and regional staff, imposed strict criteria and
requirements, making it next-to-impossible for local parent groups
to secure approval for innovative proposals to repurpose their community schools. In the case of the Chignecto-Central Regional School
Board, the superintendent and staff imposed requirements that
thwarted, at every turn, hub school proposals for three elementary
schools, River John, Maitland, and Wentworth.[58] When the George
D. Lewis Hub School Society plan was rejected in 2017 by the Cape
Breton Victoria Regional School Board, the parent group called for
the resignation of the entire elected school board.[59] Shooting down
hub school plans, on top of closing schools, burned bridges and alienated active parents in a half-dozen or more communities.

Regional school boards grew more and more distant and disconnected from local school communities. School boards consolidated and
retrenched, and superintendents gradually expanded their authority
over not only elected boards, but the whole P–12 school system. The
NSSBA and its member boards operated in a peculiar educational
bubble. When the decision to dissolve all seven English school boards
was announced, it caught the leading members of NSSBA and most
regional board chairs unawares.[60] That was also symptomatic of the
general malaise and insularity that afflicted elected boards right across
Canada. The dissolution of Nova Scotia's school boards may turn out
to be a turning point in the evolution of educational governance. The
CAQ under François Legault appear determined to eliminate Quebec
school boards and replace them with "regional centres of education,"

much like those in Nova Scotia. A Manitoba school system review, initiated in January 2019 and guided by Dr Avis Glaze, has put elected school boards, once again, under the microscope. Restoration of elected boards in PEI provides a glimmer of hope. How to "better encourage and facilitate local input and engagement" in a "coordinated and relevant education system" has emerged as a critical issue not only in Manitoba, but elsewhere.[61]

Epilogue

Re-engineering Education

Flip the System and Build from the Schools Up

The centralized and overly bureaucratic School System has had its day and needs to be replaced, province by province, right across Canada. Cage-busting leadership will be required to transform our schools into responsive and responsible social institutions that, first and foremost, serve students, families, and communities. The nub of the problem lies in the current structure of provincial and school district governance, which reinforces and supports centralized, bureaucratic school administration. What is needed is a complete rethink of education governance and a commitment to clear away the obstacles to a more responsible, locally accountable school system that puts student needs first. Without re-engineering education governance from the schools up, this is not going to happen.

Today's education centres are worlds unto themselves, most often situated far from the true centre of the whole educational enterprise. In September 2010, Atlantic Canada's largest school board, the Halifax Regional School Board, moved its Central Administrative Office from downtown Dartmouth to a corporate industrial park in Burnside, on the city's outskirts. The decision to expand the central office to 73,000 square feet for some $1 million more in annual leasing costs was justified on the grounds that the board had, it was only then revealed, accumulated a $4.3 million surplus for this purpose. Few at the time questioned the move, nor what it signified as a concrete example of the so-called "controlling politics" of the "new managerialism" in public education.[1]

Centralizing the administration was assumed to be necessary to advance what former OISE professor Dr Ben Levin championed as "macro-directions" and presumably to minimize the dissonance and local resistance emanating from "micropolitics" in the schools. Then–Chair of the Board Irvine Carvery defended the move as sound financially and claimed that then–Chief Superintendent Carole Olsen saw the need for a much bigger central headquarters to facilitate large scale professional development activities. With the passage of the *Education Reform (2018) Act* on 9 March 2018, the Halifax Regional School Board was shorn of its elected trustees and renamed the Halifax Regional Centre for Education (HRCE). Chief Superintendent Elwin LeRoux was appointed Regional Executive Director of Education of HRCE, and made accountable only to the provincial education authority.[2] Some forty years after the advent of decentralized democratic governance in the form of School-Based Management, this school district, like many across North America, remained wedded to system-wide management of virtually every aspect of educational service.

THE PROMISE OF SCHOOL-COMMUNITY GOVERNANCE

Entrusting education to those closest to students harkens back to the Common School vision, and school-community governance is far from a new idea. A modern variation known as School-Based Management (SBM) arrived in Canada in the early 1970s when an American educator, Dr Rolland Jones, began experimenting with the concept as Superintendent of the Edmonton Public School Board. Described as "a visionary 20 years ahead of his times," he favoured local decision-making and espoused "site-based budgeting."[3] From 1976 until 1995, his successor Michael Strembitsky and school planner Alan Parry effectively dismantled a centrally managed school system and operationalized school-based decision-making. A determined team of administrators led by Strembitsky implemented a robust plan that shifted more responsibility to local schools, increasing local budget allocations to schools from 2 percent to 82 percent of provincial education dollars. While not perfect, the decentralized approach, in the words of Board Chair Joan Cowling, was "a dramatic improvement in the way schools were administered" and more attuned to school-level needs.

The Edmonton model was further developed by Strembitsky's successor, Superintendent Angus McBeath. School choice was introduced and implemented along with site-based budgeting.[4] Students and parents were offered their choice of schools within the city, and by 2003, 62 percent of high schoolers and 54 percent of junior high students attended schools outside their attendance zones. A depopulating, decaying high school was transformed into an arts academy and its enrolment rebounded, largely at the expense of competing private schools. An energy conservation initiative, entrusted to local schools, netted $2 million a year in savings. Publishing school-by-school student achievement results improved overall test scores. While it was a top-down reform initiative, the key to its success, according to McBeath, lay in the strong support it engendered among "allies outside the educational system."[5]

After a flurry of SBM initiatives in the mid-1990s, including in some school districts in Ontario and Nova Scotia, school administrators pulled back from the whole approach. Centralization and administrative build-up proved to be powerful forces, strengthened by the consolidation of school boards, the introduction of system-wide testing, the proliferation of special programs, and the spread of program consultants. Student loads per teacher, called Total Student Loads (TSLs) by William G. Ouchi, actually rose in junior and senior high schools. Superintendents acquired more power by increasing the size of their headquarters staffs and created more non-teaching positions, and this, in turn, led teachers to abandon the classroom. A 1997 American research study revealed that only 43 percent of district employees were regularly engaged in classroom teaching.[6]

The Edmonton Education Model attracted many public accolades but few followers in the ranks of North American educational administration. In his 2008 book *Making Schools Work*, Ouchi, a leading UCLA management professor, reported that Edmonton had "the best-run schools" compared to those of many other North American cities.[7] He credited Edmonton's educational leadership in school-based management with engineering a "revolution" and charting the way for other school systems to escape educational mediocrity and under-performance.

While North American educational leaders still shy away from School-Based Management, it is now undergoing a renaissance in the developing world, where school systems are seeking immediate "turn-around" educational reforms. Since 2003, the World Bank has been particularly active in supporting and funding SBM initiatives in countries such as Kenya, Indonesia, Nepal, and Senegal. A recent international study, commissioned by the World Bank (2011), claimed that "education is too complex to be efficiently produced and distributed in a centralized fashion." In spite of some successes, the study found "ambiguous results" in countries where "elite capture" was a problem and "teachers and unions" resisted ceding more control to "parents and community members."[8]

Senior administrators who promote the latest educational panacea known as "distributed leadership" remain surprisingly resistant to a more democratic, school-level decision-making model.[9] Yet more open-minded educators such as New Yorker Thomas Whitby, initiator of #edchat, and Australian researcher Bruce Johnson continue to muse about the unsettling impact of centralizing administration on the quality and tone of teaching and learning in schools.

Sympathetic observers such as Whitby express concern over teacher-administrators who get swept up in the "Education Center world" and managerial matters and lose touch with the classroom.[10] In Australia, Johnson contends that bureaucratic managerialism has been used to "construct a seemingly irresistible top-down juggernaut of reform that largely excludes the possibility or desirability of local agency." School-Based Management has considerable appeal because it fosters a "positive politics" of negotiation, collaboration, and conflict resolution to address "issues of local concern in schools." He longs for the day when teachers, as well as parents, can enjoy a more "positive framework" with ongoing opportunities to participate in the "school improvement journey."[11]

THE NEW ZEALAND VISION –
SELF-MANAGED SCHOOLS

The most ambitious venture aimed at establishing school-level governance originated in the mid-1980s and completely transformed the New Zealand school system. Concerned over the state of education, and the unresponsiveness of the country's ten education boards, the David Lange Labour government (1984–89) embraced the reinvention of government and education reform with gusto and determination. In July 1987, this government appointed a five-person national education task force, headed by Brian Picot, a well-known supermarket magnate. The task force worked in collaboration with the NZ Treasury and the State Services Commission (SSC), as part of a whole-of-government commitment to reinventing public services, tapping into the entrepreneurial spirit of business. Its mandate was to review management structures and cost-effectiveness, but did not include curriculum, teaching, or effectiveness. In nine months the commission received input from over 700 people or organizations and then released its earth-shaking report.[12]

The Picot task force's report, *Administering for Excellence: Effective Administration in Education*, released in May 1988, was highly critical of the Department of Education, which it claimed was both inefficient and unresponsive. It recommended a system where each school would be largely independent, governed by a board consisting mainly of parents, although subject to review and inspection by specialized government agencies. The government accepted many of the recommendations in their response *Tomorrow's Schools* (1988), which provided a blueprint for transformative education reform.[13] Secondary schools already managed their own budgets, and the reform extended that responsibility to all primary schools.

The revamped New Zealand structure gave parents a much greater role in school governance. Each school's parents were authorized to elect their own board of trustees, the new legal entity entrusted with the educational and financial well-being of the school. The policy embraced freedom of choice by allowing parental choice of school, based upon the assumption that competition among schools would spur improvement. The Department of Education was broken up into a Ministry of Education and what became the Education Review Office, the Qualifications Agency, and several smaller units. The massive structural reform set out to improve the flexibility and responsiveness of schools to their students and to improve educational opportunities.[14]

A few key Picot recommendations were set aside by the New Zealand government. The concept of a coordinating Education Policy Council was dropped. The task force conceived of the school charter as a contract between school boards, the local community, and central authority. After a review by the ssc, the school-level boards of trustees were made responsible to the Minister of Education, who gained the power to dismiss boards. The recommendation of the task force to provide funding to the boards for payment of salaries, rather than have teachers paid by the government, was initially rejected. Later reintroduced on a voluntary trial basis, the proposed policy of paying staff salaries out of block grants was not implemented by most boards.[15]

The main gains from the *Tomorrow's Schools* initiative were apparent once the formidable implementation challenges were over. New partnerships between boards of trustees and school professionals were usually working well and benefiting students. School-level boards were becoming more representative of parents. Women made up

52 percent of the members. For the first time, women were as likely as men to chair their board. Parent satisfaction levels remained high at around 80 percent, the same as before the reforms. Those who worked for schools took enjoyment and pride in their work, compensating for increases in their workload. Self-managed schools exhibited a renewed interest in continuing professional development and a growing focus on integrated school development.[16]

Implementing self-managed schools also produced a few vital lessons. The extent and speed of restructuring sparked resistance from education professionals who felt excluded from major decisions. Over the first decade, funding levels declined under a more fiscally conservative National Party government. By 1999, 87 percent of principals and 65 percent of trustees said their budget was inadequate, compared with only 20 percent of each in 1989. Boards of trustees reported spending most of their time on funding and property. Funding per student grew by 4.4 percent from 1990 to 1999. School fundraising increased markedly. The increase in locally raised funds was more consistent and much larger than the increase in government funding. Some 38 percent of schools raised more than $15,500, compared with 10 percent in 1989. Though NZ school education remained legally free, 74 percent of schools asked parents to pay a voluntary fee, and 69 percent of these asked for more than $20 a child, up from 29 percent in 1989. Schools in low socio-economic areas and with high Māori enrolment were likely to have gained least from the reforms. Decentralization of decision-making was a success as principals and schools gained far more autonomy. While principals and teachers advocated for more consistent focus on acquiring resources, staff workload, and student support issues, the governing councils prioritized policy-making, property management, and finances.[17]

Twenty-five years on, New Zealand remained the leading exemplar of self-managed schools. Back in 2012, Cathy Wylie, lead researcher at NZCER, produced *Vital Connections*, a comprehensive study of the *Tomorrow's Schools* reform.[18] The disruptive effects of massive reform left many newly constituted boards struggling with their expanded governance responsibilities. After what Wylie described as "a lost decade," New Zealanders gradually accepted the decentralized model. The School Trustees Association maintained that school-level boards needed more support, although it rejected any return to "archaic" regional education boards. Enhanced school-based governance was welcomed by most parents, even though they spent a "mucky decade" trying to manage property and finances. Promising educational advances were achieved in the late 1980s, but – over time – school governing boards tended to be enmeshed in wrestling with local policy and administrative matters. Up to one out of five school councils were given corrective reports each year, and some 15 to 20 percent of school principals reported "personality clashes" with their boards. Decentralizing decision-making, Wylie concluded, was not sufficient, in and of itself, to produce school improvement. She proposed boards be managed by one of twenty district authorities, to ensure schools and teachers were supported, challenged, and linked together in a professional community. Those authorities would have the final sign-off on appointing principals, instead of school boards. Like most New Zealand educators, Wylie urged the NZ government to look at a system refresh rather than a return to "archaic" regional boards in any shape or form.[19]

BUILDING A MADE-IN-CANADA MODEL OF LOCAL DEMOCRATIC GOVERNANCE

No current school governance model here in Canada provides a suitable framework, so we would be well-advised to look further afield and to create a homemade model that best serves students and better serves the public interest. In doing so, we will see the possibilities for a Community-School Governance Model borrowing elements from the Edmonton Public Schools and New Zealand, both of which have implemented School-Based Management (SBM) and school-level governing councils.[20] A 1994 Nova Scotia paper, *Restructuring the System*, points us in the right direction with a school-based democratic model designed to "expand our education horizons and strengthen public accountability" for schools, parents, and communities.[21] The Edmonton model of SBM, initiated in Edmonton Public Schools in 1976, has stood the test of time. Alberta Education published a School-Based Decision-Making Guide in 1997 and opened the door to other boards adopting school-based budgeting. In 2003, when the World Bank started championing SBM in developed countries across the globe, a feature story in *Time* Magazine described Edmonton's public schools as "the most imitated public school system in North America." Superintendent Darrel Robertson, in an August 2016 *Edmonton Journal* news story, reported that school-based decision-making was still going strong in the district. It remained the core philosophy because it successfully "empowers and engages staff, students and parents."[22]

Today's Edmonton Public Schools remain the best exemplar of the success of school-based management. With a total budget of $1.2 billion, the Edmonton system serves 98,900 students across 213 schools, all operating under school-based budgeting.[23] School principals and governing councils enjoy far greater autonomy, and the system budget for 2017–18 allocated some $656 million in block funding to the schools, representing 67.5 percent of the budget. When school-generated revenues are included, the proportion allocated to the schools inches up to 70.2 percent. Looking more closely at the budget, it is clear that the central office targets school allocations, earmarking funds for special needs children (levels 4–8), First Nations, Métis, and Inuit Education (FNMI), and international students, as well as Plant Operation and Maintenance.[24] Once the regional school board approves the budget, much of it is still allocated to local schools. When each school sets its budget each spring, central office finance staff assemble the overall district budget to be approved by the school board. One change made in recent years is the policy of reserving funds at central office to allow the system to respond to urgent needs popping up throughout the school year.

The fundamental test of any initiative would be its efficacy in turning the school system right side up and building from the school level up, not the top down. Turning the situation around does require structural change to set right a system where a closely knit educational leadership class have co-opted the educational agenda to preserve and protect their interests rather than serve the needs of children, teachers, parents, or local communities.[25] Reversing the flow of policy inputs will not happen unless and until a model is developed that fosters and develops school community-based decision-making.[26] Instead of relying upon school district consolidation to achieve cost efficiencies, pursue greater potential efficiencies through the proven strategy of joint consortia for shared services, including financial services, transportation, purchasing, networked learning, and community services.[27] Those who continue to argue for the retention of existing elected school boards on the grounds that they represent the people are, in the words of veteran Ontario educator Peter Hennessy, "missing the point" that "elective parent councils" have been established precisely because "the boards were and are out of touch with the grassroots."[28]

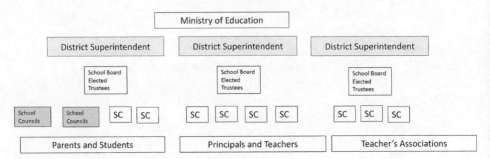

Figure 13.1 Conventional Education Decision-Making

Top-down decision-making following the established hierarchy still dominates K–12 education. Here is a schematic demonstrating the conventional, hierarchical model prevalent in provincial systems with elected trustees.

Now is the time to transform the education governance system to cure the now-visible deficit in public accountability and local democratic participation. The best course of action would be to announce a gradual, planned transition to School-Community-Based Governance, replacing the remaining regional school boards with autonomous, self-governing school councils.[29] That sets a clear direction. It vests far more authority where it belongs, in school-level councils, and paves the way for the construction of a new community-based model of education. Some regional coordination will still be required to provide some oversight, to ensure the equitable sharing of educational resources, and to ensure proper regional planning. The proposed plan recognizes the need for the further development, at a later stage, of regional coordinating bodies to be known as District Education Development Councils.

THE INITIAL STEPS – FOR IMPLEMENTATION OF COMMUNITY-SCHOOL GOVERNANCE

The most effective, accountable, and democratic Community-School Education Governance Model would embrace the following structural changes:

- Replace elected provincial or regional school boards with a school-based governance and management system, embracing Community School Governance;

- Contract school district administration or "administrative units," while designing and constructing more robust school-based governance and management;
- Establish joint district consortia for the sharing of services, including financial, facilities, transportation, and purchasing services;
- Develop and implement District Education Development Councils, composed of a majority of regional trustees, representing elected School Governing Councils, and including appointed members from municipalities, boards of trade, and universities/colleges; and
- Reinvest cost savings into school-community development and designated "education improvement zones" to address inequities at the school-community level.

A hybrid model – known as Community-School Governance – has many advantages over tinkering with the current status quo, once again. We have seen what happens when regional school boards are simply eliminated, as in the cases of New Brunswick, Prince Edward Island, and Nova Scotia – a net loss in public accountability and visible popular resistance to any and all initiatives from the centralized authority. Embracing a School Community Development approach would be far better than the current mish-mash of school governance models. School-based management and governance combined with District Education Councils, populated by trustees and municipal appointees from the community and business, is the best hope for salvaging local democratic control in public education and addressing the critical need for more effective schools.

THREE PRIORITIES IN FLIP-THE-SYSTEM REFORM

Decentralizing education is a means to an end and not an end in itself. Thirty years after the implementation of the first wave of school-based management initiatives, it is abundantly clear that self-managed schools, by themselves, are not enough to produce dramatic improvement in the quality and vitality of public education. The devolution of decision-making to the local school and community level carries with it significant benefits, but two problems remain to be solved to fully realize the vision of more democratic and effective schools. First of all, real authority, in far too many cases, is still vested in ministries of education and/or regional school administrations, limiting the freedom of action of school governing councils. Second, when decentralization is implemented, it usually applies to the management structure and process (such as site-based budgeting) but does not really impact the day-to-day teaching and learning that exert a bigger influence on school improvement.[30] Decentralization, then, is only the first piece in the overall strategy to make our schools more democratic, responsive, and accountable to parents, teachers, students, and communities.

The successes and failures of initial School-Based Management ventures provide lessons for today's school reform projects following that path. In embracing the school-based governance model, it is best to survey the situation and to prepare the ground for such large-scale reform. First and foremost, that involves working to establish the "winning" pre-conditions (i.e., the requisite school-level leadership, the capacity of teachers and community members, and an infrastructure of support). Successful ventures such as those in Edmonton and New Zealand demonstrated the capacity to prepare the school principals, embrace new teaching and learning methods, mobilize and engage parents, forge and build community partnerships, and be more open and transparent in assessment and accountability. Decentralizing education is, after all, far more than just a structural change; it is a cultural change significantly altering the normal order of things in the world of K–12 education.

Flipping the system will involve a significant shift from centralized, top-down, bureaucratic policies and practice to a more humane, teaching-centred, and democratic approach to educating children and teens. Turning the system right side up means placing students, teachers, and parents at the centre of the whole enterprise and wresting the steering wheel away from the current dominant players ensconced in the so-called education "blob" – senior bureaucrats, superintendents, education gurus, and district consultants. Simply put, taking back the schools means reclaiming the system from those who work outside of classrooms, soaking up resources and resisting school reform without contributing to student achievement.

Humanizing Education – on a Student Scale

Students should come first in our schools, and this is best achieved in smaller schools operating on a human scale. Since the early 1980s, a Human Scale Education (HSE) movement has emerged to challenge the prevailing orthodoxy. Inspired by E.F. Schumacher's 1973 classic text, *Small Is Beautiful*, and spearheaded by British small school advocates Satish Kumar, James Wetz, and Mary Tasker, the movement mounted a determined resistance to the giant UK comprehensive high schools built in the 1950s and 1960s. Disenchantment with the big comprehensive school led to the founding of the Human Scale Education Trust in 1985 and the issuing of a Practical Manifesto endorsing eight practices aimed at "humanizing" schools.[31] The eight guiding practices, originally conceived as the sides of a UK fifty-pence piece, embraced small schools (ideally learning communities of 250 to 300 students), teaching teams, cross-curricular integration, inquiry-based learning, assessment for learning, enhanced student voice, and genuine partnerships with parents. It was all a direct response to what Mary Tasker aptly described as "parental concerns that schools were too big" and "that the loss of human scale was leading to strained relations between teachers and students, teachers and parents, and between the school and the local community."[32]

Smaller schools are demonstrably better schools. Since 2006, Michael Corbett of Acadia University and his colleague Dennis Mulcahy of Memorial University have resisted the relentless march of school consolidation and been champions of a Canadian version of the Human Scale Education movement. "For many decades of the 20th century," Corbett and Mulcahy wrote in *Education on a Human Scale*, "school consolidation was considered synonymous with school improvement, despite the fact that there was virtually no evidence to support that assumption."[33] Central to the core principles of Human Scale Education are the firm beliefs that relationships are at the heart of education and that human-scale learning communities are the right sizes to build vital connections that produce fully educated persons. Perhaps the late Ted Sizer, founder of the American Coalition for Essential Schools, said it best: "You cannot teach a child well unless you know that child well."[34] That axiom applies, whatever one's ideological position.

Breaking up traditional high schools into smaller units is not the answer. From 2000 to 2009, the Bill and Melinda Gates Foundation "Small Schools" initiative poured some $2 billion into subdividing comprehensive urban high schools of 2,000 to 4,500 students into some 1,600 smaller units of a few hundred students each. That grand experiment to downsize "dropout factories" capsized when the money invested in Oregon and other states did not "improve students' achievement in a significant way."[35] Among the lessons learned was that changing established school culture in comprehensive high schools was extremely challenging, especially when so many of the subsidiary units lacked the autonomy to chart their own courses. One particular network of charter schools, however, the Knowledge Is Power Program (KIPP) schools, met most of the Human Scale Education criteria, averaging some 300 students, and were judged to have been very successful in building close student-teacher bonds and in raising the academic standards of predominantly disadvantaged students.[36] In the right school settings, smaller schools do produce superior student outcomes.

Teaching-Centred Classrooms

Teachers are clamouring for a much larger role in setting priorities and determining what happens in today's schools. That spirit was captured well in a 2016 collection of essays, *Flip the System*, edited by two Dutch teachers, Jelmer Evers and Rene Kneyber, which made the case for teachers to take the lead in reforming education. Like most of the book's contributors, the co-editors saw education under threat on a global scale by the so-called "forces of neoliberalism," exemplified in "high stakes accountability, privatization, and a destructive language of learning."[37] Instead of "being told what to achieve and how to achieve it," Evers and Kneyber urged fellow teachers to "show leadership in regard to the how and the what" of education. What did that mean in practice? Reasserting teacher agency in an educational world where many advocating "teacher leadership" were, in fact, appropriating the term as "another tool for domestication" rather than "an instrument for deregulation and professionalization." Flipping the system would move teachers to the centre of the enterprise and resemble more of "a process of emancipation than a 'system intervention.'" The voice of teachers would be given a meaningful place, instead of being just part of the "noise" reverberating through the system.[38]

The days when teachers decided on matters of curriculum and delivery without any form of accountability are over. Many in the teaching profession, however, are awakening to the impact of standardized testing and accountability in promoting and entrenching efficiency and managerialism, while eroding teacher autonomy in the school and community. Education research professor Gert Biesta has argued that the "neoliberal shift" has essentially led to the "death of the teacher" in terms of his/her freedom and capacity to contribute

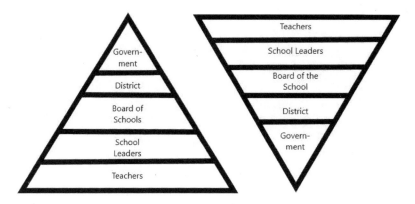

Figure 13.2 Flip the System

A diagram illustrating educational governance reform and exemplifying the concept of turning the system right side up.

meaningfully to what happens in the classroom.[39] Symptomatic of the shift is what Biesta has termed "learnification" – the emergence of a new, technocratic "language of education" where students are referred to as "learners," teaching is "facilitating learning," and school is a "learning environment." The dominance of such a language, promulgated by ministries of education and education faculties, is to subvert the real point of education – to learn *something*, to learn it *for a reason*, and to learn it *from someone*.[40]

Teachers across Canada are beginning to question the hegemony of educational change theorists and systems thinkers over our provincial school systems. The Ontario Secondary School Teachers Federation (OSSTF), under newly elected president Harvey Bischof, is in the forefront of a movement to challenge educational policy and teaching practices that are based upon unproven theories. Inspired by the work of British teacher Tom Bennett, founder of researchED UK, Bischof and the OSSTF have called into question the prevailing orthodoxy in Ontario education and found common cause with reform-minded parents.[41] Speaking at researchED Toronto in November 2017, Bischof spoke out about the need for teacher-centred education where teaching practice was based upon what works in the classroom. "The Ontario educational environment," he stated, "lacks a culture of empiricism, which leaves the education system and its practitioners vulnerable to the influence of self-appointed gurus, ideologues, and advocates who promote unproven trends and fads."

While regular teachers know instinctively what works in the class-room, Bischof claimed that "the government has virtually handed education policy-making over to advocacy groups, like People for Education, that wouldn't recognize the inside of a classroom from an educator's perspective." "For practitioners to successfully reclaim their professional autonomy," he added, "they need to be able to demonstrate that they are working from a foundation of evidence-based judgement."[42] That message not only resonated with Ontario teachers, but found favour with leading education reform advocate Michael Zwaagstra and like-minded parents in Ontario and far beyond.[43]

Engaging Parents – in Family-centric Schools

"Parent engagement" is now part of the standard educational lexicon, but, in practice, it is incredibly hard to find it exhibited in any kind of sustained fashion. That will have to change if school community-based governance is to succeed in schools across Canada. School leaders, educational consultants, and even principals tend to focus more on managing parent involvement and on mobilizing parent participation to secure more funding or for other similar purposes.[44] One of Canada's leading researchers on parent engagement, Debbie Pushor, makes a clear distinction between school-managed parent involvement and genuine parent engagement. Far too many of today's school administrators and consultants seeking parent involvement exhibit what is termed a "school-centric" way of thinking.[45] That attitude is starkly revealed in the choice of words. In the current system, parents are essentially taught to "speak the language of education" and led to believe that it is critical to their children's success. Educational leadership sessions and faculty of education programs work from the assumption that it is the responsibility of educators to "build parents' capacity" to engage with their local schools. Parents with concerns are faced with trying to navigate a system that sends the wrong signals. "I want to be engaged," one parent recently told Pushor, "but I can't go to my kids' school. I don't have the right clothes and I don't have the right words."[46]

School superintendents, consultants, and many school principals have a lot to unlearn. Thinking outside the box is challenging when one has been taught how to train parents to respect the normal pecking order and to fit into the existing school structures. The whole notion of "building capacity" implies that parents need to be taught to respect the established order conveying, in a subliminal sense, that "teacher knows best." The cumulative effect is to make parents at the school level feel like pupils rather than mature adults and to leave them with the unfortunate impression of being marginalized in school conversations. Professor Pushor is absolutely correct in advocating a completely different approach – the "family-centric" approach, embracing a philosophy of "walking alongside" parents and genuinely supporting the active engagement of the families that make up the school community.[47]

Parent engagement will be critical to the success of reinventing education at the school and community level. "Walking alongside" parents means meeting them where they are and where they actually live. School superintendents, consultants, and principals have to stop "caring for" parents and begin to "care about" them. Creating the space for true parent engagement should become a school priority, superseding existing structures designed to channel and contain parent involvement and feedback. Getting out into the community, extending a warm and genuine greeting, and working to build partnerships should come naturally and not be seen as part of a formalized parent engagement strategy. In today's world, engaging parents and families involves being flexible and culturally responsible so as to reach and better serve marginalized communities, including Indigenous families with different ways of thinking, being, and doing community conversations.[48] School community-based governance will require changes in the ways system leaders and administrators engage with parents and families as well as students and teachers.

IN SUMMATION: SEIZE THE DAY

Centralization, bureaucratization, and conformity continue to be relentless social forces sustaining the System. The conventional fast-food model of public education thrives on organizational efficiency, mass production, and uniformity. Only 35 percent of American K–8 students in 2008 walked to school, and the estimated figure in the Canadian provincial systems is much lower, perhaps one in four across Canada. Canada's largest school district, Toronto District School Board, with a $3.2 billion budget, 583 schools, and 246,000 students, is in a near-constant state of crisis and under threat of being broken up into more effective, manageable, accountable organizational units.[49] Provincial governments in New Brunswick, Newfoundland

and Labrador, Prince Edward Island, and now Nova Scotia eliminated locally elected school boards between 1996 and 2019 and moved dramatically in the direction of centralizing control over their systems. Revitalizing school-level education democracy has now become imperative in provinces with school districts covering large swaths of the country.

Centralized, bureaucratic, technology-driven education is sparking resistance among parents and teachers and in local school communities. Turning the school system right side up will require bold and committed reform leadership. Prominent education researchers and academics, most notably Corbett and British Columbia Teachers Federation (BCTF) researcher Larry Kuehn, see the "globalization of education" and attendant neo-liberal education reform as fundamental contributing factors. Global learning corporations, exemplified by Pearson International and Google, have achieved dominance through the spread of educational technology and licensed earning resources – and are finally attracting critical scrutiny.[50] Reform-minded teachers are beginning to challenge top-down educational initiatives, to cast a more skeptical eye upon prevailing educational theories, and to demand evidence demonstrating what works in the classroom. That explains, in part, the warm reception given to the British grassroots teacher movement, researchED, upon its arrival in Canada in November of 2017.[51]

The System is not going unchallenged, and the resistance comes from all positions on the political spectrum. Student testing and accountability, whatever its original intentions, has devolved into a new layer of regulatory oversight, driven by data collection, breeding a new brand of school managerialism, and producing transparency without much public accountability. Even staunch supporters of the standards and accountability movement now acknowledge that "localism" has been lost, far too many citizens feel "discounted, discombobulated and disconnected," and reformers need to "approach school reform in a manner that's sensitive to these concerns."[52] Parent advocacy organizations such as Ontario's People for Education were co-opted by provincial ministries of education and absorbed into the so-called "education blob," but they have been superseded by other, more populist parent groups, such as the Ontario Autism Coalition and the Western Initiative for Strengthening Education in Mathematics (WISE Math). Thousands of parents concerned about the spread of the "21st Century Learning" mantra, the proliferation of "Discovery Math," the decline of mathematics and literacy scores, and the erosion of teaching the fundamentals have signed petitions demanding changes in Alberta, British Columbia, and Ontario. Whether it's urban neighbourhoods in Toronto, Vancouver, Hamilton, and Moncton or rural communities from River John, Nova Scotia, to Quesnel, B C, parents and community activists have arisen in waves against the relentless advance of educational centralization and school consolidation.[53]

Reforming the System is essentially about taking back our schools. Top-down decision-making, educational managerialism, and rule by the technocrats has run its course.[54] Putting students first has to become more than a hollow promise. A new set of priorities are in order: democratize school governance, deprogram education ministries and school districts, and listen more to parents and teachers in the schools. Design and build smaller schools at the centre of urban neighbourhoods and rural communities. Let's focus our energies on what's really fundamental: regaining control over our schools, rebuilding social capital, and revitalizing local communities.[55] Rediscovering education on a human, student scale, embracing evidence-based policy and practice, and revitalizing local education democracy have never been more urgent. With this book comes a call to turn the system right side up and to chart a more constructive path forward.

Notes

INTRODUCTION

1 Paul Cappon, "Canada Must Stop Being 'A School that Never Issues Report Cards,'" *The Globe and Mail*, 4 December 2013. For a prime example of Canadian educational boosterism, see Sean Coughlan, "How Canada Became an Education Superpower," *BBC News*, 2 August 2017.

2 The origins of the centralized, bureaucratic System are identified and analyzed in Paul W. Bennett, "Consolidation, Bureaucracy and the Public Schools: The Formation of the Modern Bureaucratic Education State, 1920–1993," *Canadian Issues / Thèmes canadiens* (Spring 2014): 16–22. See also David Graeber, *The Utopia of Rules* (Brooklyn, NY: Melville House, 2016), 3–21, for an anthropological analysis of the gradual integration of liberalism into corporate bureaucratic culture.

3 Donald J. Peurach, David K. Cohen, Maxwell M. Yurkofsky, and James P. Spillane, "From Mass Schooling to Education Systems: Changing Patterns in the Organization and Management of Instruction," *Review of Research in Education* 43 (March 2019): 33–4.

4 Carl Hendrick, "Bureaucracy Is Sucking the Life out of Teaching," *Spiked*, 1 September 2015; Larry Cuban, *Inside the Black Box of Classroom Practice: Change without Reform in American Education* (Cambridge, MA: Harvard Education Press, 2013), 10–13, 77–98, 155–88.

5 Max Weber, *Weber: Political Writings*, ed. Peter Lassman, trans. Ronald Speirs (Cambridge: Cambridge University Press, 1994), xvi.

6 Peter Baehr, "The 'Iron Cage' and the 'Shell as Hard as Steel': Parsons, Weber, and the *Stahlhartes Gehäuse* Metaphor in the Protestant Ethic and the Spirit of Capitalism," *History and Theory* 40, no. 2 (May 2001): 153–69.

7 George Martell, *The Politics of the Canadian Public School* (Toronto: James Lorimer & Sons, 1974); David Clandfield, "The School as a Community Hub: A Public Alternative to the Neo-Liberal Threat to Ontario Schools," in Clandfield and Martell, eds., *Our Schools/Our Selves* (Special Issue: School as Community Hub: Beyond Education's Iron Cage, Summer 2010): 5–74.

8 Jennifer Lewington and Graham Orpwood, *Overdue Assignment: Taking Responsibility for Canada's Schools* (Toronto: John Wiley and Sons, 1993), 42–53.

9 Caroline Alphonso, "Ontario Liberals to Pay $39 Million to Several Education Groups," *The Globe and Mail*, 18 April 2018; Dean Bennett, "Alberta Announces Sweeping 6-Year Overhaul of School Curricula at a Cost of $64M," *Global News Edmonton*, 15 June 2016.

10 Caroline Alphonso and Jeff Gray, "Head of Ontario High School Teachers Union Vows to 'Cultivate Resistance' ahead of Labour Negotiations," *The Globe and Mail*, 15 August 2019; Jamie Mauracher, "Premier Says Teachers Unions 'Declared War' on the Ford Government," *Global News*, 17 April 2019.

11 Former US Education Secretary William Bennett coined the term "the blob" and it first appeared in a March 1987 *Education Week* interview story. See R. Walker, "Bennett: Test Gains at 'Dead Stall,'" *Education Week*, 2 March 1987. See also Jim Dueck, *Education's Flashpoints: Upside Down or Set-Up to Fail* (Lanham, MD: Rowman & Littlefield, 2015), 188.

12 Peter Clancy, "Public and Post-Secondary Education: Structural Change and Embedded Clienteles," in Clancy et al., *The Savage Years: The Perils of Reinventing Government in Nova Scotia* (Halifax: Formac Publishing, 2000), ch. 6.

13 David Osborne and Ted Gaebler, *Reinventing Government: How the Entrepreneurial Spirit Is Transforming the Public Sector* (Don Mills, ON: Addison-Wesley, 1992).

14 See Jelmer Evers and Rene Kneyber, eds., *Flip the System: Changing Education from the Ground Up* (London: Routledge, 2016).

15 Eric Kalenze, *Education Is Upside-Down: Reframing Reform to Focus on the Right Problems* (Lanham, MD: Rowman & Littlefield, 2014).

16 On the fusion of public and private systems and the spectre of "total bureaucratization," see Graeber, *The Utopia of Rules*, 17–21.

17 Frederick M. Hess, *The Cage-Busting Teacher* (Cambridge, MA: Harvard Education Press, 2013), 1–3, 30–3.

18 See Pedro De Bruyckere, Paul A. Kirschner, and Casper Hulshof, *Urban Myths about Learning and Education* (Cambridge, MA: Academic Press,

2015); Daisy Christodoulou, *Seven Myths about Education* (New York: Routledge, 2014); and Daniel T. Willingham, *Why Don't Students Like School?* (San Francisco, CA: Jossey-Bass, 2009).

19 See Donald J. Peurach, David K. Cohen, and James P. Spillane, "Governments, Markets and Instruction: Considerations for Cross-national Research," *Educational Administration* (March 2019), doi: 10.1108/JEA-09-2018-0172. See also B. Rowan, "The Ecology of School Improvement: Notes on the School Improvement Industry in the United States," *Journal of Educational Change* 3: 283–389.

20 Founder of researchED Tom Bennett's new series of teacher guides, launched in 2019 with the first title, *Education Myths* (Melton, Woodbridge, UK: John Catt Educational, 2019), is bringing evidence-based research directly to classrooms. On the arrival of researchED in Canada, see Randy Banderob, "Tom Bennett and the researchED Revolution," *OSSTF Education Forum Magazine*, 26 October 2017. For a book capturing the spirit of researchED, see Michael Zwaagstra, *A Sage on the Stage: Common Sense Reflections on Teaching and Learning* (Melton, Woodbridge, UK: John Catt Educational, 2020).

CHAPTER ONE

1 The best-known diagnoses of the "crisis" in Canadian public education identify the sources of stress in the system, but tend to propose radically different policy cures. See Jennifer Lewington and Graham Orpwood, *Overdue Assignment: Taking Responsibility for Canada's Schools.* (Toronto: John Wiley and Sons, 1993); Charles Ungerleider, *Failing Our Kids: How We Are Ruining Our Public Schools* (Toronto: McClelland & Stewart, 2003); and Michael C. Zwaagstra, Rodney A. Clifton, and John C. Long, *What's Wrong with Our Schools and How We Can Fix Them* (Lanham, MD: Rowman & Littlefield, 2010).

2 Kelly Gallagher-MacKay and Nancy Steinhauer, *Pushing the Limits: How Schools Can Prepare Our Children Today for the Challenges of Tomorrow* (Toronto: Doubleday Canada, 2017), especially 7–9, 228–9.

3 Gallaher-Mackay and Steinhauer, "How Schools Can Stop Killing Creativity," *The Walrus*, 12 September 2017.

4 Paul W. Bennett, "Building on Illusions: Why 'Preparing Students for Jobs That Don't Exist Yet' Is Problematic," *EDCan Network*, 26 September 2017.

5 Paul W. Bennett, "Turning Around Our Schools," *Progress Magazine* 17, no. 2 (2010): 26–9.

6 Stephen B. Lawton, *Busting Bureaucracy to Reclaim Our Schools* (Montreal, QC: IRPP, 1995), 32–6, 62.

7 Joe Freedman, *The Charter School Idea: Breaking Educational Gridlock* (Red Deer, AB: Society for Advancing Educational Research, 1995), 70–5.

8 Richard G. Neal, *School-Based Management* (Bloomington, IN: National Educational Service, 1991), 2–15; Peter Coleman, "Improving Schools by School-Based Management," *McGill Journal of Education* 19, no. 1 (Winter 1984): 25–41.

9 See Larry Cuban, *Inside the Black Box of Classroom Practice* (Cambridge, MA: Harvard Education Press, 2013).

10 Lewington and Orpwood, *Overdue Assignment*, 50–1.

11 Amanda Cooper and Ben Levin, "Some Canadian Contributions to Knowledge Mobilization," *Evidence & Policy* 6, no. 3 (2010): 351–69.

12 Dennis Raphael, "Accountability and Educational Philosophy: Paradigms and Conflict in Ontario Education," *Canadian Journal of Education* 18, no. 1 (1993): 30.

13 Jim Dueck, *Education's Flashpoints: Upside Down or Set-Up to Fail* (Lanham, MD: Rowman & Littlefield, 2015), 92–117.

14 Zwaagstra et al., *What's Wrong with Our Schools*, 157–64.

15 R.D. Gidney, *From Hope to Harris: The Reshaping of Ontario's Schools* (Toronto: University of Toronto Press, 1999), 185.

16 Lewington and Orpwood, *Overdue Assignment*, 3.

17 See Debbie Pushor, "Parent Engagement: Creating a Shared World," research paper (Toronto: Ontario Education Research Symposium, 18–20 January 2007).

18 See Doug Hart and Arlo Kempf, *Public Attitudes Toward Education in Ontario 2018: The 20th OISE Survey of Educational Issues* (Toronto: University of Toronto / Ontario Institute for Studies in Education, June 2018), 2, 7–13.

19 Lewington and Orpwood, *Overdue Assignment*, 6.

20 Zander Sherman, *The Curiosity of School: Education and the Dark Side of Enlightenment* (Toronto: Viking Canada, 2012), 268–9, 332.

21 Lewington and Orpwood, *Overdue Assignment*, 9.

22 Canadian Education Association, *Teaching the Way We Aspire to Teach; Now and in the Future* (Toronto: Canadian Education Association and the Canadian Teachers Federation, 2012), 3, 23–4.

23 See Angela MacLeod and Sazid Hasan, *Where Our Students Are Educated: Measuring Student Enrolment in Canada – 2017* (Vancouver, BC: Barbara Mitchell Centre, Fraser Institute, June 2017), 3, 6, 7, 15.

24 Michael Corbett, "From Shinjuku to River John: The Neoliberal Juggernaut, Efficiency, and Small Rural Schools," *Alberta Journal of Educational Research* 60, no. 4 (Winter 2014): 620.

25 Toronto District School Board, "About Us," 2016, http://www.tdsb.on.ca/About-Us (accessed 19 December 2019).

26 Kristin Rushowy, "Could Possible Shakeup Break Up the TDSB?" *The Toronto Star*, 12 January 2015.

27 Stephen Maher, "There Are Two Doug Fords. Which One Will Govern?" *Maclean's*, 7 June 2018.

28 See Ontario PC Party Platform 2018, "Plan for the People." The "promise package" was posted online at https://www.ontariopc.ca/plan_for_the_people (accessed 4 December 2019).

29 Jeffrey Simpson, "How Ontario Became Ford Nation," *The Globe and Mail*, 8 June 2018.

30 Ontario PC Party Platform 2018, "Plan for the People," section on "Education."

31 J. Paul Grayson, James Côté, Liang Chen, Robert Kennedy, and Sharon Roberts, *Academic Skill Deficiencies in Four Ontario Universities: A Call to Action* (Toronto: York University, April 2019), https://skillsforuniversitysuccess.info.yorku.ca/files/2019/04/04-26-2019-AcademicSkills.pdf. See also Barbara Kay, "Universities Shine a Light on Ontario's Failing Schools," *National Post*, 1 May 2019.

32 James E. Côté and Anton L. Allahar, *Ivory Tower Blues: A University System in Crisis* (Toronto: University of Toronto Press, 2007), 19–30.

33 Lewington and Orpwood, *Overdue Assignment*, 27.

34 See Theme Issue, "Small Rural Schools," *Alberta Journal of Educational Research* 60, no. 4 (Winter 2014); and Paul W. Bennett, *The Last Stand: Schools, Communities and the Future of Rural Nova Scotia* (Halifax: Fernwood Publishing, 2013).

35 Paul W. Bennett, "Alberta Gov't Putting Spin on Survey Results," *The Edmonton Journal*, 11 April 2017; Nova Scotia, *Disrupting the Status Quo: Nova Scotians Demand a Better Future for Every Student*, Report of the Minister's Panel on Education, Myra Freeman, Chair (Halifax: DOEECD, October 2014), 1–2.

CHAPTER TWO

1 Paul W. Bennett, *Vanishing Schools, Threatened Communities: The Contested Schoolhouse in Maritime Canada, 1850–2010* (Halifax and

Winnipeg: Fernwood Publishing, 2011), 9. See also Kristen Jane Green, "The Macdonald Robertson Movement 1899–1909," PhD thesis (Vancouver, BC: University of British Columbia, Educational Studies, 2003), 16–17, 26–34, 145–6.

2 Jon Young, Benjamin Levin, and Dawn Wallin, *Understanding Canadian Schools: An Introduction to Educational Administration*, 4th ed. (Scarborough, ON: Nelson, 2006), ch. 2.

3 Bennett, *Vanishing Schools, Threatened Communities*, 10, 54–5, 111–12, 117–21, 177.

4 Paul W. Bennett, "Consolidation, Bureaucracy and the Public Schools: The Formation of the Modern Bureaucratic Education State, 1920–1993," *Canadian Issues / Thèmes canadiens* (Spring 2014): 16–22.

5 Ian McKay, "The Liberal Order Framework: A Prospectus for the Reconnaissance of Canadian History," *Canadian Historical Review* 81 (2000): 617–45.

6 Earlier versions of this chapter were presented at the Canadian Society for the Study of Education (CSSE) Conference, 26 May 2014, at the Canadian Congress of Humanities and Social Sciences, Brock University, St Catharines, ON; and at the Association for Canadian Studies in the United States (ACSUS) Biennial Conference, October 2015, in Las Vegas, NV.

7 Ontario Royal Commission on Learning, *For the Love of Learning*, Report of the Royal Commission on Learning (Toronto: Queen's Printer, 1995). See also Dennis Raphael, "Accountability and Educational Philosophy: Paradigms and Conflict in Ontario Education," *Canadian Journal of Education* 18, no. 1 (1993): 29–35, 42; and Alberta Education, "Restructuring and Refinancing Education" (Edmonton: Alberta Education, February 1995), 12.

8 Robert S. Patterson, "Society and Education during the Wars and Their Interlude," in J. Donald Wilson, Robert M. Stamp, and Louis-Philippe Audet, eds., *Canadian Education: A History* (Scarborough, ON: Prentice-Hall of Canada, 1970), 368–9.

9 Patterson, "Society and Education," 369–70; Hugh A. Stevenson, "Developing Public Education in Post-War Canada to 1960," in Wilson et al., *Canadian Education*, 387–8.

10 Jack K. Masson and Edward C. LeSage, *Alberta's Local Governments: Politics and Democracy* (Edmonton: University of Alberta Press, 1994), 103–10. A poster exhibited at the 1936 Consolidation College attempted to show the benefits of the new system of consolidation for "country children" (Public Archives of Alberta, Photo Collection, A 7065).

11 Bennett, *Vanishing Schools, Threatened Communities*, 48–56.

12 John M. Paton, *The Role of Teachers' Organizations in Canadian Education* (Toronto: W.J. Gage, 1962), 2, 34; John H. Hardy, *Teachers' Organizations in Ontario: An Historical Account of Their Past in Ontario Educational Development, and Their Influence on the Teacher and Teaching, 1840–1938* (Toronto: University of Toronto, 1939), 43. See also Barbara Richter, *It's Elementary: A Brief History of Ontario's Public Elementary Teachers and Their Federations, Part 2: Early 1800s to 1944* (Toronto: Ontario Elementary Teachers' Federation of Ontario, December 2006), 4.

13 Richter, *It's Elementary, Part 2*, 4. On the origin of the OSSTF, see "Courage – The Formation of OSSTF/FEESO in 1919," Historical Vignette, *100 Years Strong 1919–2019* Series (Toronto: OSSTF, 2019), https://www.osstf.on.ca/news/100-years-strong/historical-vignettes/courage_the-formation-of-osstf-feeso-in-1919.aspx (accessed 11 July 2019).

14 Canadian Teachers' Federation, "History of CTF," https://www.ctf-fce.ca/en/Pages/About/History-of-CTF.aspx (accessed 11 July 2019).

15 Doris French, *High Button Bootstraps* (Toronto: Ryerson Press, 1968), 53, 105; Richter, *It's Elementary, Part 2*, 7–8. See also Robert Thomas Dixon, *Be a Teacher: A History of the Ontario English Catholic Teachers' Association 1944–1994* (Toronto: OECTA, 1994), 12.

16 A.O. Aalborg, "New Year's Message, 1960," cited in Aalborg, "The History of Teacher Education in Alberta," *The ATA Magazine* 44, no. 3 (1963): 26–30.

17 Alberta Teachers Association, "About the ATA/History," https://www.teachers.ab.ca/About%20the%20ATA/WhoWeAre/History/Pages/History.aspx (accessed 28 June 2019).

18 See, for example, E.L. Morphet., R.L. Johns, and T.L. Reller, *Educational Organization and Administration* (Englewood Cliffs, NJ: Prentice Hall, 1967), 269–71.

19 Atlantic Development Board, *Profiles in Education in the Atlantic Provinces*, Background Study No. 5 (Ottawa: Atlantic Development Board, 1969), 240–3. Reprinted in Douglas Lawr and Robert Gidney, eds., *Educating Canadians: A Documentary History of Public Education* (Toronto: Van Nostrand Reinhold Ltd, 1973), 250–1.

20 Manitoba Historical Society, "Memorable Manitobans: Wesley Crawford Lorimer (1913–2010)," http://www.mhs.ca (accessed 21 January 2018).

21 George E. Flower, *How Big Is Too Big? Problems of Organization and Size in Local School Systems* (Toronto: W.J. Gage Limited, 1964).

22 George E. Flower, "Local Government and Education," *Nova Scotia Journal of Education* (December 1967): 6–11.

23 John K. Galbraith, *The New Industrial State* (Boston, MA: Houghton Mifflin, 1967).

24 Jim McNiven, "The Impact of School Reorganization on Rural Lifestyles," in Eric Ricker, ed., *Educational Development in Atlantic Canada* (Halifax: Dalhousie Department of Education, 1978).

25 Robin S. Harris, *Quiet Evolution: A Study of the Education System of Ontario* (Toronto: University of Toronto Press, 1967).

26 R.D. Gidney, *From Hope to Harris: The Reshaping of Ontario's Schools* (Toronto: University of Toronto Press, 1999), 37–53.

27 Bennett, *Vanishing Schools, Threatened Communities*, 114.

28 Robert M. Stamp, "Government and Education in Post-War Canada," in Wilson et al., *Canadian Education*, 449–50.

29 "Nova Scotia's Comprehensive School System," *Journal of Education* (October 1966): 17–21; "Amalgamation of School Boards," *Journal of Education* (May 1970): 10–19.

30 Bennett, *Vanishing Schools, Threatened Communities*, 115.

31 Edward MacDonald, *If You're Stronghearted: Prince Edward Island in the Twentieth Century* (Charlottetown: Prince Edward Island Museum and Heritage Foundation, 2000), 271–2.

32 Verner Smitheram, "Development and the Debate over School Consolidation," in *The Garden Transformed: Prince Edward Island, 1945–1980* (Charlottetown: Ragweed Press, 1982), 185–200.

33 MacDonald, *If You're Stronghearted*, 272.

34 Norman Henchey, "Quebec Education: The Unfinished Revolution," *McGill Journal of Education* 7 (1972): 7, 95–118. See also Henry Milner, *The Long Road to Reform: Restructuring Education in Quebec* (Montreal, QC: McGill-Queen's University Press, 1986).

35 Frère Untel, *The Impertinences of Brother Anonymous* (Montreal, QC: Harvest House, 1962).

36 Ibid., 23, 28–36, 47, 61, 63, 121.

37 D.A. Burgess, "Reorganizing the School System in Quebec," *Education Canada* 22, no. 4 (1982): 12–16, 21.

38 William J. Smith, *Themes and Traditions in Quebec Education: A Sourcebook for Educators* (Montreal, QC: McGill University Office of Research on Education Policy, 1995), 41–60.

39 Henchey, "Quebec Education," 102.

40 Joan M. Payzant, *Second to None: A History of Public Education in Dartmouth, Nova Scotia* (Dartmouth, NS: Dartmouth Historical Association, 1991), 94–105.

41 Bennett, *Vanishing Schools, Threatened Communities*, 117.

42 Peter McCreath, "Current Developments in Education in Atlantic Canada," in Douglas Meyers, ed., *The Failure of Educational Reform in Canada* (Toronto: McClelland and Stewart, 1973), 168–9.

43 Michael B. Katz, "Class, Bureaucracy and Schools," in Myers, ed., *The Failure of Educational Reform*, 15–28.

44 See Willard Brehaut, "Trends in the History of Ontario Education," in Hugh Oliver, Mark Holmes, and Ian Winchester, eds., *The House that Ryerson Built: Essays in Education to Mark Ontario's Bicentennial* (Toronto: OISE Press, 1984), 7–18.

45 Katz, "Class, Bureaucracy and Schools," 15–28.

46 Jean Cochrane, "The Ontario School House," in Oliver et al., eds., *The House that Ryerson Built*, 19, 28–9; Fred G. Barrett, *Rural Schools of Annapolis County, Vol. I and II: The One Room School Was an Institution* (Bridgetown, NS: Valley Seniors in Sight and Sound, 1993), 87–9.

47 Richard Wilbur, "Education in the Robichaud Era," *The Mysterious East* (September 1970): 4–8.

48 Dorothy Elderkin Lawrence, ed., *Tales Told Out of School* (Liverpool, NS: Retired Teachers' Association, Nova Scotia Teachers Union, 1995), Preface and 57.

49 Berton Robinson and John Cook, *Nova Scotia: Three Hundred Years in Education* (Halifax: Nova Scotia Teachers Union, 1968).

50 William B. Hamilton, *A Guide to Public Education in Nova Scotia* (Halifax: Atlantic Institute of Education, 1979).

51 Thomas Fleming and B. Hutton, "School Boards, District Consolidation, and Educational Governance in British Columbia, 1872–1995," *Canadian Journal of Educational Administration and Policy* 10 (14 January 1997).

52 Stan Persky, *Son of Socred* (Vancouver, BC: North Star Books, 1979), 138.

53 British Columbia Provincial School Review Committee, *Let's Talk About Schools: A Report to the Minister of Education and the People of British Columbia* (Victoria: Queen's Printer, 1985), 8; British Columbia Royal Commission on Education, *A Legacy for Learners* (Victoria: Queen's Printer, 1988), 10, 261.

54 Yvonne M. Martin, "Parental Participation Policy for Schools: A Comparative Legislative Analysis of Reform and Dynamic Conservatism in British Columbia, Alberta, and Quebec," in Yvonne Martin and R.J.S. MacPherson, eds., *Restructuring Administrative Policy in Public Schooling* (Calgary, AB: Detselig, 1993), 128; Royal Commission of Inquiry into the Delivery of Programs and Services in Primary, Elementary, Secondary Education, *Our Children Our Future: Summary Report* (St John's: Government of Newfoundland and Labrador, 1992), 11.

55 Ontario Royal Commission on Learning, *For the Love of Learning* (Report of the Royal Commission on Learning), 50; Alberta Education, "Restructuring and Refinancing Education" (Edmonton: Alberta Education, February 1995), 12.

56 Martin, "Parental Participation Policy for Schools," 130–1; "School Councils Signal Shift in Power Structure," *Canadian Principal* 6, no. 5 (1995): 1–4; Michael Fullan and Joanne Quinn, "School Councils – Non-event or Capacity Building for Reform?" *Orbit* 27, no. 4 (1996): 2–5.

57 See Tino Bordinaro and William J. Smith, *Themes and Traditions in Quebec Education* (Montreal, QC: Office of Research on Education Policy, McGill University, 1995), 89.

58 Gary J. Anderson and Janyne M. Rahming, "The Education Project: From Policy to Practice," *McGill Journal of Education* 18, no. 2 (Spring 1982): 94–5, 101–3.

59 Norman Henchey and Donald A. Burgess, *Between Past and Future: Quebec Education in Transition* (Calgary, AB: Detselig, 1987), 82.

60 Rosalind Zinman, "Developments and Directions in Multicultural/Intercultural Education, 1980–1990, The Province of Quebec," *Canadian Ethnic Studies* XXXIII, no. 2 (1991): 65–76.

61 Gidney, *From Hope to Harris*, 221–2.

62 Raphael, "Accountability and Educational Philosophy: Paradigms and Conflict in Ontario Education," 29–35, 42.

63 See Jennifer Lewington and Graham Orpwood, *Overdue Assignment: Taking Responsibility for Canada's Schools* (Toronto: John Wiley and Sons, 1993); and Stephen B. Lawton, Joseph Freedman, and Heather-Jane Robertson, *Busting Bureaucracy to Reclaim Our Schools* (Montreal, QC: Institute for Research on Public Policy, 1995). For a more conventional interpretation, see Gidney, *From Hope to Harris*, 221–4; and Ken Osborne, *Education: A Guide to the Canadian School Debate – or Who Wants What and Why?* (Toronto: Penguin / McGill Institute Book, 1999), 14–15.

64 Andrew Nikiforuk, *School's Out: The Catastrophe in Public Education and What We Can Do About It* (Toronto: MacFarlane Walter Ross, 1993); William Robson, *Could Do Better: What's Wrong with Public Education in Ontario – and How to Fix It* (Toronto: Coalition for Education Reform, 1994).

65 Quebec Ministry of Education, *Joining Forces: Plan of Action on Educational Success* (Quebec: MEQ, 1992), 23–32; Smith, *Themes and Traditions in Quebec Education*, 91–4.

66 Quebec Ministry of Education, *Moving Ahead* (Quebec: MEQ, 1993), as cited in Smith, *Themes and Traditions in Quebec Education*, 97–9.
67 Brian O'Sullivan, "Global Change and Educational Reform in Ontario and Canada," *Canadian Journal of Education* 24, no. 3 (1999): 315–19.
68 See Peter Clancy, "Public and Post-Secondary Education: Structural Changes and Embedded Clienteles," in Peter Clancy, James Bickerton, James Haddow, and Ian Stewart, eds., *The Savage Years* (Halifax: Formac Publishers, 2000), 140–2, 152–7. See also Nova Scotia Department of Education, *Restructuring Nova Scotia's Education System: Preparing All Students for a Lifetime of Learning* (Halifax: NSDE, 1994).

CHAPTER THREE

1 The whole saga of Maureen Somers-Beebe and Parents for Education is reconstructed in Andrew Nikiforuk, *School's Out: The Catastrophe in Public Education and What to Do about It* (Toronto: Macfarlane, Walter and Ross, 1993), 19–21.
2 See Carol Copple, *Developmentally Appropriate Practice in Early Childhood Programs* (Washington, DC: NAEYC, 1987), a popular guide produced for the National Association for the Education of Young Children (NAEYC) and widely used by Primary Division teachers in the early 1990s.
3 Andrew Nikiforuk, *If Learning Is So Natural, Why Am I Going to School? A Parent's Guide* (Toronto: Penguin Books, 1994).
4 Nikiforuk, *School's Out*, 22.
5 See Garrett Harden, "Tragedy of the Commons," *Science* 182 (1968): 1243–8. See also Garrett Harden and John Baden, eds., *Managing the Commons* (San Francisco, CA: W.H. Freeman, 1977).
6 Nikiforuk, *School's Out*, 82.
7 Theodore R. Sizer, *Horace's Compromise: The Dilemma of the American High School* (Boston, MA: Houghton Mifflin Company, 1984), 20–1. See also James Traub, "Sizers Hope," *The New York Times*, 2 August 1996, for an explanation of the "conspiracy of the least."
8 Nikiforuk, *If Learning Is So Natural*, 289–90.
9 Ibid., 8–9.
10 William Robson, *Could Do Better: What's Wrong with Public Education in Ontario and How to Fix It* (Toronto: The Coalition for Education Reform, 1994), 1–2, 5–34.
11 Ibid., and the sequel, *Could Still Do Better!* (Toronto: CER, August 1999).

12 Jennifer Lewington and Graham Orpwood, *Overdue Assignment* (Toronto: John Wiley & Sons, 1993), 123.

13 Robson, *Could Do Better*, 35–53.

14 Lewington and Orpwood, *Overdue Assignment*, 127.

15 See, for example, Harold Stephenson and James Stigler, *The Learning Gap* (New York: Summit Books, 1992); and Alberta Chamber of Resources, *International Comparisons in Education – Curriculum, Values and Lessons* (Edmonton: Chamber of Resources, 1991).

16 Peter C. Emberley and Waller R. Newell, *Bankrupt Education: The Decline of Liberal Education in Canada* (Toronto: University of Toronto Press, 1994), 30–50.

17 See Gerald Grant, "The World We Created at Hamilton High," *Surface/ University of Syracuse Magazine* (September 1988): 30–3.

18 Nikiforuk, *School's Out*, 58–9.

19 Denis Cassivi, *Education and the Cult of Modernism: A Personal Observation* (Sydney, NS: Angeline Press, 1981).

20 R.D. Gidney, *From Hope to Harris: The Reshaping of Ontario's Schools* (Toronto: University of Toronto Press, 1999), 224.

21 See Peter Clancy, James Bickerton, Rodney Haddow, and Ian Stewart, eds., *The Savage Years: The Perils of Reinventing Government in Nova Scotia* (Halifax: Formac Publishing, 2000).

22 Peter Clancy, "Nova Scotia: Fiscal Crisis and Party System Transition," in Bryan M. Evans and Charles E. Smith, eds., *Transforming Provincial Politics: The Political Economy of Canada's Provinces and Territories in the Neoliberal Era* (Toronto: University of Toronto Press, 2015), 77–109.

23 See John Ibbitson, *Promised Land: Inside the Mike Harris Revolution* (Scarborough, ON: Prentice-Hall Canada, 1997); and Sid Noel, ed., *Revolution at Queen's Park: Essays on Governing Ontario* (Toronto: James Lorimer, 1997).

24 Gidney, *From Hope to Harris*, 234–5.

25 *The Globe and Mail*, 16 and 23 August 1995, cited in Gidney, *From Hope to Harris*, 236.

26 See Bill 30, *An Act to Establish the Education Quality and Accountability Office*, Chapter 11 (Statutes of Ontario, 1996).

27 See Bill 31, *An Act to Establish the Ontario College of Teachers*, Chapter 12 (Statutes of Ontario, 1996); and Ontario College of Teachers, *Professionally Speaking* newsletter, September 1995 to December 1996.

28 Ontario Ministry of Education, *School Councils: A Guide for Members, 2001, Revised 2002* (Toronto: MOE, 2002), 2.1–2.2.

29 Gidney, *From Hope to Harris*, 244–7, 257–64.

30 Joe Freedman, *Failing Grades: Canadian Schooling in a Global Economy* (Red Deer, AB: Society for Advancing Educational Research, 1993).
31 See Alison Taylor, *The Politics of Educational Reform in Alberta* (Toronto: University of Toronto Press, 2001).
32 Joe Freedman, *The Charter School Idea: Breaking Educational Gridlock* (Red Deer, AB: Society for Advancing Educational Research, 1995).
33 Shawna Ritchie, *Innovation in Action: An Examination of Charter Schools in Alberta* (Calgary, AB: Canada West Foundation, January 2010), 1–6.
34 Larry Kuehn, "The Globalization of Education: Implications for Canada," in Ed Finn, ed., *Canada After Harper* (Toronto: Lorimer Publishers, 2015), 218–19.
35 Neil Selwyn, *Distrusting Educational Technology: Critical Questions for Changing Times* (New York: Routledge, 2014), 27. For a recent historical analysis of the incursion of commercialism into Canadian schools, see Catherine Gidney, *Captive Audience: How Corporations Invaded Our Schools* (Toronto: Between the Lines, 2019).
36 See Maude Barlow and Heather-Jane Robertson, *Class Warfare: The Assault on Canada's Schools* (Toronto: Key Porter Books, 1994).
37 See Stephen Ball, "Voices / Political Networks and a Global Neoliberal Curriculum," *ATA Magazine* 93, no. 4 (2009).
38 Jason Clemens, Milagros Palacios, Jane Loyer, and Frazier Fathers, *Measuring School Choice and Competition in Canadian Education* (Vancouver, BC: Fraser Institute, February 2014), 1–2.
39 Paul Cappon, *What Is the Future of Learning in Canada?: Final Report of the Canadian Council on Learning* (Ottawa: CCL, 2011); Anne-Marie Tobin, "Canadian Council On Learning Report: Students Falling Behind International Peers, National Body Needed," *HuffPost*, 11 October 2011, http://www.huffingtonpost.ca/2011/10/11/canadian-council-on-learning-report_n_1004449.html.
40 Kuehn, "The Globalization of Education," 222–3.
41 Donald Gutstein, "Pearson's Plan to Control Education: Report to the BC Teachers' Federation" (Vancouver, BC: BCTF, 30 June 2012), 1–2.
42 C21 Canada, *Shifting Minds: A 21st Century Vision of Public Education for Canada*, May 2012, http://www.c21canada.org/wp-content/uploads/2012/11/Shifting-Minds-Revised.pdf (accessed 6 December 2019).
43 Paul W. Bennett, "Digital Learning in Canadian K–12 Schools: A Review of Critical Issues, Policy and Practice," in Ann Marcus-Quinn and Triona Hourgan, eds., *Handbook on Digital Learning for K–12 Schools* (Basle, Switzerland: Springer International, 2017), 295.

44 Ibid., 295–6.

45 Ibid., 297, 302.

46 See Phil McRae, "Rebirth of the Teaching Machine," ATA *Magazine* 3, no. 4 (2009).

47 See, for example, Nova Scotia, Council to Improve Classroom Conditions, *Report of the Council to Improve Classroom Conditions* (Halifax: Nova Scotia Education and NSTU, 28 April 2017), 1–2, 15–18, 25–6.

48 Kuehn, "The Globalization of Education," 230–1.

CHAPTER FOUR

1 Sir Ken Robinson is the best-known contemporary critic of the so-called "factory model" in North American public education. See, for example, *Bring On the Learning Revolution!* (TED Talk, 2010), https://www.youtube.com/watch?v=r9LeIXa3U_I (accessed 8 January 2020).

2 The most effective and sustained recent critique of the repetitive, self-defeating cycle of education reform is Frederick M. Hess, *The Same Thing Over and Over: How School Reformers Get Stuck in Yesterday's Ideas* (Cambridge, MA: Harvard University Press, 2010). See also American expert on teaching machines Audrey Watters, curator of HackEducation.com, on the history of attempts to automate teaching and its most recent iteration, Pearson Education's "personalized learning" initiative: http://books.audreywatters.com (accessed 8 December 2019).

3 See Larry Cuban, *Inside the Black Box of Classroom Practice: Change without Reform in American Education* (Cambridge, MA: Harvard Education Press, 2013); and David Tyack and Larry Cuban, *Tinkering toward Utopia: A Century of Public School Reform* (Boston, MA: Harvard University Press, 1997).

4 L. Gulick and L. Urwick, eds., *Papers on the Science of Administration* (New York: Institute of Public Administration, 1937), cited in Craig Howley, Jerry Johnson, and Jennifer Petrie, *Consolidation of Schools and Districts: What the Research Says and What It Means* (Boulder, CO: National Education Policy Center, February 2011), 3.

5 A.C. Ornstein, "School Consolidation vs. Centralization: Trends, Issues, and Questions," *Urban Review* 25, no. 2 (1993): 167–74; L.G. Bjork and J. Blasé, "The Micropolitics of School District Decentralization," *Educational Assessment, Evaluation and Accountability* 21, no. 3 (2009): 195–208.

6 D. Brasington, "Size and School District Consolidation: Do Opposites Attract?" *Economica* 70 (2003): 673–90.

7 Anthony H. Normore, "The Edge of Chaos: School Administrators and Accountability," *Journal of Educational Administration* 42, no. 1 (2004): 56–77.
8 Lorna Earl, "Assessment and Accountability," *Orbit* 29, no. 1 (1998): 23–8. See also Kenneth Leithwood and Lorna Earl, "Educational Accountability Effects: An International Perspective," *Peabody Journal of Education* 75, no. 4 (2000): 1–8.
9 See Barbara Kohm and Beverly Nance, *Principals Who Learn: Asking the Right Questions, Seeking the Best Solutions* (Alexandria, VA: ASCD, 2007), ch. 10. See also Tina M. Trujillo, "The Disproportionate Erosion of Local Control: Urban School Boards, High Stakes Accountability, and Democracy," *Educational Policy* 27, no. 2 (March–April 2013): 334–59.
10 William Duncombe and John Yinger, "The Benefits and Costs of School District Consolidation: What Recent Research Reveals about Potential Cost Savings," *The School Administrator* 67, no. 5 (May 2010): 10–17.
11 Paul W. Bennett, *Vanishing Schools, Threatened Communities: The Contested Schoolhouse in Maritime Canada* (Halifax: Fernwood Publishing, 2011); Michael Corbett, "From Shinjuku to River John: The Neoliberal Juggernaut, Efficiency, and Small Rural Schools," *Alberta Journal of Educational Research* 60, no. 4 (Winter 2014): 619–28.
12 Gerald Galway, Bruce Sheppard, John Wiens, and Jean Brown, "The Impact of Centralization on Local School District Governance in Canada," *Canadian Journal of Educational Administration and Policy* no. 145 (18 September 2013).
13 Prince Edward Island, Education Governance Commission, *Charting the Way: A Discussion Paper* (Charlottetown: PEI Education Governance, October 2011).
14 William Duncombe and John Yinger, "Does School Consolidation Cut Costs?" working papers (Syracuse, NY: Syracuse University, 2005 and 2007). Updated and published in *Education Finance and Policy*.
15 Duncombe and Yinger, "The Benefits and Costs of School District Consolidation," 13–15.
16 Howley et al., *Consolidation of Schools and Districts*, 9.
17 Duncombe and Yinger, "The Benefits and Costs of School District Consolidation," 15–17.
18 Howley et al., *Consolidation of Schools and Districts*, 12.
19 See Bennett, *Vanishing Schools, Threatened Communities*, 1, 117–21, 169–81; and Paul W. Bennett, "The Triumph of the Modern *Bureaucratic Education State* 1920–1993," Association for Canadian Studies, *Canadian Issues* (Spring 2014): 16–22.

20 Paul W. Bennett, "School Consolidation in Maritime Canada: The Educational Legacy of Edgar L. Morphet and His Disciples," *Country School Journal* 5 (2017): 31–47.

21 Stuart Grauer and Christina Ryan, "Small Schools: The Myths, Reality and Potential of Small Schools," *Community Works Journal*, 5 December 2016, https://medium.com/communityworksjournal/small-schools-the-myths-reality-and-potential-of-small-schools-76a566c42f6e (accessed 8 January 2020). See also The Rural School and Community Trust, "School Size: Research Based Conclusions" (Arlington, VA: The Rural School and Community Trust, 2003), https://www.ruraledu.org/user_uploads/file/schoolsize.pdf (accessed 8 January 2020).

22 James Conant, *The American High School Today* (New York: McGraw Hill, 1959).

23 Lorna Jimerson, *The Hobbit Effect: Why Small Works in Public Schools* (Washington, DC: Rural School and Community Trust, August 2006).

24 Barbara Kent Lawrence et al., *Dollars & Sense: The Cost Effectiveness of Small Schools* (Cincinnati, OH: Knowledge Works Foundation, 2002).

25 Craig B. Howley, "Don't Supersize Me: The Relationship of Construction Cost to School Enrollment in the U.S.," *Educational Planning* 17, no. 2 (2008): 23–40, http://isep.info/wp-content/uploads/2015/03/17-2_3Dont SupersizeMe.pdf (accessed 8 January 2020).

26 Thomas Toch, "Small Is Still Beautiful," *Washington Monthly* (July/August 2010), https://hechingerreport.org/small-schools-are-still-beautiful/ (accessed 8 January 2020).

27 Betsy Hammond, "Portland, Oregon: All the Advantages and Nothing to Show for It," *Washington Monthly* (July/August 2010), A13–A15, https://www.issuelab.org/resources/9283/9283.pdf (accessed 8 January 2020).

28 Valerie E. Lee and Julia B. Smith, *Restructuring High Schools for Equity and Excellence* (New York: Teachers College Press, 2001), 157.

29 Sarah Garland, "New York City: Big Gains in the Big Apple," *Washington Monthly* (July/August 2010), https://hechingerreport.org/new-york-city-big-gains-in-the-big-apple/ (accessed 8 January 2020).

30 Toch, "Small Is Still Beautiful."

31 Barbara Kent Lawrence et al., *Dollars & Sense II: Lessons from Good, Cost-Effective Small Schools* (Cincinnati, OH: Knowledge Works Foundation, 2005).

32 Toch, "Small Is Still Beautiful."

33 Robert D. Putnam, *Bowling Alone: The Collapse and Revival of American Community* (New York: Touchstone Books, 2001), 26–7, 187–8, 404–6.

34 *CBC News Calgary*, "School Board Starts Move into New Building,"
2 March 2011; Brian Labby, "Calgary Board of Education Pays 'Absurd'
Rent for Admin Building under Secret Contract," *CBC News Calgary*,
3 October 2017.

35 See Samantha Craggs, "Work in Progress on Hamilton's New Education
Centre," *CBC News Hamilton*, 9 April 2013; Ryan McGreal, "Crestwood
Plan: Bad Decision Based on a Flawed Process," *Raise the Hammer*,
14 February 2012, https://www.raisethehammer.org/article/1542/crestwood_
plan:_bad_decision_based_on_a_flawed_process; and Paul W. Bennett,
"Edifices and Students: The Halifax Board's Move to Costly New
Headquarters," *Halifax Magazine* (September 2010).

36 *CBC News Calgary*, "School Board's New Home Called Too Costly,"
28 September 2010; Labby, "Calgary Board of Education Pays 'Absurd'
Rent."

37 Ryan Rumbolt, "Provincial Audit Finds CBE Made $9.1M Mistake,"
Calgary Herald, 6 April 2018.

38 Avis Glaze, *Raise the Bar: A Coherent and Responsive Education
Administrative System for Nova Scotia* (Halifax: Nova Scotia Department
of Education and Early Childhood Development, January 2018), 10, 18,
31. See also Jack Julian, "Top 38 School Board Admins Earned Almost
$5M – but Dissolution 'Not about Savings,'" *CBC News Nova Scotia*,
26 January 2018.

39 Anna Yeatman, *Bureaucrats, Technocrats, Femocrats: Essays on the
Contemporary Australian State* (Sydney, NSW: Allen and Unwin, 1990);
P. O'Brien and B. Down, "What Are Teachers Saying about the New
Managerialism?" *Journal of Educational Inquiry* 3, no. 1 (2002): 111–33;
Janet Newman, "Bending Bureaucracy: Leadership and Multi-level
Governance," in P. Du Gay, ed., *The Values of Bureaucracy* (Oxford, UK:
Oxford University Press, 2005), 191–211.

40 Bruce Johnson, "Local School Micropolitical Agency: An Antidote to the
New Managerialism," *Hawke Research Institute, Working Paper Series,
No. 26* (Magill, SA: University of South Australia, 2004).

41 Kathleen Lynch, "New Managerialism: The Impact on Education,"
Concept 5, no. 3 (Winter 2014): 5–6.

42 Charles Ungerleider, *Failing Our Kids: How We Are Ruining Our Public
Schools* (Toronto: McClelland and Stewart, 2003), 238–54.

43 Ibid., 221–2.

44 Heinz-Deiter Meyer, "The New Managerialism in Education Management:
Corporatization or Organizational Learning?" *Journal of Educational
Administration* 40, no. 6 (2002): 534–49.

45 Michael Corbett, "The Edumometer: The Commodification of Learning from Galton to the PISA," *Journal for Critical Education Policy Studies* 6, no. 1 (2008).

46 Michael Corbett and Ann Vibert, "Mediating Plastic Literacies and Placeless Governmentalities: Returning to Corporeal Rurality," in B. Green and M. Corbett, eds., *Rethinking Rural Literacies* (New York: Palgrave Macmillan, 2013).

47 Michael Corbett, "Rural Futures: Development, Aspirations, Mobilities, Place, and Education," *Peabody Journal of Education* 91, no. 2 (2016): 270–82.

48 Michael Corbett, "We Have Never Been Urban: Modernization, Small Schools, and Resilient Rurality in Atlantic Canada," *The Journal of Rural and Community Development* 9, no. 3 (2014): 186–202.

49 David A. Gruenewald, "Foundations of Place: A Multidisciplinary Framework for Place Conscious Education," *American Educational Research Journal* 40, no. 3 (2003): 619–54; Michael Corbett, *Learning to Leave: The Irony of Schooling in a Coastal Community* (Halifax: Fernwood Publishing, 2008), 272–3.

50 Michael Corbett, "Rural Education: Some Sociological Provocations for the Field," *Australian and International Journal of Rural Education* 25, no. 3 (2015): 9–25.

51 Lynch, "New Managerialism," 7–8.

52 Ben Williamson, "Governing Software: Networks, Databases and Algorithmic Power in the Digital Governance of Public Education," *Learning, Media and Technology* 40, no. 1 (2015): 83–105.

CHAPTER FIVE

1 See Aimee Howley and Craig Howley, "Rural School Busing," ERIC *Digest*, ED459969, 2001-12-00 (December 2001): 1–2.

2 *The Magic School Bus*, PBS Kids / Scholastic Entertainment, 10 September 1994 – 6 December 1997, 52 episodes, 25 minutes each, based upon the original Scholastic book series of the same name by Joanna Cole and Bruce Degen, and the sequel *The Magic School Bus Rides Again*, Netflix, 29 September 2017 – 13 April 2018, 39 episodes, 25 minutes each. See also Michael Corbett, "We Have Never Been Urban; Modernization, Small Schools, and Resilient Rurality in Atlantic Canada," *Journal of Rural and Community Development* 9, no. 3 (2014): 186–7, 194–5.

3 Paul W. Bennett and Derek M. Gillis, *Education on Wheels: Seizing Cost and Energy Efficiency Opportunities in Student Transportation* (Halifax: AIMS, January 2015).

4 Paul W. Bennett, *The Last Stand: Schools, Communities and the Future of Rural Nova Scotia* (Halifax: Fernwood Publishing, 2013), 29–32.

5 Alberta School Boards Association, *At the Breaking Point: Alberta's Student Transportation System* (Edmonton: ASBA, May 2008), 3.

6 Safe Routes to School National Partnership, *Buses, Boots, Bicycles: Exploring Collaboration between Safe Routes to School and School Busing Professionals to Get Students to School Safely and Healthily* (Oakland, CA: SRSNP, 2014); Jeffrey M. Vincent, Carrie Makarewicz, Ruth Miller, Julia Ehrman, and Deborah L. McKoy, "Beyond the Yellow Bus: Promising Practices in Maximizing Access to Opportunity Through Innovations in Student Transportation" (Berkeley, CA: University of California, Center for Cities + Schools, 2014).

7 National Center for Safe Routes to School, "How Students Get to School: School Travel Patterns from 1969 to 2009" (Chapel Hill, NC: NCSRS, 2011).

8 Bennett and Gillis, *Education on Wheels*, 9.

9 Rolland Cilliers, "Fewer Schools Mean Longer Bus Rides in Rural Ontario," *Almaguin News*, 2 April 2014.

10 Canadian Education Association, *Student Transportation in Canada: Facts and Figures* (Toronto: CEA, 1987)

11 *School Bus Fleet* Magazine, Annual Reports, "Canadian Pupil Transportation Data, 2007 to 2014" (June 2007 to 2014).

12 Bennett and Gillis, *Education on Wheels*, 9, 12–13.

13 Ontario, "Ontario Student Transportation Reform Project Outline" (Toronto: Ministry of Education, Government of Ontario, 2014), http://www.ipac.ca (accessed 29 November 2014).

14 Don Drummond, *Public Services for Ontarians: A Path to Sustainability and Excellence* (Commission on the Reform of Ontario's Public Services), ch. 6: "Elementary and Secondary Education: Encouraging Efficient Student Transportation" (Toronto: Ministry of Finance, 15 February 2012), 220–4.

15 See, for example, *Ministry of Education Effectiveness & Efficiency Review: Student Transportation Services of Waterloo Region*, Phase 3 Review (Toronto: Deloitte, November 2008).

16 Joseph Monteiro and Benjamin Atkinson, "School Bus Transportation in Canada" conference paper, *Proceedings of the Canadian Transportation Research Forum* (Calgary, AB: Mount Royal University, 3–6 June 2012).

17 Bennett and Gillis, *Education on Wheels*, 5, 21.

18 Catherine O'Brien, "Sustainable Happiness and the Trip to School," *World Transportation Policy & Practice* 14, no. 1 (May 2008): 15–16.

19 Craig B. Howley, Aimee A. Howley, and Steven Shamblen, "Riding the School Bus: A Comparison of the Rural and Suburban Experience in

Five States," *Journal of Research in Rural Education* 17, no. 1 (Spring 2001): 41–63.

20 Beth Spence, "Long Bus Rides: Stealing the Joy of Childhood" (Charleston, wv: Challenge West Virginia, 29 February 2000).

21 Michael Fox, "Rural Transportation as a Daily Constraint in Students' Lives," *Rural Educator* 17, no. 2 (1996): 22–7.

22 Y. Lu and T. Tweeten, "The Impact of Busing on Student Achievement," *Growth and Change* 4, no. 4 (1973): 44–6; and "Reply," *Growth and Change* 7, no. 3 (1976): 48–9.

23 Howley and Howley, "Rural School Busing," 3.

24 As a leading expert, Stu Auty was instrumental influencing provincial anti-bullying policy. See Ontario, Safe Schools Action Team, *Shaping Safer Schools: A Bullying Prevention Plan* (Toronto: Ontario Government, November 2005).

25 Erika Tucker, "How Canadian Schools Are Fighting Bullying on the Bus," *Global News*, 13 May 2014.

26 See Belle Zars, "Long Rides, Tough Hides: Enduring Long School Bus Rides," Rural Policy Program, Randolf, vt: ERIC ED 432 419, 1998-00-00.

27 Richard Gilbert and Catherine O'Brien, *Child and Youth-Friendly Land Use and Transportation Planning Guidelines* (Winnipeg: Centre for Sustainable Transportation, University of Winnipeg, 2005), 15, 17.

28 Fully documented in Bennett, *The Last Stand*, 30–1.

29 Robert Strang, "Provincial Transportation Strategy" panel presentation, Annual General Meeting (Truro, ns: Community Transit–Nova Scotia, 4 June 2014).

30 Safe Routes to School National Partnership, *Buses, Boots, Bicycles*, 1; Ecology Action Centre, *Reducing Childhood Obesity by Increasing Opportunities for Active Transportation*, Discussion Brief (Halifax: EAC, November 2011).

31 Halifax Regional Centre for Education (formerly HRSB), "Student Transportation Policy and Policy Procedures. F.005: Operations Services, Approved," 2013.

32 See Ecology Action Centre, "What Do We Do?" Safe Routes Nova Scotia, http://www.saferoutesns.ca (accessed 6 October 2014).

33 Ibid.

34 Bennett and Gillis, *Education on Wheels*, 24–5.

35 The ultimate goals are clearly articulated in Safe Routes to School National Partnership, *Buses, Boots, Bicycles*.

36 Paul W. Bennett, "Education on Wheels: How School Bus Safety Gets Compromised," *The Chronicle Herald* (Halifax), 27 November 2017.

37 Nova Scotia Utility and Review Board, *Decision, in the Matter of the Motor Carrier Act and the Motor Vehicle Transport Act and Stock Transportation*, delivered by Donna J. Ring, QC (Halifax: UARB, 14 November 2017), 21–64, 176–80; Jean Laroche, "After Scathing Report, School Board Chair Says Bus Service Is Safe," CBC *News Nova Scotia*, 16 November 2017; Alexander Quon and Steve Silva, "Stock Transportation Responds after N.S. Regulator Finds It Violated Licenses," *Global News Halifax*, 17 November 2017.

38 Graeme Benjamin, "'It Was a Hot Mess': Bedford Parents Outraged after Students Left Stranded at School," *Global News Halifax*, 5 September 2019; "Education Minister to Review Stock Transportation Bus Performance," CBC *Nova Scotia / Canadian Press*, 6 September 2018.

39 Keith Doucette, "Additional 37 School Buses Will Be Added in Halifax to Improve School Bus Problem," *Star Metro Halifax*, 27 September 2018. See also Paul W. Bennett, "Why More School Buses Are Not the Answer," *The Chronicle Herald* (Halifax), 29 September 2018.

40 Andrew Rankin, "Nova Scotia Government Backs Out of Halifax Bus Contract with Stock Transportation," *The Chronicle Herald* (Halifax), 7 June 2019.

41 Andrew Rankin, "School Bus Questions – Mom: Why Use Stock Another Year?" *The Chronicle Herald* (Halifax), 11 June 2019.

CHAPTER SIX

1 Samuel E. Trosow and Bill Irwin, "It's Time to Merge Ontario's Two School Systems," *The Conversation*, 22 July 2018, https://theconversation.com/its-time-to-merge-ontarios-two-school-systems-99922 (accessed 7 January 2019).

2 Forum Research, "Majority Continue to Oppose Public Funding for Catholic Schools," *The Forum Poll*, 2 March 2016; One School System, http://www.oneschoolsystem.org/ (accessed 7 January 2019). See also CBC *Radio*, The 180, "It's Time to End Public Funding of Catholic Schools," CBC *News*, 18 June 2017.

3 Ryan Flanagan, "Is It Time to Merge the Ontario School Systems?" CTV *News*, 26 July 2018.

4 Terri-Lynn Kay Brennan, "Roman Catholic Schooling in Ontario: Past Struggles, Present Challenges, Future Directions?" *Canadian Journal of Education* 34, no. 4 (2011): 21, 23.

5 See C.B. Sissons, *Church and State in Canadian Education* (Toronto: The Ryerson Press, 1959); and Franklin A. Walker, *Catholic Education and Politics in Upper Canada* (Toronto: J.M. Dent & Sons, 1955).

6 See Robert T. Dixon, "The Ontario Separate School System and Section 93 of the British North America Act" (Toronto: Unpublished Ph.D. dissertation, University of Toronto, 1976); and Mark G. McGowan, "A Short History of Catholic Schools in Ontario" (Toronto: Ontario Catholic School Trustees Association, 2013), 2–3.

7 Robert Dixon, "William Davis and the Road to Completion in Ontario's Catholic High Schools," Canadian Catholic Historical Association, *Historical Studies* 69 (2003): 9.

8 Brennan, "Roman Catholic Schooling in Ontario," 24; Shmuel Shamai, "Jewish Resistance to Christianity in the Ontario Public School System," *Historical Studies in Education* 9, no. 2 (1997): 251–5.

9 Dixon, "William Davis and the Road to Completion," 11, 15.

10 Michael McKee, "Political Competition and the Roman Catholic Schools; Ontario, Canada," *Public Choice* 56, no. 1 (1988): 59–62.

11 Dr Henry B. Mayo, *Report of the Ottawa-Carleton Review Commission* (Toronto: Queen's Printer, 1977), 128–9.

12 Dixon, "William Davis and the Road to Completion," 19.

13 Ibid., 19–20.

14 Department of Justice, *Charterpedia, Section 29 – Denominational Schools* (Ottawa: Department of Justice Canada), https://www.justice.gc.ca/eng/csj-sjc/rfc-dlc/ccrf-ccdl/check/art29.html (accessed 7 January 2019).

15 Franklin Walker, *Catholic Education and Politics in Ontario* (Toronto: Catholic Education Foundation of Ontario, 1986), 3: 375.

16 Dixon, "William Davis and the Road to Completion," 19, 22–3.

17 Ibid., 30–2.

18 Ontario Government, "Notes for a Statement by the Honourable William G. Davis, Premier of Ontario, on Education Policy to the Legislative Assembly of Ontario," 12 June 1984.

19 Ontario Legislative Assembly, Standing Committee on Social Development, *Debates*, 20 September 1985.

20 See Claire Hoy, *Bill Davis: A Biography* (Toronto: Methuen, 1985), 265, 275; and Steve Paikin, *The Life: The Seductive Call of Politics* (Toronto: Penguin/Viking, 2001), 49.

21 Judgements of the Supreme Court of Canada, Reference re; Bill 30, *An Act to Amend the Education Act* (Ont.) Case No. 19798, Report [1987] 1 SCR 1148, 25 June 1987, https://scc-csc.lexum.com/scc-csc/scc-csc/en/item/228/index.do.

22 Dixon, "William Davis and the Road to Completion," 33.

23 William J. Smith, "Linguistic School Boards in Quebec – A Reform Whose Time Has Come," *McGill Law Journal* 39 (1994): 200–33.

24 William J. Smith, William F. Foster, and Helen M. Donahue, "The Transformation of Educational Governance in Quebec: A Reform Whose Time Has Finally Come," *McGill Journal of Education* 34, no. 3 (Fall 1999): 209.

25 Ibid., 209–10.

26 Task Force on English Education, *Report to the Minister of Education* (Montreal: TFEE/MEQ, 1992), 7.

27 Smith et al., "The Transformation of Educational Governance in Quebec," 210.

28 Ministry of Education of Quebec, *A New Direction for Success: Policy Statement and Plan of Action* (Quebec: MEQ, 1997).

29 Elaine Freeland, "Education Reform and the English Schools of Quebec," *McGill Journal of Education* 34, no. 3 (Fall 1999): 246–7.

30 Ibid., 246.

31 Don Macpherson, "Low Turnout in Quebec School Board Elections," *Montreal Gazette*, 3 November 2014.

32 Dan Delmar, "An Alternative to English-Language Boards," *Montreal Gazette*, 24 April 2016

33 Albert Kramberger, "Will West Islanders Fight to Save the English School Board?" *Montreal Gazette*, 13 December 2018. See also Elysha Enos, "Writing's on the Blackboard for Quebec School Boards as CAQ Moves to Take Away EMSB Schools," *CBC News Montreal*, 11 May 2019.

34 D. Card, M. Dooley, and A. Payne, *School Choice and the Benefits of Competition: Evidence from Ontario* (Toronto: C.D. Howe Institute, 2008).

35 Louise Brown, "Ontario Catholic Elementary Schools Quietly Admitting Students of All Faiths," *The Toronto Star*, 29 August 2014.

36 Konrad Yakabuski, "The Catholic Funding Debate Needs to Be Schooled by Facts," *The Globe and Mail*, 14 February 2018.

37 David R. Johnson, *Ontario's Best Public Schools, 2009–2011* (Toronto: C.D. Howe Institute, June 2012); Louise Brown, "Catholic Schools More Often Score Better than Public Schools, New C.D. Howe Report Shows," *The Toronto Star*, 7 June 2012.

38 Yvan Guillemette, *Breaking Down Monopolies: Expanding Choice and Competition in Education* (Toronto: C.D. Howe Institute, 2007), 7.

39 Caroline Alphonso, "In Push for Funding, Ontario's Catholic Schools Enrolling More Non-Catholics," *The Globe and Mail*, 12 February 2018.

40 Yakabuski, "The Catholic Funding Debate."

41 Ashley Martin, "Long-Running Theodore Court Case Decides Non-Catholic Students Won't Be Funded to Attend Catholic Schools," *The Leader-Post* (Regina), 20 April 2017.

42 Sean Fine, "Saskatchewan to Invoke Charter Clause over Catholic School Funding," *The Globe and Mail*, 1 May 2017.

43 Paul W. Bennett, "Premier Wall Was Right to Maximize Parental Choice in the Schooling System," *The National Post*, 8 May 2017.

44 Government of Saskatchewan, "'Notwithstanding Clause Invoked to Protect Parents' and Students' Rights," news release, 8 November 2017.

45 Heather Polischuk, "Sask. Court of Appeal Reserves Decision on School Funding Case," *The Star Phoenix* (Saskatoon), 14 March 2014.

46 Elementary Teachers' Federation of Ontario, "EFTO Extremely Concerned at Loss of 11,000 Mainly Non-Catholic Students from Public Education System to Catholic Schools," media release, 16 February 2018.

47 See Beth Green and Stephanie Schoenhoff, *Lessons for Ontario: Education Diversity across Canada* (Hamilton, ON: Cardus Education, 2015), 7–9.

48 Deani Van Pelt, "Why Ontario Needs Its Religious Schools," *Ottawa Citizen*, 26 February 2018.

49 See Derek J. Allison, Deani van Pelt, and Sazid Hasan, *A Diverse Landscape: Independent Schools in Canada* (Vancouver, BC: Fraser Institute, 2016).

50 See Robson Fletcher, "Why Does Alberta Still Have a Separate Catholic School System?" *CBC News Calgary*, 21 April 2018; and Serena Shaw, "Catholic Schools Add Diversity and Choice," *Edmonton Journal*, 3 January 2019.

51 Beth Green and Deani Van Pelt, "Parents Want, and Deserve, Educational Options," *The Toronto Star*, 13 March 2018; Van Pelt, "Why Ontario Needs Religious Schools."

CHAPTER SEVEN

1 Deani Van Pelt, "School Enrolment in Canada – a Snapshot," *Fraser Forum*, 5 July 2017. See also Angela MacLeod and Sazid Hasan, *Where Our Students Are Educated: Measuring Student Enrolment in Canada – 2017* (Vancouver, BC: Barbara Mitchell Centre, Fraser Institute, June 2017).

2 See a revealing Toronto District School Board report on the popularity of programs of choice from French Immersion to Alternative School Programs in a major metropolitan school system: Ehran Sinay, *Programs of Choice in the TDSB* (Toronto: TDSB, June 2010), 1–7.

3 Gordon Porter, "Are We Star Gazing? Can Canadian Schools Really Be Equitable and Inclusive?" *Canadian Education Association* blog,

7 December 2011, https://inclusiveeducationcanada.files.wordpress. com/2013/07/are-we-stargazing.png (accessed 8 January 2020).

4 See Michael Gauvreau, *The Catholic Origins of Quebec's Quiet Revolution, 1931–1970*, McGill-Queen's Studies in the History of Religion, Series Two, no. 41 (Montreal, QC: McGill-Queen's University Press, 2005).

5 See Gérard Bouchard, *Interculturalism: A View from Quebec*, trans. Howard Scott, foreword by Charles Taylor (Toronto: University of Toronto Press, 2015).

6 Alex Ballingall, "How Secularism Became Quebec's Religion: The Distinct Path to Bill 21," *The Toronto Star*, 5 April 2019.

7 MacLeod and Hasan, *Where Our Students Are Educated*, 2.

8 Ibid., 3.

9 Aaron Hutchins, "Just Say 'Non': The Problem with French Immersion," *Maclean's*, 22 March 2015.

10 "Bilingualism Translates into Higher Earnings, Study Finds," *University of Guelph News*, 31 August 2010.

11 J. Douglas Willms, "The Case for Universal French Instruction," *Policy Brief*, Canadian Research Institute for Social Policy, University of New Brunswick, April 2008.

12 Sinay, *Programs of Choice in the TDSB*, 21.

13 Hutchins, "Just Say 'Non.'"

14 Wayne MacKay, *Connecting Care and Challenge: Tapping Our Human Potential. Report on Inclusive Education Programming and Services* (Fredericton: New Brunswick Department of Education, January 2006), https://www2.gnb.ca/content/dam/gnb/Departments/ed/pdf/K12/mackay/ ReportOnInclusiveEducationSummaryDocument.pdf (accessed 8 January 2020).

15 Porter, "Are We Star Gazing?"

16 Yude M. Henteleff, "Full Inclusion Is Not in the Best Interest of Children with Learning Disabilities," Policy Paper, Learning Disabilities Association of Canada (LDAC), October 2002; and "Meaningful Access as an Integral Part of the Right to Equal Access in Education," presentation (St John's, NL: Learning Disabilities Association of Newfoundland and Labrador, 9 April 2013), http://www.ldanl.org/lda/pdf/Henteleff-MeaningfulAccess. pdf.

17 LDAC Policy Statement on Educational Inclusion for Students with Learning Disabilities, updated 17 November 2008, http://www.ldao.ca/ wp-content/uploads/LDAO-Policy-Statement-on-Educational-Inclusion.pdf (accessed 8 January 2020).

18 Anne Price and Mary Cole, "Best Practices in Teaching Students with Learning Disabilities," Calgary Learning Centre, 6 February 2009, reprinted in Nova Scotia Department of Education, *Tuition Support Program Review 2009* (Halifax: Nova Scotia Education, 2009), https://studentservices.ednet.ns.ca/sites/default/files/Tuition_Support_Program_Review_2009.pdf (accessed 11 December 2019).

19 Bernard Richard, *Connecting the Dots: A Report on the Condition of Youth At-Risk and Youth with Complex Needs in New Brunswick* (Fredericton: Ombudsman and Child and Youth Advocate Office, January 2008), https://www.ombudnb.ca/site/images/PDFs/ConnectingtheDots-e.pdf (accessed 8 January 2020).

20 Gordon Porter and Angela AuCoin, *Strengthening Inclusion, Strengthening Schools: An Action Plan for Growth* (Fredericton: Department of Education and Early Childhood Development, June 2012), https://www.gnb.ca/legis/business/pastsessions/57/57-2/LegDocs/2/en/StrengtheningInclusion-e.pdf (accessed 8 January 2020).

21 Paul W. Bennett, *Building a Bigger Tent: Serving All Special Needs Students Better in New Brunswick's Inclusive Education System* (Halifax: Atlantic Institute for Market Studies, June 2012), http://www.aims.ca/site/media/aims/Building%20a%20Bigger%20Tent.pdf (accessed 11 December 2019).

22 Harold L. Doherty, "Building a Bigger Tent Is a Badly Needed Critical Analysis," *Facing Autism in New Brunswick* blog, 20 June 2012, http://autisminnb.blogspot.ca/2012/06/building-bigger-tent-is-badlyneeded.html.

23 Paul W. Bennett, *A Provincial Lifeline: Expanding the Nova Scotia Tuition Support Program* (Halifax: Atlantic Institute for Market Studies, February 2012).

24 Bennett, *Building a Bigger Tent*, "Recommendations."

25 *CBC News New Brunswick*, "AIMS Says Students with Learning Disabilities Need Financial Help," 27 May 2015.

26 Paul W. Bennett, *Extending the Educational Lifeline: The Tuition Support Program and Its Benefits for Special Needs Students* (Halifax: Atlantic Institute for Market Studies, May 2015), http://www.aims.ca/site/media/aims/AIMS_ExtendingEdu_MY26-F4.pdf (accessed 8 January 2020).

27 *CBC Information Morning Moncton*, "Learning Outside the Box" Series, Rebecca Bulmer, 27 May 2015, https://www.cbc.ca/informationmorningmoncton/2015/05/27/the-cost-of-learning-disabilities/ (accessed 8 January 2020).

28 Bennett, *Extending the Educational Lifeline.*

29 Holly Conners, "'Inclusion' Is the Classroom Challenge Teachers Are Too Afraid to Talk About, Educator Says," CBC *News Cape Breton*, 2 December 2016.

30 See Bernie Froese-Germain, Richard Riel, and Bob McGahey, "Class Size and Student Diversity: Two Sides of the Same Coin," Canadian Teachers' Federation, *Perspectives*, Issue 6 (February 2012); and Paul W. Bennett, "Inclusion, Class Composition and Teaching in Today's Classrooms," presentation (Washington, DC: researchED Washington, 29 October 2016).

31 British Columbia Teachers Federation, "British Columbia Annual Class Size and Composition Data, 2006–2018," https://bctf.ca/IssuesInEducation.aspx?id=5530 (accessed 8 January 2020).

32 Canadian Council on Learning, "Making Sense of the Class Size Debate," Lessons in Learning (14 September 2005), http://www.ccl-cca.ca/pdfs/LessonslnLearning/Sep-14-05-Makingsense-of-the-class-sizedebate.pdf.

33 Canadian Teachers' Federation, *The Voice of Canadian Teachers on Teaching and Learning* (Ottawa: CTF, October 2011).

34 Bernie Froese-Germain, Richard Riel, and Bob McGahey, "Class Size and Student Diversity: Two Sides of the Same Coin," *Teacher Voice, Summary of Research Findings* (Ottawa: CTF, 2012).

35 Bennett, "Inclusion, Class Composition and Teaching," researchED Washington, October 2017. See also Paul W. Bennett and Heather Cumming, "Inclusion and Class Composition: Moving from Theory to Research-Based Policy and Practice," researchED Toronto, 11 November 2017.

36 CBC *News New Brunswick*, "NBTA Claims Teachers Donning Kevlar in Classrooms," 4 March 2016.

37 Tracy Sherlock, "Class Size, Composition Slightly Worse in B.C. despite $400-Million Fund," *The Vancouver Sun*, 15 February 2016.

38 Peter O'Neil and Tracy Sherlock, "Court Ruling to Force Hiring of Hundreds of Teachers in B.C.," *The Vancouver Sun*, 10 November 2016.

39 Tracy Sherlock, "What Does This Mean for Classrooms?" *The Vancouver Sun*, 10 November 2016.

40 CBC *News British Columbia*, "BCTF Supreme Court Victory: How Does It Help Students with Learning Disabilities?" 6 September 2017.

41 Nova Scotia, Commission on Inclusive Education, *Students First, Report of the Commission on Inclusive Education, March 20/8*, Commissioners Sarah Shea, Adela Njie, and Monica Williams (Halifax: CII, 2018), 5, 9–10, 17.

42 Alex Ballingall, "How Sectarianism Became Quebec's Religion: The Distinct Path to Bill 21," *The Toronto Star*, 5 April 2019. See also Darryl

Leroux, "Quebec Nationalism and the Production of Difference: The
Bouchard-Taylor Commission, the Herouxville Code of Conduct and
Quebec's Immigrant Immigration Policy," *Quebec Studies* 49 (Spring/
Summer 2010): 107–26.

43 Jasmin Zine, "Muslim Youth in Canadian Schools: Education and the
Politics of Religious Identity," *Anthropology & Education Quarterly* 32,
no. 4 (December 2001): 399–425; Zine, "Unsettling the Nation: Gender,
Race and Muslim Cultural Politics in Canada," *Studies in Ethnicity and
Nationalism* 9, no. 1 (2009): 146–63.

44 Jonathan Montpetit, "The Big Question about Democracy Lurking behind
Quebec's Secularism Bill," *CBC News Montreal*, 12 May 2019; Les
Perreaux, "Quebec Passes Bill Banning Public Servants from Wearing
Religious Symbols," *The Globe and Mail*, 16 June 2019.

45 Philip Authier, "Legault Defends Plan to Ban Religious Symbols, Abolish
School Boards," *Montreal Gazette*, 13 December 2018; Ballingall, "How
Secularism Became Quebec's Religion."

46 Jerome Melancon, "Liberty, Equality, Laicity: Quebec's Charter of Values
and the Reframing of Politics," *Canadian Political Science Review* 9, no. 3
(2015): 35–71.

47 Jacques Boissinot, "Quebec's Couillard Rejects Push for Ban on Official's
Religious Headwear," *The Globe and Mail*, 14 February 2017; "Quebec
Weighing Legal Options as Judge Suspends Face Covering Ban," *The
Globe and Mail*, 29 June 2018.

48 "Ban on Sikh Kirpan Overturned by Supreme Court," *CBC News*,
2 March 2006. For the case summary and court decision, see Supreme
Court Judgements, *Balvir Singh Multani (on behalf of Garbaj Singh
Multani) v. Commission scolaire Marguerite-Bourgeoys and Attorney
General of Quebec*, 2006 SCC 6, [2006] 1 SCR 256. Case No. 30322,
2 March 2006.

49 Jonathan Montpetit, "What We Can Learn from Herouxville, the Quebec
Town that Became Shorthand for Intolerance," *CBC News Montreal*,
25 January 2017.

50 "Montreal YMCA Drops Tinted Windows after Members Protest," *CBC
News Montreal*, 19 March 2007.

51 Gerard Bouchard and Charles Taylor, *Building the Future: A Time for
Reconciliation* (Quebec: Government of Quebec, 2008), 18.

52 Ibid., 20–2.

53 Perreaux, "Quebec Passes Bill Banning Public Servants from Wearing
Religious Symbols."

54 *CBC News Montreal*, "Bill 21 Must Be Seen in Context of Islamophobia, Charles Taylor Says," 8 May 2019, https://www.cbc.ca/news/canada/montreal/bill-21-must-be-seen-in-context-of-islamophobia-charles-taylor-says-1.5127852.

55 Jason Magder, "A New Poll Shows Support for Bill 21 Based upon Anti-Islam Sentiment," *Montreal Gazette*, 30 May 2019.

56 Zine, "Muslim Youth in Canadian Schools." See also Maham Abedi, "Quebec Face-Coverings Ban Leaves Muslims Fearful: 'Life Will Get Harder,'" *Global News*, 19 October 2017.

57 Navid Bakali, "Islamophobia in Quebec Secondary Schools: Inquiries into the Experiences of Muslim Male Youth Post 9/11," in M. Mac an Ghaill and C. Haywood, eds., *Muslim Students, Education and Neoliberalism* (London: Palgrave Macmillan, 2017), 145–59.

58 Janice Dickson, "Legault Backs Education Minister's Comment, Says Malala Yousafzai 'Couldn't Teach' in Quebec with Head Scarf," *The Globe and Mail*, 8 July 2019.

59 Sidhartha Banerjee, "Quebec's Largest School Board Refuses to Apply Bill 21 before 'Proper Consultation,'" *Global News Montreal*, 20 June 2019; "Bill 21 Won't Apply to Us, Quebec's English School Boards Say," *CBC News Montreal*, 14 May 2019.

60 Ballingall, "How Secularism Became Quebec's Religion."

61 Yvan Lamonde, *L'heure de vérité. La laïcité québécoise à l'épreuve de l'histoire* (Montreal, QC: Del Busso, 2010), 64–5, 78, 96, 122–3, 128–9, 183. See also Kevin McDonough, Bruce Maxwell, and David Waddington, "Teachers, the State and Religious Symbols: A Question of Professional Ethics," *Theory and Research in Education* 13, no. 3 (2015): 249–66.

CHAPTER EIGHT

1 Tim Falconer, *Watchdogs and Gadflies: Activism from Marginal to Mainstream* (Toronto: Penguin/Viking, 2001), 70–1.

2 Malkin Dare, "Experiential Learning Advocates Have Had It Wrong for Decades," *HuffPost Blog*, 2 August 2016.

3 Malkin Dare, *How to Get the Right Education for Your Child* (Waterloo, ON: OQE-SAER Publications, 2008).

4 Ibid., 8.

5 Michael C. Zwaagstra, Rodney A. Clifton, and John C. Long, *What's Wrong with Our Schools and How We Can Fix Them* (Lanham, MD: Rowman & Littlefield, 2010), 6–7. For the origin of the term "romantic

progressivism," see E.D. Hirsch, Jr, *The Schools We Need and Why We Don't Have Them* (New York: Doubleday, 1996), 71–9.

6 Frederick M. Hess, *The Same Thing Over and Over Again: How School Reformers Get Stuck in Yesterday's Ideas* (Cambridge, MA: Harvard University Press, 2010), 101.

7 Zwaagstra et al., *What's Wrong with Our Schools*, 17.

8 Hess, *The Same Thing Over and Over Again*, 101–2.

9 See Ken Osborne, *Education: A Guide to the Canadian School Debate* (Toronto: Penguin Books, 1999), 10–11.

10 On the cycle of faddism in North American school reform, see Diane Ravitch, *Left Back: A Century of Battles over School Reform* (New York: Touchstone Books, 2000), 328, 440–3; Amy Binder, *Contentious Curricula* (Princeton, NJ: Princeton University Press, 2004); and Paul W. Bennett, "Turning Around Our Schools," *Progress Magazine* 17, no. 2 (2010): 26–30.

11 See Caroline Winterer, *The Culture of Classicism: Ancient Greece and Rome in American Intellectual Life, 1780–1910* (Baltimore, MD: Johns Hopkins University Press, 2002).

12 Martin Robinson, *Trivium 21c: Preparing Young People for the Future with Lessons from the Past* (Carmarthen, UK: Independent Thinking Press, 2013). See also Martin Robinson, *Curriculum: Athena versus the Machine* (London: Crown House Publishing, 2019), a sequel that reaffirms the enduring value of the pursuit of wisdom and a content-rich curriculum for our current age.

13 Plato, *The Republic of Plato*, trans. B. Jowett (London: Oxford University Press, 1881), 233, cited in Hess, *The Same Thing Over and Over*, 107.

14 Terrence E. Cook, "Rousseau: Education and Politics," *Journal of Politics* 37 (February 1975): 108.

15 See Nel Noddings, *Philosophy of Education* (Boulder, CO: Westview Press, 1995), 18.

16 Laurel N. Tanner, "The Meaning of Curriculum in Dewey's Laboratory School (1896–1904)," *Journal of Curriculum Studies* 23, no. 2 (1991): 101–17.

17 Gerald L. Gutek, *Education and Schooling in America* (Englewood Cliffs, NJ: Prentice-Hall, 1983), 61–2.

18 Donalda Dickie, *The Enterprise in Theory and Practice* (Toronto: W. J. Gage, 1940). See also Rebecca Preigert Coulter, "Getting Things Done: Donalda J. Dickie and Leadership Through Practice," *Canadian Journal of Education* 28, no. 4 (2005): 669–99.

19 Osborne, *Education: A Guide to the Canadian School Debate*, 43–4.

20 Paul W. Bennett, "The Ontario Hall-Dennis Report, Fifty Years On: What Sparked the Passion and Fierce Resistance?" *voicED Canada* blog, 31 January 2018.

21 E.D. Hirsch, Jr, *Cultural Literacy: What Every American Needs to Know* (Boston, MA: Houghton Mifflin, 1987).

22 E.D. Hirsch, Jr, "The 21st-Century Skills Movement," Test of Presentation at Common Core, 24 February 2009, cited in Hess, *The Same Thing Over and Over*, 114. See also Hirsch, *The Schools We Need*.

23 Mark Holmes, *The Reformation of Canada's Schools: Breaking the Barriers to Parental Choice* (Kingston, ON: McGill-Queen's University Press, 1998).

24 See Alfie Kohn, *The Schools Our Children Deserve: Moving Beyond Traditional Classrooms and "Tougher Standards"* (Boston, MA: Houghton Mifflin, 1999).

25 Joe Bower, *for the love of learning* blog, 2004–16, http://joe-bower. blogspot.ca/. See also Joe Bower and P.L. Thomas, eds., *De-Testing and De-Grading Schools: Authentic Alternatives to Accountability and Standardization*, introduction by Alfie Kohn (New York: Peter Lang Publishing, 2013).

26 Paul Inchauspé, *Reaffirming the Mission of Our Schools: Report of the Task Force on Curriculum* (Quebec: Ministère de l'éducation, 1997).

27 Claude Lessard, "The Challenge of Reform," in "15 Years After the Quebec Education Reform: Critical Reflections" (*Education Canada* Theme Issue 2012, edited by Ron Canuel), posted online 14 December 2014, https://www.edcan.ca/articles/15-years-after-the-quebec-education-reform-critical-reflections/.

28 Paul W. Bennett, "What Can Be Learned from Quebec's Math Prowess?" *Policy Options Politiques* (23 October 2018), https://policyoptions.irpp. org/magazines/october-2018/what-can-be-learned-from-quebecs-math-prowess/.

29 See Robert Green, "Quebec's Ongoing Education Policy Disaster," *Montreal Gazette*, 15 February 2015.

30 See Charles Ungerleider, *Failing Our Kids: How We Are Ruining Our Public Schools* (Toronto: McClelland & Stewart, 2003), 8–9, 105–25. For an American perspective, see Diane Ravitch, *Left Back: A Century of Failed School Reforms* (New York: Simon & Schuster, 2000), 13–18, 465–7.

31 Rudolf Flesch, *Why Johnny Can't Read – and What You Can Do about It* (New York: Harper, 1955).

32 Ibid., 17, 84–5.

33 Jeanne S. Chall, *Learning to Read: The Great Debate* (New York: McGraw-Hill, 1967).

34 Frank Smith, *Understanding Reading: A Psychoanalytic Analysis of Reading and Learning to Read* (New York: Holt, Rinehart, and Winston, 1971), 2. See also Smith, *Psycholinguistics and Reading* (New York: Holt, Rinehart and Winston, 1973); and Smith, "Learning to Read: The Never-Ending Debate," *Phi Delta Kappan* 73, no. 6 (February 1992): 432–5, 438–41.

35 See Ken Goodman, *What's Whole in Whole Language?* (Portsmouth, NH: Heinemann, 1986).

36 National Center for Education Statistics, National Assessment of Educational Progress, *NAEP 1994 Reading Report Card for the Nation and the States* (Washington, DC: US Department of Education, 1996), 56–7, 145, 153; Malkin Dare, "More than Meets the Eye?" *OQE Forum* (March 1998).

37 Dare, *How to Get the Right Education for Your Child*, 10.

38 See Janet S. Gaffney and Billie Askew, eds., *Stirring the Waters: The Influence of Marie Clay* (Portsmouth, NH: Heinemann, 1999). For a critical literature review of RR, see Melissa Farrall, "Reading Recovery: What Do School Districts Get for Their Money? A Review of the Research," *Wrightslaw*, IDEA 2004, http://www.wrightslaw.com/info/read.rr.research.farrall.htm (revised 17 January 2018).

39 Paul W. Bennett, "Early Reading Instruction: Why Has Reading Recovery Survived?" *Educhatter* blog, 10 March 2011.

40 Paul W. Bennett, "Better Approach Needed to Correct Reading Deficits," *The Chronicle Herald* (Halifax), 1 February 2013. For the latest results, see Nova Scotia Department of Education and Early Childhood Development, Student Results, 2016–2017 Nova Scotia Assessment Reading and Writing in Grade 3 and Grade 6 (Halifax: NSDE, 2018), https://plans.ednet.ns.ca/sites/default/files/documents/2016-2017_RW3-EN_Results.pdf (accessed 11 December 2019).

41 Bruce R. Vogeli, "The Rise and Fall of the New Math," Inaugural Lecture (New York: Teachers College, Columbia University, 1976), 4–17, cited in Ravitch, *Left Back*, 438–9.

42 Morris Kline, *Why Johnny Can't Add: The Failure of the New Math* (New York: St. Martin's Press, 1973).

43 National Council of Teachers of Mathematics, *Curriculum and Evaluation Standards for School Mathematics* (Reston, VA: NCTM, 1989).

44 *Creating a Climate for Change: Math Leads the Way – Perspectives on Math Reform* (New York: Public Agenda, 1993), 8.

45 Marianne M. Jennings, "Rainforest Algebra and MTV Geometry," *The Textbook Letter* (November–December 1996).

46 See Lynne Cheney, "Creative Math or Just Fuzzy Math?" *The New York Times*, 11 August 1997; and Martin Gardiner, "The New New Math," *The New York Times Review of Books*, 24 September 1998.

47 Cynthia Reynolds, "Why Is It Your Job to Teach Your Kid Math?" *Maclean's*, 13 March 2012; Anna Stokke, "Why Our Kids Fall Behind in Math," *Winnipeg Free Press*, 16 September 2011.

48 Nick Martin, "Basic Arithmetic Back in Class: Manitoba Kids to Learn to Do Math the Old Way," *Winnipeg Free Press*, 18 June 2013.

49 "Frustrated Professors Convince Elementary Schools to Step Back from 'New Math' and Go 'Back to Basics,'" *The National Post*, 13 September 2013. See also "Decline of Canadian Students' Math Skills the Fault of 'Discovery Learning,'" *The National Post*, 27 May 2015.

50 Kelly Gallagher-MacKay and Nancy Steinhauer, *Pushing the Limits: How Schools Can Prepare Our Children Today for the Challenges of Tomorrow* (Toronto: Doubleday Canada, 2017).

51 Paul W. Bennett, "Building on Illusions," *EdCan Network: Edwire* (Canadian Education Association), 26 September 2017.

52 BBC World News Service, "Have 65% of Future Jobs Not Yet Been Invented?" 29 May 2017, http://www.bbc.co.uk/programmes/po53ln9f.

53 See Michael Sefcik, "Intellectual Engagement, Good Grades, and 'Doing School,'" *Education Canada* (Winter 2013).

54 Ash Kelly, "Should Schools Hold Back Students?" *The Globe and Mail*, 25 September 2015.

55 Popular and provocative curriculum critiques can be found in John Taylor Gatto, *Dumbing Us Down: The Hidden Curriculum of Compulsory Schooling* (Philadelphia, PA: New Society Publishers, 1992); and Maureen Stout, *The Feel-Good Curriculum: The Dumbing Down of America's Kids in the Name of Self-Esteem* (New York: Perseus Books, 2000)

56 Charles Ungerleider, *Failing Our Kids: How We Are Ruining Our Public Schools* (Toronto: McClelland & Stewart, 2003), 105.

57 Ontario Ministry of Education, *Achieving Excellence: A Renewed Vision for Education in Ontario* (Toronto: Ministry of Education, April 2014), https://www.oise.utoronto.ca/atkinson/UserFiles/File/Policy_Monitor/ON_01_04_14_-_renewedVision.pdf (accessed 8 January 2020).

58 Frederick M. Hess, *The Cage Busting Teacher* (Cambridge, MA: Harvard Education Press, 2015), 3–11. See also Laura Elizabeth Pinto, "Fear and Loathing in Neoliberalism: School Leader Responses to Policy Layers," *Journal of Educational Administration and History* 47, no. 2 (2015): 140–54.

59 Bob Davis, *Whatever Happened to High School History? Burying the Political Memory of Youth* (Toronto: James Lorimer 1995). See also Leon Fink, "Losing the Hearts and Minds, or How Clio Disappeared from Canadian Public Schools," *Labour / Le Travail* 43 (Spring 1999): 211–15; and Paul W. Bennett, "Saving an Endangered Subject: High School History in Ontario Schools, 1960–2010," *Education Matters* 4, no. 1 (2016): 51–65.

60 Desmond Morton, "History Teaching in Canada: The Past Does Not Change but Its Interpretation Can Alter Radically," *Policy Options* 1 (1 November 2002); Penney Clark, "Clio in the Curriculum: Vindicated at Last," *Canadian Issues* (Spring 2013): 42–6.

61 Christopher Dummitt, "History Lessons, Cast in Bronze," *The Globe and Mail*, 28 October 2015; Paul Axelrod, "Instead of Renaming Buildings, Why Not Truly Improve Indigenous Lives?" *The Conversation*, 28 August 2017; Wendy Stueck and Caroline Alphonso, "Changing History," *The Globe and Mail*, 3 September 2017.

62 Ungerleider, *Failing Our Kids*, 106–7.

63 For a prime example of the pressing needs, see Stan Kutcher, "Classroom Curriculum Can Improve Mental Health Care," *The Chronicle Herald* (Halifax), 11 February 2015.

64 Ontario Secondary School Teachers Federation, "Harvey Bischof Speaks at researchED Conference, OSSTF/FEESO Plans Its Own," *OSSTF Update*, 24 November 2017. ·

CHAPTER NINE

1 Ontario People for Education, *Measuring What Matters* (Toronto: P4E, 2013–18), https://peopleforeducation.ca/measuring-what-matters/ (accessed 11 December 2019).

2 See the OECD Letter initiated by Alfie Kohn and a host of educators opposing the PISA international testing program published in *The Guardian*: "OECD and PISA Tests Are Damaging Education Worldwide – Academics," *The Guardian*, 6 May 2014, https://www.theguardian.com/education/2014/may/06/oecd-pisa-tests-damaging-education-academics.

3 People for Education, "Measuring What Matters: Moving from Theory to Practice," Summary Report (Toronto: People for Education, 2015), ch. 1, https://peopleforeducation.ca/report/measuring-what-matters-moving-from-theory-to-practice/#chapter1 (accessed 11 December 2019).

4 Ontario Ministry of Education, *A Learning Province: Public Engagement on Education Assessment in Ontario* (Toronto: MOE, September 2017).

5 Paul W. Bennett, "Stealth Assessment: Where Is Ontario's Student Well Being Assessment Initiative Heading?" presentation (Toronto: *researchED Canada*, Ontario 2018 Conference, 14 April 2018).

6 Ontario Premier's Office and Ministry of Education, *Ontario: A Learning Province, Findings and Recommendations from the Independent Review of Assessment and Reporting* (March 2018), released 24 April 2018.

7 Caroline Alphonso, "What a Ford Government Means for Ontario Classrooms," *The Globe and Mail*, 8 June 2018.

8 Dan T. Willingham, "'Grit' Is Trendy, but Can It Be Taught?" *American Educator* (American Federation of Teachers Magazine) (Summer 2016), https://www.aft.org/ae/summer2016/willingham.

9 Paul Tough, *How Children Succeed; Grit, Curiosity and the Hidden Power of Character* (New York: Houghton Mifflin Harcourt, 2012), 61–76.

10 Angela Duckworth, *Grit: The Power of Passion and Perseverance* (New York: Simon and Schuster, 2016).

11 Andrea Gordon, "Annie Kidder and People for Education Have Made a Mark on Ontario Schools, but Have They Become Part of the System?" *The Toronto Star*, 2 September 2017.

12 Paul W. Bennett, "Measuring What Matters: Can Social-Emotional Skills Be Effectively Taught – or Reliably Measured?" *Educhatter* blog, 9 July 2016.

13 Ibid.

14 Ontario People for Education, *Measuring What Matters: Defining the Competencies*, https://peopleforeducation.ca/mwm-defining-the-competencies/.

15 Ontario People for Education, *Measuring What Matters: Identifying What Matters*, https://peopleforeducation.ca/mwm-identifying-what-matters/ (accessed 11 December 2019).

16 See the "MWM Project Description" posted by David Hagen Cameron on Research Gate, https://www.researchgate.net/project/Measuring-What-Matters (accessed 11 December 2019).

17 David Cameron, "Measuring What Matters: Finding Congruence of Measurement and Assessment of Broad Areas of Student Success at Central and Local Levels," presentation to the Association of Educational Researchers of Ontario (AERO) Conference, Etobicoke, ON, 2 December 2016, http://www.aero-aoce.org/uploads/6/6/0/0/6600183/cameron_2016.pdf.

18 Paul W. Bennett, "Measuring What Matters Conundrum: Will Social and Emotional Learning (SEL) Assessments Meet the Reliability Test?" *Educhatter* blog, 29 October 2017.

19 Bennett, "Measuring What Matters: Can Social-Emotional Skills Be Effectively Taught – or Reliably Measured?"

20 Willingham, "'Grit' Is Trendy, but Can It Be Taught?"

21 Kate Zernicke, "Testing for Joy and Grit? Schools Nationwide Push to Measure Students' Emotional Skills," *The New York Times*, 29 February 2016; Jenny Anderson, "Testing Kids for 'Grit' Is a Big Mistake, Says the World's Foremost Authority on It," *Quartz*, 1 March 2016. See also Angela Duckworth and David Scott Yeager, "Measurement Matters Assessing Personal Qualities Other Than Cognitive Ability for Educational Purposes," *Educational Researcher*, 1 May 2015.

22 David Beer, "Cambridge Analytica: The Data Analytics Industry Is Already in Full Swing," *The Conversation*, 23 March 2018, http://theconversation.com/cambridge-analytica-the-data-analytics-industry-is-already-in-full-swing-93873; Ben Williamson, "Why Education Is Embracing Facebook-Style Personality Profiling for Schoolchildren," *The Conversation*, 29 March 2018, https://theconversation.com/why-education-is-embracing-facebook-style-personality-profiling-for-schoolchildren-94125.

23 Ben Williamson, *Big Data in Education: The Digital Future of Learning, Policy and Practice* (Thousand Oaks, CA: Sage Publishers, 2017).

24 Ontario People for Education, "Ontario Considering Changes to Assessment and Measurement" (Toronto: P4E, 2018), https://peoplefor education.ca/research/ontario-considering-changes-to-assessment-and-measurement/ (accessed 11 December 2019).

25 See Sam Sellar, Greg Thompson, and David Rutkowski, *The Global Education Race: Taking the Measure of PISA and International Testing* (Edmonton: Brush Education, 2017).

26 Williamson, "Why Education Is Embracing Facebook-Style Personality Profiling."

27 William Davies, "Short Cuts," *London Review of Books* 40, no. 7 (5 April 2018): 20–1.

28 Ben Williamson, "PISA for Personality Testing – The OECD and the Psychometric Science of Social-Emotional Skills," *Code Acts in Education*, 16 January 2018, https://codeactsineducation.wordpress.com/2018/01/16/pisa-for-personality-testing/ (accessed 19 January 2018).

29 Valerie Shute, "Stealth Assessment in Computer-Based Games to Support Learning," in S. Tobias and J.D. Fletcher, eds., *Computer Games and Instruction* (Charlotte, NC: Information Age Publishers, 2011); Valerie Shute and Matthew Ventura, *Stealth Assessment: Measuring and Supporting Learning in Video Games* (Boston, MA: The MIT Press, 2013).

30 James Heckman, "Cognitive Skills Are Not Enough," Public Address to Business and Policy Leaders, Chicago, IL, 16 December 2010, https://heckmanequation.org/resource/cognitive-skills-are-not-enough/; Tim Kautz, James J. Heckman, Ron Diris, Baster Weel, and Lex Borghans, *Fostering and Measuring Skills: Improving Cognitive and Non-Cognitive Skills to Promote a Lifetime of Success* (Paris: OECD Education, 2014), 7–8.

31 Williamson, "PISA for Personality Testing."

32 Bennett, "Stealth Assessment."

33 Council of Ministers of Education, "CMEC Moves Forward on Pan Canadian Education Initiatives," News Release, 8 July 2016; and "CMEC Pan-Canadian Global Competencies Descriptions," http://www.ontario directors.ca/CODETLF/docs/tel/PanCanadian_Global_Competencies_ Backgrounder_EN.PDF (accessed 5 February 2018).

34 Office of the Premier, Government of Ontario, "Updated Curriculum, New Report Cards Coming to Ontario Schools," news release, 6 September 2017.

35 Kathryn Ecclestone and Denis Hayes, "The Dangerous Rise of Therapeutic Education," *spiked review of books*, 27 June 2008, http://www.spiked-online.com/review_of_books/article/5391#.WsOt9IjwaM8 (accessed 5 February 2018).

36 Williamson, "Why Education Is Embracing Facebook-Style Personality Profiling"; Bennett, "Stealth Assessment."

37 Ministry of Education, *A Learning Province*, 4.

38 Paul W. Bennett, "Student Assessment Review: Where Is Ontario's 'Learning Province' Agenda Heading?" *Educhatter* blog, 17 December 2017.

39 Daisy Christodoulou, British student assessment expert, January 2017, cited in Bennett, "Stealth Assessment."

40 Education Quality and Accountability Office (EQAO), *EQAO: Ontario's Provincial Assessment Program Its History and Influence, 1996–2012* (Toronto: EQAO, 2013), http://www.eqao.com/en/about_eqao/about_the_ agency/communication-docs/EQAO-history-influence.pdf (accessed 9 January 2020).

41 Graham Orpwood and Emily Sandford Brown, *Closing the Numeracy Gap: An Urgent Assignment for Ontario* (Toronto: College Student Achievement Project, October 2015).

42 See EQAO, *Provincial Elementary School Report, 2017*, Results of the Assessments of Reading, Writing and Mathematics, Primary Division (Grades 1–3) and Junior Division (Grades 4–6).

43 Ministry of Education, *A Learning Province*, 6–7.
44 EQAO, *Modernizing EQAO to Better Support Student Learning* (EQAO, November 2017); Nora Marsh, CEO, EQAO, "Memorandum to Directors of Education, Superintendents and Principals," 24 January 2018.
45 Kristin Rushowy, "Report Card, Curriculum Changes on the Way in Ontario," *The Toronto Star*, 6 September 2017; Bennett, "Stealth Assessment."
46 Paul Black and Dylan Wiliam, "Inside the Black Box: Raising Standards through Classroom Assessment," *Phi Delta Kappan* 80, no. 2 (October 1998): 139–48.
47 University of Cambridge, Faculty of Education, *ORBIT: The Open Integrated Resource Bank for Interactive Teaching*, Summary of Assessment for Learning Research, http://oer.educ.cam.ac.uk/wiki/Assessment_for_Learning_Research_Summary (accessed 1 March 2020).
48 Daisy Christodoulou, *Making Good Progress? The Future of Assessment for Learning* (Oxford, UK: Oxford University Press, 2017).
49 See Bennett, "Stealth Assessment," and the full summary at *Educhatter*, 16 April 2018.
50 MOE, *Ontario: A Learning Province* (March 2018), 6, 7–8, 10–11.
51 Anya Kamenetz, "Social and Emotional Skills: Everybody Loves Them, But Still Can't Define Them," *NPR Ed Blog*, 14 August 2017, https://www.npr.org/sections/ed/2017/08/14/542070550/social-and-emotional-skills-everybody-loves-them-but-still-cant-define-them (accessed 5 February 2018).
52 Paul W. Bennett, "The Growth Mindset: Carol Dweck's Learning Theory and Its Canadian Mutation," *EdCan Network: Edwire*, 3 April 2017, https://www.edcan.ca/articles/the-growth-mindset/ (accessed 9 January 2020).
53 MOE, *Ontario: A Learning Province* (March 2018), 6, 7–8, 10–11; "Ontario Schools Should Keep Standardized Tests," *Toronto Star*, Editorial, 30 April 2018.
54 Ontario News, Office of the Premier, "Respecting Parents by Holding Unprecedented Consultation into Education Reform," News Release; and "Consultation into Education Reform," background notes, 22 August 2018.
55 Allison Jones, "Ontario Marks Whirlwind, 'Lightning Speed' Year since Premier Doug Ford's Election," *The Globe and Mail*, 5 June 2019.
56 "Doug Ford: Year One: A Recap of Ontario's Tumultuous 12 Months," *The Globe and Mail*, 20 June 2019. See the succinct Education issues summary at https://www.theglobeandmail.com/canada/article-doug-ford-year-one-ontario-premier-explainer/ (accessed 7 July 2019).

57 EQAO, "EQAO Agrees that Further Discussion Is Required regarding the
    Recommendations of the Premier's Education Advisors," Media Release,
    24 April 2018.

58 EQAO, "Supporting Student Learning through Assessment and
    Accountability," submission to the Public Consultation on Education,
    December 2018.

59 EQAO, "EQAO Welcomes Dr. Cameron Montgomery, Chair of Its Board
    of Directors," Media Release, 14 February 2019. For a helpful back-
    grounder, see Caroline Alphonso, "Ford Government Appoints Failed PC
    Candidate as First Full-time EQAO Chair," *The Globe and Mail*,
    19 February 2019.

60 EQAO, "EQAO CEO Resigns to Return to Local Focus in District School
    Board," media release, 12 November 2019.

61 People for Education, *The New Basics for Public Education*, Annual
    Report on Ontario's Publicly Funded Schools 2018 (Toronto: People
    for Education, 2018), 1–2, https://peopleforeducation.ca/wp-content/
    uploads/2018/06/AnnualReport18_Web.pdf (accessed 9 January 2020).

62 Caroline Alphonso, "UCP Leader Jason Kenney Proposes Changes to
    School Testing in Alberta," *The Globe and Mail*, 9 April 2019; Janet
    French, "Alberta Government Will Bring Back Grade 3 Provincial
    Achievement Tests," *Edmonton Journal*, 25 June 2019.

63 British Columbia Ministry of Education, "Core Competencies: Building
    Student Success – BC's New Curriculum" (Victoria: Government of
    British Columbia, 2017), https://curriculum.gov.bc.ca/competencies
    (accessed 12 January 2020); Sue Bannister, "Competency Framework –
    A Fresh Perspective" and "Traits and Competencies," *Successful
    Learners* website, https://successfullearners.ca/competency-framework/
    competencies/ (accessed 9 January 2020). For a primer on C21 Canada
    and its advocacy of 21st-century skills and competencies, see C21
    Canada, "C21 Canada Research," http://c21canada.org/c21-research/
    (accessed 12 January 2020), and *Shifting Minds 3.0: Redefining the
    Learning Landscape in Canada*" (2015), http://www.c21canada.org/wp-
    content/uploads/2015/05/C21-ShiftingMinds-3.pdf (accessed 9 January
    2020).

CHAPTER TEN

1 Kristin Rushowy, "Ontario High School Graduation Rates Highest Ever,"
   The Toronto Star, 8 May 2017.

2 Joanne Laucius, "Ontario High School Graduation Rates Are the Highest
   Ever," *Ottawa Citizen*, 6 May 2016.

3 J. Paul Grayson, James Côté, Liang Chen, Robert Kennedy, and Sharon Roberts, *Academic Skill Deficiencies in Four Ontario Universities: A Call to Action* (Toronto: York University, April 2019), 8.

4 See Laucius, "Ontario High School Graduation Rates"; and Arik Motskin, "The Vast Disparity in Canada's High School Graduation Rates," *The 10 and 3* blog, 11 August 2015.

5 See Charles Ungerleider, *Failing Our Kids: How We Are Ruining Our Public Schools* (Toronto: McClelland and Stewart, 2004), 8–10; and Sean Whetstone, "Understanding Attainment, Achievement and Statistics Commonly Used," *School Governing* blog, 14 April 2011, http://school governing.blogspot.ca/2011/04/understanding-attainment-achievement. html.

6 Paul W. Bennett, "The Attainment – Achievement Gap: What Do Rising Canadian Graduation Rates Actually Prove?" *Educhatter* blog, 30 June 2013.

7 Council of Ministers of Education, Canada (CMEC), "Canadian Education Systems Perform Well in New International Report," News Release, 25 June 2013; Julia Lawrence, "Graduation Rates on Track to Hit 90% by 2020, Study Claims," *Education News* blog, 26 February 2013.

8 OECD Education Office, *Education at a Glance 2013*, https://read.oecd-ilibrary.org/education/education-at-a-glance-2013_eag-2013-en#page1 (accessed). See also the critical review of PISA results in relation to Ontario student performance standards in James E. Côté and Anton L. Allahar, *Ivory Tower Blues: A University System in Crisis* (Toronto: University of Toronto Press, 2007), 21–2.

9 Canadian Council on Learning, *Good News: High School Dropout Rate Is Falling*, Lessons in Learning Series (Ottawa: CCL, December 2005), http://en.copian.ca/library/research/ccl/lessons_learning/good_news_hs_dropout_falling/good_news_hs_dropout_falling.pdf (accessed 12 December 2019).

10 John Richards, "Our High School Dropout Rate Is Falling, but We Can Still Do Better," *The National Post*, 17 January 2011.

11 Nick Purdon and Leonardo Palleja, "The 'Millennial Side Hustle,' Not a Stable Job, Is the New Reality for University Grads," *CBC News*, 12 March 2017.

12 See Paul W. Bennett, "A Big Disconnect in Our Schools," *The Chronicle Herald* (Halifax), 16 February 2016.

13 Bill Mah, "Alberta High School Graduation Rates on the Rise among Disadvantaged Groups, Province Says," *Edmonton Journal*, 7 September 2016.

14 Canadian Council on Learning, "Good News."

15 Bennett, "A Big Disconnect in Our Schools."

16 James E. Côté and Anton L. Allahar, *Lowering Higher Education: The Rise of the Corporate Universities and the Fall of Liberal Education* (Toronto: University of Toronto Press, 2011), 39–40.

17 Ontario Ministry of Education, memorandum from Ben Levin, Deputy Minister of Education, to School Boards, May 2009, cited in Côté and Allahar, *Lowering Higher Education*, 40–3.

18 Joanne Laucius, "Pressured to Pass: A Roundtable Discussion," *Ottawa Citizen*, 25 April 2009. See also Jon Cowans, "Why Johnny Can't Fail," *Education Forum* 32, no. 3 (2006): 16–19; and "Credit Integrity: How Johnny Can Succeed," *Education Forum* 33, no. 2 (2007): 18–21.

19 Moira Macdonald, "Our Kids Are Smart ... Really, but Some Teachers Are Frustrated," *The Toronto Sun*, 19 May 2009. See also Margaret Wente, "We Pretend to Teach 'em, They Pretend to Learn," *The Globe and Mail*, 18 April 2009.

20 Ontario Confederation of University Faculty Associations (OCUFA), "Students Less Prepared for University Education," *Quality Matters*, 6 April 2009.

21 See CBC Radio, *Cross Country Checkup*, 12 April 2009; CBC, *Sunday Edition*, 10 May 2009; and Côté and Allahar, *Lowering Higher Education*, 40–1, 43.

22 See Damian Cooper, *Plan Teach Assess* website and full biography, including his 2007 book, *Talk About Assessment*, http://www.planteachassess.com/damian-cooper/ (accessed 12 December 2019). Two other Ontario proponents of Assessment for Learning reform were Ken O'Connor and Lorna Earl, veterans of the Toronto District School Board.

23 Côté and Allahar, *Lowering Higher Education*, 44.

24 Chantalie Allick, "Cheating Students Get Second Chance in Newfoundland," *The Toronto Star*, 22 October 2011.

25 David Staples, "Suspended Teacher Lynden Dorval Is a Hero for Standing Up for High Standards in the Classroom," *The Edmonton Journal*, 31 May 2012.

26 CBC News Edmonton, "Lynden Dorval, Fired for Giving Zeros, 'Treated Unfairly,' Appeal Board Rules," 29 August 2014; Editorial, "Teacher Is a Hero, Never Was a Zero," *Calgary Herald*, 19 December 2014.

27 Janet French, "Are Teachers Inflating Grades? Critics Say Yes, School Boards Say No," *Edmonton Journal*, 27 February 2017.

28 Josh Dehaas, "Why Alberta's Education System Is Better," *Maclean's*, 28 November 2011.

29 Jim Dueck, *Education's Flashpoints: Upside Down or Set-Up to Fail*
    (Lanham, MD: Rowman & Littlefield, 2015), 97–107.
30 Michael Woods, "Making the Grade: Standard Tests Could Solve Grade
    Inflation Problem, Expert Says," *The Queen's Journal* (Kingston, ON),
    19 September 2008.
31 Robert Laurie, "Setting Them Up to Fail? Excellent School Marks Don't
    Necessarily Lead to Excellent Exam Marks," *AIMS Commentary*, 3 May
    2007; Matt McClure, "National Standard Sought for Exams," *Calgary
    Herald*, 29 November 2011; Nova Scotia, Department of Education
    and Early Childhood Development, *Accountability Report, 2015–2016*
    (Halifax: DOEECD, 2016), 22.
32 Zane Schwartz, "High-School Grade Inflation Balloon Ready to Pop,"
    The Globe and Mail, 29 March 2013.
33 Patrick Cain, "One University's Secret List to Judge Applicants by Their
    High Schools – Not Just Their Marks," *Global News*, 13 September 2018.
    For detailed analyses of school-by-school downgrades, see Conrad
    Collaco, "When Your 'A' Becomes a 'C' – Ontario University Downgrades
    Marks from Some High Schools," *CBC News Hamilton*, 18 September
    2018; and Joanne Laucius, "Grade Inflation? University of Ottawa's
    'Secret List' Suggests It's Not the Case with Ottawa Schools," *Ottawa
    Citizen*, 20 September 2018.
34 Andrew Parkin and Noel Baldwin, *Persistence in Post-Secondary
    Education in Canada: The Latest Research* (Toronto: Canada Millennium
    Scholarship Foundation, 2009), 1–13.
35 Michael Zwaagstra, "How Canada's Schools Promote Failure in
    University – and Life," Frontier Centre for Public Policy Commentary,
    28 September 2009.
36 Ibid.
37 "OCUFA Survey Shows Students Less Prepared for University," *Ontario
    University Report* 3, no. 1 (April 2009).
38 J. Paul Grayson, James Côté, Liang Chen, Robert Kennedy, and Sharon
    Roberts, *Academic Skill Deficiencies in Four Ontario Universities: A Call
    to Action* (Toronto: York University, April 2019), 5–6, https://skillsfor
    universitysuccess.info.yorku.ca/files/2019/04/04-26-2019-AcademicSkills.
    pdf (accessed 5 May 2019).
39 Barbara Kay, "Universities Shine a Light on Failing Schools," *National
    Post*, 1 May 2019.
40 Nova Scotia Department of Education, *Disrupting the Status Quo: Nova
    Scotians Demand a Better Future for Every Student*, Report of the

Minister's Panel on Education, Chair of Review Panel Myra Freeman (October 2014).

41 Government of Nova Scotia, *From School to Success: Clearing the Path*, Nova Scotia Transition Task Force (21 June 2016).

42 Jean Laroche, "Nova Scotia Should Create 'Gap Year' Program, Teach Work Ethic in School: Task Force," CBC *News Nova Scotia*, 21 June 2016.

43 Nova Scotia Department of Education, *Disrupting the Status Quo*, 31–5.

44 Ken Coates, "Are Too Many of Our Kids Going to University?" *National Post*, 29 April 2015.

45 Bentley University, *PreparedU Project on Millennial Preparedness* (Waltham, MA: Bentley University, 2014), https://www.slideshare.net/BentleyU/prepared-u-project-on-millennial-preparedness (accessed 12 December 2019).

46 McKinsey & Company, *Youth in Transition: Bridging Canada's Path from Education to Employment* (Toronto: McKinsey & Company, April 2015).

47 Ibid., 8–13.

CHAPTER ELEVEN

1 Sheree Fitch, "Maybe It Takes a Child to Raise a Village," *Breathe, Stretch, Write!* blog, 3 September 2013, http://www.shereefitch.com/blog/2013/9/3/maybe-it-takes-a-child-to-raise-a-village.html.

2 Amanda Jess, "Renowned Children's Author Sheree Fitch Inspired by River John in Latest Work," *The News* (New Glasgow, NS), 1 February 2017.

3 Paul W. Bennett, *The Last Stand: Schools, Communities and the Future of Rural Nova Scotia* (Halifax: Fernwood Publishing, 2013), 85.

4 Fitch, "Maybe It Takes a Child to Raise a Village."

5 Amy MacKenzie, "River John Hopes to Develop Successful Community Hub in School," *The News* (New Glasgow, NS), 26 March 2013.

6 Paul W. Bennett, "Board Sabotaging Hub Schools, Rural Spirit," *The Chronicle Herald* (Halifax), 18 February 2015.

7 Chignecto-Central Regional School Board, "Hub School Proposal Submission Format and Scoring Table," (Truro, NS: CCRSB, 22 January 2015), and Business Case Guidelines.

8 Margaret Atwood, "Friends Who Care – Thank You, Margaret Atwood," Letter to the Board, *Breathe, Stretch Write!* blog, 2 April 2015, http://www.shereefitch.com/blog/2015/4/2/friends-who-care-thank-you-margaret atwood.html.

9   Aaron Beswick, "Hub Model Effort 'Hard Labour,'" *The Chronicle Herald* (Halifax), 17 April 2017.

10 Francis Campbell, "Hub Schools 'Set Up for Failure,'" *The Chronicle Herald* (Halifax), 11 June 2015.

11 Carol Dunn, "Board Declines Meeting with River John Committee on Hub Proposal," *The News* (New Glasgow, NS), 31 July 2015. See also Letter from Education Minister Karen Casey, "Ministerial Points of View," *The Chronicle Herald* (Halifax), 9 July 2015.

12 Francis Campbell, "River John Keeps Battling for School," *The Chronicle Herald* (Halifax), 31 October 2015.

13 Michael Corbett, "From Shinjuku to River John: The Neoliberal Juggernaut, Efficiency, and Small Rural Schools," *Alberta Journal of Educational Research* 60, no. 4 (Winter 2014): 620.

14 Ibid.

15 See E.P. Cubberley, *Rural Life and Education: A Study of the Rural School Problem as a Phase of the Rural-Life Problem* (Boston, MA: Houghton Mifflin, 1922).

16 CBC *Radio Nova Scotia*, "Education Minister Stands Firm on Hub Schools," CBC *Information Morning Halifax*, 12 June 2015.

17 Ontario Ministry of Education, *Guide to Pupil Accommodation Reviews* (Toronto: Government of Ontario, March 2015), http://www.edu.gov. on.ca/eng/funding/1516/2015B9appenAEN.pdf (accessed 9 January 2020).

18 Prince Edward Island, Public Schools Branch, *Board Governance Policy*, 19 September 2016, 1.

19 Chignecto-Central Regional School Board, *Staff Technical Report for the Northwest Pictou County School Review Process* (Truro, NS: CCRSB, 27 March 2017), 3–4.

20 "School Board Keeping Grades P–12 Students in Pictou," *The Chronicle Herald* (Halifax), 7 April 2017; Anjuli Patil, "Pictou Academy Building to Close, but the Name Is Sticking Around," CBC *News Nova Scotia*, 7 April 2017.

21 Paul W. Bennett, "School Consolidation in Maritime Canada: The Educational Legacy of Edgar L. Morphet and his Disciples," *Country School Journal* 5 (January 2017): 31–47.

22 "Edgar L. Morphet, University of California, In Memorium, 1991," http:// content.edlib.org (accessed 5 August 2010). See also E.L. Morphet, R.L. Johns, and T.L. Reller, *Educational Organization and Administration* (Englewood Cliffs, NJ: Prentice Hall, 1967), 269–71.

23 Dick Chambers, *School Closures in British Columbia: Past Present and Future* (Vancouver, BC: British Columbia School Trustees Association, 2007), v–vii, 65–73.
24 Craig B. Howley, "Don't Supersize Me: The Relationship of Construction Cost to School Enrollment in the U.S.," *Educational Planning* 17, no. 2 (2008), 23–40.
25 Barbara Kent Lawrence et al., eds., *Dollars and Sense II: Lessons from Good, Cost-Effective Small Schools* (Cincinnati, OH: KnowledgeWorks Foundation, 2005).
26 Michael Corbett and Dennis Mulcahy, *Education on a Human Scale: Small Rural Schools in a Modern Context*, Municipality of Cumberland County, Research Report 061 (Wolfville, NS: Acadia Centre for Rural Education, 2006), 8–11, 127–36.
27 See Rural School and Community Trust, "School Size: Research Based Conclusions," (Arlington, VA: Rural School and Community Trust, 2003), on better academic results.
28 Barbara Kent Lawrence et al., eds., *Dollars and Sense: The Cost Effectiveness of Small Schools* (Cincinnati, OH: KnowledgeWorks, 2002), 11–12.
29 Corbett, "From Shinjuku to River John," 621.
30 Pepper Parr, "Academic Researchers Question the PAR Process and Suggest Smaller Schools Work Better," *Burlington Gazette*, 28 October 2016, http://www.burlingtongazette.ca/academic-researchers-question-the-par-process-and-suggest-smaller-schools-work-better/. See also Bennett, *The Last Stand*; and Michael Corbett, *Alberta Journal of Educational Research*, Special Edition.
31 Paul W. Bennett, "School Closures and Community Renewal: Where Do 'Old School' Review Processes Fall Short?" *Educhatter* blog, 20 February 2017; Karen Howlett, "Ontario Moves to Speed Up Process for Closing Schools," *The Globe and Mail*, 5 April 2015.
32 "Ontario Alliance Against School Closures Open Letter to Education Ministry," reprinted in *Cornwall Free News*, 28 October 2016, http://cornwallfreenews.com/2016/10/28/ontario-alliance-against-school-closures-open-letter-to-education-ministry-oct-28-2016/.
33 Paul W. Bennett, "Stop the Consolidation Train," *The Guardian* (Charlottetown), 11 February 2017.
34 Geoff Bartlett, "Whitborne Elementary Closure Saga Continues with Public Meeting in St. John's," *CBC News NL*, 10 August 2016.

35 Jeremy Eaton, "First Day of School, Possibly the Last One at Whitborne Elementary," CBC News NL, 8 September 2016.

36 Newfoundland and Labrador English School District, *Board Meeting Minutes*, Special Meeting of the Board, 20 September 2017, https://www.nlesd.ca/includes/files/minutes/doc/1475510087200.pdf.

37 Daybreak North, "Quesnel Kersley Elementary Parents Protest Potential Closure," CBC News BC, 10 February 2016.

38 Liam Britten, "School Closures in Penticton, Osoyoos and Summerland Trigger Protests," CBC News BC, 30 March 2016.

39 Tracy Sherlock and Rob Shaw, "B.C. Rural Schools Slated to Close Tossed a Lifeline," The *Vancouver Sun*, 15 June 2016.

40 Audrey McKinnon, "B.C. Ministry Releases Report on Rural Education after Being Accused of Burying It," CBC News British Columbia, 14 March 2018, including a link to the draft report.

41 Susan Burgess, "School Closures Will Turn Villages into Ghost Towns, Rural Residents Warn," CBC News Ottawa, 28 March 2017.

42 Community Schools Alliance, founded by Doug Reycraft of Ontario's Middlesex County, championed the cause of saving small rural schools, which evolved in 2016–17 into the Ontario Alliance Against School Closures. *The Local Schools Matter* Facebook campaign was championed by Marcus Ryan of Zorra Township: https://www.communityschoolsalliance.ca/ (accessed 9 January 2020).
   Ontario Alliance Against School Closures, *Local Schools Matter*, Facebook group, Marcus Ryan, curator, Zorra Township, ON, https://www.facebook.com/oaasc/ (accessed 4 April 2017).

43 Elyse Skura, "12 UCDSB Schools Set to Close Following 'Devastating' Vote," CBC News Ottawa, 24 March 2017.

44 "Upper Canada District School Board Votes to Close Rothwell-Osnabruck Secondary, S.J. MacLeod Public Schools," *Standard-Freeholder* (Cornwall, ON), 23 March 2017.

45 Ontario Ministry of Education, *Guide to Pupil Accommodation Reviews* (Toronto: MOE, February 2015), http://www.edu.gov.on.ca/eng/policyfunding/pupilreview.html (accessed 4 April 2017).

46 Burgess, "School Closures Will Turn Villages into Ghost Towns."

47 Colin Butler, "Chapman's Ice Cream Wants to Buy Local School to Keep It Open," CBC News Kitchener-Waterloo, 23 November 2016.

48 "Group Calling on Minister of Education to Halt School Closures," *The Post* (Hanover, ON), 26 October 2016, including letter from Susan MacKenzie, chair of Ontario Alliance Against School Closures.

49 Burgess, "School Closures Will Turn Villages into Ghost Towns."

50 Prince Edward Island, Department of Education and Early Childhood Development, Public Schools Branch, *Board Governance Policy*, 19 September 2016; Bob Andrews, *School Review – Better Learning for All*, 23 September 2016.

51 Sara Fraser, "5 School Closures Recommended in P.E.I. Report on Public Schools," *CBC News PEI*, 10 January 2017.

52 Prince Edward Island, Department of Education and Early Childhood Development, Public Schools Branch, *Draft Recommendations for School Review Process*, 11 January 2017, https://www.princeedwardisland.ca/en/news/feedback-invited-school-review-recommendations (accessed 5 April 2017).

53 Mitch MacDonald, "Hundreds of Supporters Form Human Chain around Georgetown Elementary," *The Charlottetown Guardian*, 29 January 2017.

54 Kevin Curley, "Parents Demand a School Closure Moratorium," *The Eastern Graphic* (Montague, PEI), 15 February 2017.

55 Alan Buchanan, "Community with a Capital 'C,'" *The Charlottetown Guardian*, 30 January 2017.

56 Teresa Wright, "Public Schools Branch Calls for Closure of St. Jean and Georgetown," *The Charlottetown Guardian*, 4 April 2017.

57 Prince Edward Island, Department of Education and Early Childhood Development, Public Schools Branch, *Original Recommendations for All Families of Schools*, 3 April 2017.

58 Kevin Yan, "No Schools Will Close, Says P.E.I. Premier," *CBC News PEI*, 4 April 2017.

59 Sarah MacMillan, "Georgetown Community Celebrates School Announcement," *CBC News PEI*, 4 April 2017.

60 See Hernan Cuervo, *Understanding Social Justice in Rural Education* (London: Palgrave, 2016). See also Cuervo, "Problematizing the Relationship between Rural Small Schools and Communities: Implications for Youth Lives," *Alberta Journal of Educational Research* 60, no. 4 (2014): 643–55.

61 Barbara Barter, "Education Reform: The Effects of School Consolidation on Teachers and Teaching," *Alberta Journal of Educational Research* 60, no. 4 (2014): 674–90.

62 David Clandfield, "The School as a Community Hub: A Public Alternative to the Neo-Liberal Threat to Ontario Schools," in Clandfield and George Martell, eds., *Our Schools / Our Selves*, Special Issue: "School as Community Hub: Beyond Education's Iron Cage" (Summer 2010): 5–74.

63 Paul W. Bennett, "Petite Riviere: How School Reviews Go Wrong," *The Chronicle Herald* (Halifax), 25 March 2017.

64 Stephen Kimber, "Education: The Byzantine, Bizarre and Just Plain Nonsense," *Halifax Examiner*, 27 February 2017.

65 Tom Ayers, "School Board Not Appealing Ruling to Keep Petite Riviere, Pentz Schools Open," *The Chronicle Herald* (Halifax), 21 February 2018.

66 Kristin Rushowy, "Chapman's Ice Cream Melts Hearts in Battle to Save School," *The Toronto Star*, 5 April 2017.

67 Sheree Fitch, "River John SOS – The Things We Do," *Breathe, Stretch, Write!* blog, 6 February 2015, http://sheree-fitch-gnnk.squarespace.com/blog/2015/2/6/river-john-sos-the-things-we-do.html (accessed 11 February 2015).

CHAPTER TWELVE

1 Thomas Fleming, "Provincial Initiatives to Restructure Canadian School Governance in the 1990s," *Canadian Journal of Educational Administration and Policy* 11 (1997); Bruce Sheppard, Gerald Galway, Jean Brown, and John Wiens, *School Boards Matter: Report of the Pan-Canadian Study of School District Governance* (Ottawa: Canadian School Boards Association, 2013).

2 Michael Corbett, "From Shinjuku to River John: The Neoliberal Juggernaut, Efficiency, and Small Rural Schools," *Alberta Journal of Educational Research* 60, no. 4 (Winter 2014): 619–28.

3 Avis Glaze, *Raise the Bar: A Coherent and Responsive Education Administrative System for Nova Scotia* (Halifax: Nova Scotia Department of Education and Early Childhood Development, January 2018).

4 Louise Brown and Kristin Rushowy, "School Boards Behaving Badly: TDSB Is Not Alone," *Toronto Star*, 9 January 2015; David MacKinnon, *School District Governance: Theoretical and Conceptual Foundations*, policy paper (Dartmouth, NS: Nova Scotia School Boards Association [NSSBA], May 2016).

5 Gerald Galway, "School Boards in Canada: Outworn Relics of the Past or Champions of Local Democracy?" presentation to Nova Scotia School Boards Association (Dartmouth, NS: NSSBA, November 2016); Glaze, *Raise the Bar*, 23–6.

6 T.R. Williams, "Educational Governance," unpublished paper prepared for the Panel on the Role of Government, Centre for Policy Studies, Queen's University, Kingston, ON, 2003.

7 Louise Brown, "Secret Life of a Trustee: Behind the Scenes, School Board Reps Are Busy Putting Out Fires," *Toronto Star*, 5 December 2014; Brown and Rushowy, "School Boards Behaving Badly"; Claude Lessard

and André Brassard, "Education Governance in Canada: Trends and Significance, AERA Policy Paper, 2005," http://www2.crifpe.ca/html/ chaires/lessard/pdf/AERAgouvernanceang3.pdf (accessed 12 December 2019).

8 Louise Brown, "Donna Quan to End Tumultuous Term at TDSB," *Toronto Star*, 16 November 2015.

9 Kate Howlett, "Embattled TDSB Director Donna Quan Resigning, Joining York University," *The Globe and Mail*, 16 November 2015; Brown, "Donna Quan to End Tumultuous Term."

10 Martin Regg Cohn, "Dump Our Trustees, Dissolve Our School Boards," *Toronto Star*, 26 November 2014.

11 Joseph Brean, "After Years of Amalgamation, Are Canada's School Boards Too Big to Succeed?" *National Post*, 31 December 2015.

12 Lisa Johnson, "Vancouver School Board Fired by B.C. Education Minister," *CBC News British Columbia*, 17 October 2016.

13 Roslyn Goldner, *Confidential Report of External Examiner in the Matter of an Investigation Pursuant to School District 39 (Vancouver) Harassment in the Workplace Policy* (Vancouver, BC: Goldner Law Corporation / WorkSafe BC, 17 February 2017).

14 Karin Larsen, "Vancouver School Board Workplace Made Toxic by Trustee Behaviour, Report Finds," *CBC News British Columbia*, 3 March 2017; Lawrie McFarlane, "School Trustees' Harassment Must Stop," *Times-Colonist* (Victoria), 17 March 2017.

15 "Vancouver Re-elects Four Former School Trustees Fired by the Province," *CTV News Vancouver*, 15 October 2017.

16 Patti Bacchus, "Vancouver School Board By-election Set for October 14 and No, 'I'm Not Running,'" *Vancouver Observer*, 4 August 2017.

17 Emily Lazatin, "Education Minister Denies Pressure from Government Has VSB Considering School Closures," *Global News 980 CKNW*, 26 February 2019; Patti Bacchus, "Here's a Problem Education Minister Rob Fleming Can Fix," *Georgia Straight* (Vancouver, BC), 9 May 2019.

18 Noor Javed and Kristin Rushowy, "Markham Principal Who Apologized for Anti-Muslim Facebook Posts Now on Leave," *Markham Economist & Sun*, 29 November 2016.

19 Javed and Rushowy, "Draft Plan to Tackle York School Board Woes Called 'Disappointing,'" *Toronto Star*, 11 January 2017.

20 Caroline Alphonso, "Ontario's Education Minister Orders Review of York Region School Board," *The Globe and Mail*, 26 January 2017.

21 Martin Regg Cohn, "Dismantle Our Boards, Ditch Our Trustees," *Toronto Star*, 1 February 2017.

22 Randall Denley, "We Should Combine School Boards and Cut Trustees,"
   Ottawa Citizen, 1 February 2017.
23 "Half of School Boards in Quebec to Be Eliminated," CTV *News
   Montreal*, 19 November 2014.
24 Marlene Jennings, *Final Report of the Election Systems Study Panel*
   (Montreal, QC: Quebec English School Boards Association and partners,
   September 2015).
25 "Jennings Panel Endorses Elected School Boards – Panel Proposes New
   Voting Procedures," news release, Quebec English School Boards
   Association, 16 September 2015.
26 See Quebec National Assembly, *Bill 86, An act to modify the organization
   of school boards*, 1st Session, 41st Legislature, 2015, introduced by
   François Blais, Minister of Education, Higher Education and Research.
27 Jesse Feith, "Bill 86: Quebec to Scrap Contentious Education Reform,
   Propose Consensus-Based Legislation," *Montreal Gazette*, 13 May 2016.
28 Philip Authier, "Quebec School Board Elections Could Be Delayed until
   2020," *Montreal Gazette*, 26 April 2018.
29 Philip Authier, "Minister's Tough Stance on School Board Reform Sparks
   War of Words," *Montreal Gazette*, 18 December 2018.
30 Elysha Enos, "Writing's on the Blackboard for Quebec School Boards as
   CAQ Moves to Take Away EMSB Schools," CBC *News Montreal*, 11 May
   2019.
31 See Paul W. Bennett, *Education Restructuring: Curing the Accountability
   and Democratic Deficit*, research report, Atlantic Institute for Market
   Studies, February 2018.
32 Paul W. Bennett, *Vanishing Schools, Threatened Communities: The
   Contested Schoolhouse in Maritime Canada, 1850–2010* (Halifax:
   Fernwood Publishing, 2011), 135–6.
33 Lawrence Bezeau, "Structural Reform of the New Brunswick System of
   Education," research study report (Fredericton: UNB, Centre of Education
   Administration, 5 December 2000).
34 James Foster, "Three DEC Members Step Down," *Moncton Times &
   Transcript*, 21 July 2009.
35 Paul MacNeil, "Demise of a Board: Backroom Politics and the Firing
   of the Eastern School Board," *The Eastern Graphic* (Montague, PEI),
   20 April 2011; CBC *News Prince Edward Island*, "School Board Fired
   by Education Minister," 22 February 2011.
36 CBC *News Prince Edward Island*, "P.E.I.'s English Language School Board
   to Be Dissolved," 5 November 2015; and "P.E.I. English Language School
   Board's Last Stand," 6 November 2015.

37 Michael Fullan and Mary Jean Gallagher, *A Focus on the Future: Education Improvement in Prince Edward Island*, 31 March 2016.
38 CBC *News Prince Edward Island*, "We Need Elected Trustees: Board Questioned at Latest Schools Review Meeting," 3 February 2017; Paul W. Bennett and Leif Helmer, "School Reviews, Hub Schools, and School-Centred Community Enterprise," testimony at Standing Committee on Education and Economic Development, Prince Edward Island Legislative Assembly, *Hansard*, 15 February 2017, 55–65; "Now Is Not the Time to Close P.E. I. Schools: MacLauchlan," *Charlottetown Guardian*, 4 April 2017.
39 Kevin Yarr, "Elected School Boards Returning to P.E.I.," CBC *News*, 4 December 2019, https://www.cbc.ca/news/canada/prince-edward-island/pei-school-board-elected-education-1.5383650.
40 Gerald Galway, "Democracy Cookbook: Re-democratizing School Governance in Newfoundland and Labrador," *The Telegram* (St John's), 20 November 2017.
41 Brenda Kelleher-Flight, "Newfoundland and Labrador Reduces Number of School Boards," GDP *Consulting* blog, 28 March 2013.
42 Newfoundland and Labrador Department of Education, "Backgrounder – Budget 2013," 26 March 2013; "Regions Will Have Strong Educational Presence under Provincial School Board: Minister," 18 April 2013.
43 Diane Crocker, "School Board Association Not Weighing In on Consolidation," *The Western Star* (Corner Brook, NL), 17 April 2013.
44 Newfoundland and Labrador English School Board, *District Overview* (St John's: NLESB, 2018), https://www.nlesd.ca/about/districtoverview.jsp (accessed 20 February 2018).
45 Peter Clancy et al., *The Savage Years: The Perils of Reinventing Government in Nova Scotia* (Halifax: Formac Publishing, 2000), 140–69.
46 Don Trider, "Leadership in a Turbulent Policy Environment – Implications for School Leaders: Evidence from the Field," unpublished paper (Montreal, QC: American Educational Research Association, January 1999).
47 Paul W. Bennett, "Three Ways to Remodel School Boards," *The Chronicle Herald* (Halifax), 10 December 2014; Glaze, *Raise the Bar*.
48 Paul W. Bennett, "Fixing the Education Accountability Gap," *The Chronicle Herald* (Halifax), 4 December 2015.
49 Nova Scotia Department of Education and Early Childhood Development, *Disrupting the Status Quo: Nova Scotians Demand a Better Future for Every Student*, report of the Minister's Panel on Education, Myra Freeman, Chair (Halifax: DOEECD, October 2014).

50 Jean Laroche, "Nova Scotia to Dissolve Elected School Boards in Favour of Advisory Council," CBC News Nova Scotia, 24 January 2018.
51 Paul W. Bennett. "School Board Reform: A Better Cure for the Democratic Deficit," presentation brief to Nova Scotia Assembly, Law Amendments Committee, 20 November 2012.
52 T.R. Williams, "Educational Governance," Unpublished Paper prepared for the Panel on the Role of Government, Centre for Policy Studies, Queen's University, Kingston, ON, 2003; P. Bradshaw and R. Osborne, "School Boards: Emerging Governance Challenges," *Education Canada* 50, no. 1 (2010): 46–9.
53 Angus McBeath, "Choice, Accountability and Performance in Public Schools: How Edmonton Does It and Why," Presentation (Halifax: AIMS and SAEE, 11 July 2003); Charles Cirtwill, "Should We SAC the Province's School Boards?" *The Chronicle Herald* (Halifax), 6 November 2007.
54 Bennett, *Vanishing Schools, Threatened Communities*, 175–6; Bennett, "School Board Reform."
55 Paul W. Bennett, "Board Reform: Better Cure for the Democratic Deficit," *The Chronicle Herald* (Halifax), 22 November 2012; Glaze, *Raise the Bar*, 11.
56 Nova Scotia, Office of the Auditor General, *Report of the Auditor General to the Nova Scotia House of Assembly* (Halifax: OAG, December 2014). See also Jean Laroche, "Tri-County School Board's Problems Known before Audit: Province," CBC News Nova Scotia, 11 February 2015.
57 Nova Scotia, Office of the Auditor General, *Report of the Auditor General to the Nova Scotia House of Assembly*, December 2014 and November 2015.
58 Paul W. Bennett, *The Last Stand: Schools, Communities and the Future of Rural Nova Scotia* (Halifax: Fernwood Publishing, 2013); Michael Corbett and Leif Helmer, "Hub Schools: Education Brass Must Join Cause," *The Chronicle Herald* (Halifax), 18 March 2015.
59 Wendy Martin, "Residents Say Board Should Resign over Closure of Louisbourg's Only School," CBC News Nova Scotia, 9 June 2017.
60 Laroche, "Nova Scotia to Dissolve Elected School Boards."
61 Bartley Kives, "Are Fewer School Boards an Answer to What Ails Education in Manitoba?" CBC News Manitoba, 15 February 2019; Government of Manitoba, *Manitoba's Commission on Kindergarten to Grade 12 Education: Public Consultation Discussion Paper* (Winnipeg: Manitoba Government, April 2019), 3, 6, 14.

EPILOGUE

1 Paul W. Bennett, "Edifices and Students," *Halifax Magazine* (September 2010); Bruce Johnson, "Local School Micropolitical Agency: An Antidote to New Managerialism," Hawke Research Institute, Working Paper Series, No. 2 (Magill, SA: University of South Australia, 2004).

2 Halifax Regional Centre for Education, "HRSB's New Name: Halifax Regional Centre for Education," Notice, 27 March 2018, https://www. hrce.ca/news/2018/03/27/hrsbs-new-name-halifax-regional-centre-education. See also Caroline Alphonso, "Nova Scotia Dissolving School Boards into One Appointed Advisory Council," *The Globe and Mail*, 29 March 2018; and Taryn Grant, "Nova Scotia Announces Members of Advisory Council on Education," *Star Metro Halifax*, 27 September 2018.

3 Peter Coleman, "Improving Schools by School-Based Management," *McGill Journal of Education* 19, no. 1 (1984).

4 Angus McBeath, "Choice, Accountability and Performance in the Public Schools: How Edmonton Does It and Why It Works," address (Halifax: Atlantic Institute for Market Studies, Halifax Club, 11 July 2003).

5 Angus McBeath, "The Edmonton Model," *CBC Radio: Atlantic Voice*, 26 September 2011, https://www.cbc.ca/atlanticvoice/mind-the-gap/ 2011/09/26/the-edmonton-model-interview-with-angus-mcbeath/ (accessed 9 January 2020).

6 Jay Mathews, "Beware of the Easy School Fix," *The Washington Post*, 26 September 2008.

7 William G. Ouchi, *Making Schools Work: A Revolutionary Plan to Get Your Children the Education They Need* (New York: Simon & Schuster, 2008).

8 Barbara Bruns, Deon Filmer, and Harry Anthony Patrinos, *Making Schools Work: New Evidence on Accountability Reforms* (Washington, DC: The World Bank, 2011), 87.

9 Eleni Natsiopoulou and Vicky Giouroukakis, "When Teachers Run the School," *Educational Leadership* 67, no. 7 (April 2010), http://www.ascd. org/publications/educational-leadership/apr10/vol67/num07/When-Teachers-Run-the-School.aspx (accessed 9 January 2020).

10 Tom Whitby, *My Island View* blog, https://tomwhitby.wordpress.com/ author/tomwhitby/ (accessed 18 December 2019).

11 Johnson, "Local School Micropolitical Agency," 23.

12 See Cathy Wylie, *School Governance in New Zealand: How Is It Working?* (Wellington: New Zealand Council for Educational Research, 2007).

13 Benjamin Levin, *Reforming Education: From Origins to Outcomes* (New York: Routledge, 2001).

14 Cathy Wylie, "Tomorrow's Schools after 20 Years: Can a System of Self-Managing Schools Live Up to Its Initial Aims?" (Wellington: University of Victoria, 2009).

15 G. Butterworth and S. Butterworth, *Reforming Education: The New Zealand Experience, 1984–1996* (Palmerston North, NZ: Dunmore Press, 1998).

16 Cathy Wylie, "Impact of Education Reforms," Series of research reports, 1990–99, New Zealand Council for Educational Research (NZCER), https://www.nzcer.org.nz/category/research-project/impact-education-reforms (accessed 11 July 2019).

17 Ibid.

18 Cathy Wylie, *Vital Connections: Why We Need More than Self-Managed Schools* (Wellington: NZCER, 2012).

19 Jody O'Callaghan, "Tomorrow's Schools 'Lost a Decade,'" *The Dominion Post* (Wellington), 4 December 2012.

20 Richard G. Neal, *School-Based Management: Detailed Guide for Successful Implementation* (Bloomington, IN: National Educational Service, 1991); Bruce Sheppard, "Implementing Change: A Success Story," unpublished paper (St John's: Faculty of Education, Memorial University of Newfoundland, Fall 1995); L. Gordon, "Controlling Education: Agency Theory and the Reform of New Zealand Schools," *Educational Policy* 9, no. 1 (1995): 54–74.

21 Nova Scotia Department of Education, *Restructuring Nova Scotia's Education System: Preparing All Students for a Lifetime of Learning* (Halifax: NSDE, 1994).

22 Janet French, "Michael Strembitsky: The Brains behind School-Based Budgeting," *Edmonton Journal*, 27 August 2016. See also French, "Retired Edmonton Superintendent Bets He Can Overhaul Massive Las Vegas School System," *Edmonton Journal*, 27 August 2016.

23 Edmonton Public Schools, "Facts and Stats," EPSB website, https://epsb.ca/ourdistrict/facts/ (accessed 28 March 2018).

24 Edmonton Public Schools, "Budget Recommendation Report," Darrel Robertson, Superintendent of Schools, to Board of Trustees, 28 November 2017 and Attachments, including Total Allocations, and Direct School Allocations.

25 Jim Dueck, *Education's Flashpoints: Upside Down or Set-Up to Fail* (Lanham, MD: Rowman & Littlefield, 2015), vii–xii, 110.

26 Peter Hennessy, *From Student to Citizen: A Community-Based Vision for Democracy* (Toronto: White Knight Books, 2006), 184–94.

27 Craig Howley, Jerry Johnson, and Jennifer Petrie, *Consolidation of Schools and Districts: What the Research Says and What It Means* (Boulder, CO: National Education Policy Center, February 2011); Paul W. Bennett and Derek M. Gillis, *Education on Wheels: Seizing Cost and Energy Efficiency Opportunities in Student Transportation* (Halifax: AIMS, January 2015).

28 Hennessy, *From Student to Citizen*, 228.

29 Paul W. Bennett, *Re-engineering Education: Curing the Democratic and Accountability Deficit in Nova Scotia* (Halifax: AIMS, February 2018), 16–22.

30 Michael Fullan and Nancy Watson, "School-Based Management: Reconceptualizing to Improve Student Outcomes," policy paper, "Improving Learning Outcomes in the Caribbean" Conference (New York: The World Bank, August 1999), 1.

31 Mary Tasker, "Human-Scale Education: History, Values and Practice" (Lisbon, Portugal: Calouste Gulbenkian Foundation, December 2008), 3. See also Satish Kumar, "Human-Scale Education: Inventing a School that Meets Real Needs," *The Green Teacher* (Spring 2004); and "Schools on a Human Scale" (London: 21 Trust/School 21, 2013), http://www.21trust. org (accessed 12 June 2015).

32 Tasker, "Human-Scale Education," 4.

33 Michael Corbett and Dennis Mulcahy, "Education on a Human Scale" (Wolfville, NS: Acadia Centre for Rural Education, 2006).

34 Theodore Sizer, founder of Coalition of Essential Schools, quoted in Tasker, "Human-Scale Education," 8.

35 David Marshak, "Why Did the Gates Small-High-Schools Program Fail? Well, Actually It Didn't," *Education Week*, 19 February 2010.

36 Thomas Toch, "High Schools: Small Is Still Beautiful," *Washington Monthly* (July 2010), https://hechingerreport.org/small-schools-are-still-beautiful/ (accessed 8 January 2020).

37 Jelmer Evers and Rene Kneyber, "Introduction," in Evers and Kneyber, *Flip the System: Changing Education from the Ground Up* (London: Routledge, 2016), 1–7.

38 J. Ranciere, *Dis-agreement: Politic and Philosophy* (Minneapolis: University of Minnesota Press, 1999), cited in Evers and Kneyber, *Flip the System*, 7.

39 Gert Biesta, *The Beautiful Risk of Education* (Boulder, CO: Paradigm Publishers, 2013).

40 Gert Biesta, "Good Education and the Teacher: Reclaiming Educational Professionalism," in Evers and Kneyber, *Flip the System*, 80–3.

41 Randy Banderob, "Tom Bennett and the researchED revolution," *Education Forum*, OSSTF Teacher Magazine (26 October 2017).

42 "Harvey Bischof Speaks at researchED Conference, OSSTF/FEESO Plans Its Own," *OSSTF News Brief*, November 2017, https://osstfupdate. ca/2017/11/24/harvey-bischof-speaks-at-researched-conference-osstffeeso-plans-its-own/ (accessed 18 May 2018).

43 See Michael Zwaagstra, "Teacher's Unions Should Resist Education Fads," 1 May 2018, http://michaelzwaagstra.com/?p=621 (accessed 18 May 2018).

44 Debbie Pushor, "Parent Engagement: Creating a Shared World," research paper (Toronto: Ontario Education Research Symposium, 18–20 January 2007), 2–11. See also D. Pushor and M. Murphy, "Parent Marginalization, Marginalized Parents: Creating a Place for Parents on the School Landscape," *Alberta Journal of Educational Research* 50, no. 3 (2004): 221–35.

45 M.A. Lawson, "School-Family Relations in Context: Parent and Teacher Perceptions of Parent Involvement," *Urban Education* 38, no. 1 (2003): 77–133; Debbie Pushor, "Family-centric Schools: Creating a Place for All Parents," *Education Canada* (December 2017): 17–19.

46 A parent's perspective cited in Pushor, "Family-centric Schools," 17.

47 Debbie Pushor, "Walking Alongside: A Pedagogy of Working with Parents and Families in Canada," in L. Orland Barak and C. Craig, eds., *International Teacher Education: Promising Pedagogies* (Bingley, UK: Emerald Group Publishing, 2015), 233–51.

48 Pushor, "Family-centric Schools," 18–19.

49 Aaron Harris, "Fix Board or Be Broken Up, Toronto Trustees, Staff Warned," *The Toronto Star*, 4 December 2015; John Lorinc, "Class Dismissed: Do We Really Need School Board Trustees?" *The Walrus*, 15 October 2015; Joseph Brean, "After Years of Amalgamation, Are Canada's Schoolboards Too Big to Succeed?" *National Post*, 31 December 2015.

50 Larry Kuehn, "The Globalization of Education and the Implications for Canada," in Ed Finn, ed., *Canada after Harper* (Toronto: Lorimer Books, 2015), 223–8.

51 "On the Road to researchED Ontario: Interview with Tom Bennett and Harvey Bischof, hosted by Stephen Hurley" (VoicED Canada, April 2018), https://soundcloud.com/voiced-radio/the-road-to-researched-ontario-tom-bennett-and-harvey-bischof (accessed 17 May 2018).

52 See Frederick M. Hess and Andy Smarick, "Localism and Education: Pluralism, Choice and Democratic Control," in Joel Kotkin and Ryan Streeter, eds., *Localism in America: Why We Should Tackle Our Big Challenges at the Local Level* (Washington, DC: American Enterprise Institute, February 2018), 68–73.

53 Kelly Gallagher-Mackay and Nancy Steinhauer, *Pushing the Limits: How Schools Can Prepare Our Children for the Challenges of Tomorrow* (Toronto: Doubleday Canada, 2017), 209–29; David Staples, "Dump Discovery Math and Bring Back Standard Rules," *Edmonton Journal*, 14 January 2017; Michael Corbett and Leif Helmer, "Contested Geographies: Competing Constructions of Community and Efficiency in Small School Debates," *Geographical Research* 55, no. 1 (February 2017): 47–57.

54 The faltering of "Big Reform" in the United States in the 2010s and the shortcomings of "technocratic engineering" are identified in Robert Pondiscio, "Ed Reform's Lost Decade: Twilight of the Technocrats," *Flypaper* (Thomas B. Fordham Institute Weekly Magazine), 18 December 2019, https://fordhaminstitute.org/national/commentary/ed-reforms-lost-decade-twilight-technocrats (accessed 9 January 2020).

55 See Paul W. Bennett, *Vanishing Schools, Threatened Communities: The Contested Schoolhouse in Maritime Canada, 1850–2010* (Halifax: Fernwood Publishing, 2011), 177–81.

Index